GREAT THINKERS, GREAT IDEAS

GREAT THINKERS, GREAT IDEAS

AN INTRODUCTION TO WESTERN THOUGHT

SECOND EDITION

VINCENT J. FALCONE

CRANBURY PUBLICATIONS

Acknowledgment is made to the authors and publishers listed below for their permission to use the material reprinted in this book:

A Glossary of Literature and Composition, Lazarus, A., and Smith, W.H., Copyright © NCTE, 1983
The Christian Philosophy of St. Thomas Aquinas, Gilson, Etienne, trans. by Lynch, L.E.M., Copyright © Random House, Inc., 1956
The Great Issues of Politics, An Introduction to Political Science, Lipson, Leslie, Copyright © Prentice Hall Inc., 1954

Library of Congress Cataloging-in-Publication Data

Falcone, Vincent J., 1934-
    Great thinkers, great ideas : an introduction to Western thought / Vincent J. Falcone. -- 2nd ed.
        p.   cm.
    Originally published: Croton-on-Hudson : North River Press, 1988. With new introd.
    ISBN 0-9629323-1-0 : $9.95
    1. Philosophy. 2. Political science. 3. Economics. I. Title.
[B72.F26 1992]
190--dc20   92-7554
                                                         CIP

Printed in the United States of America
Second printing - 1999

Cranbury Publications
2230 Chesterbrook Court
Naples FL 34109

For June, Steve, Maryellen and Sue

CONTENTS

PART 3
Political Theory: The Relationship
of Man and the State

PART 4
Economic Theory: An Introduction

ACKNOWLEDGEMENTS

This revised edition is in large part the result of input provided by former students who have commented on the value of the text, and the help it has provided in a variety of courses that they have taken. Also many friends, colleagues and acquaintances have used the book to introduce themselves to, or reacquaint themselves with, the great ideas. Those who used the book as a beginning primer have validated my hope that complex ideas could be simply stated and easily understood. I remain indebted to my colleagues and friends—those who initially advised me—Peter Donase, Edward Kovacs, Stewart Hulbert, and Raol Wolf. I thank, once again, those who continue to advise and instruct me—especially Dr. Richard C. Harper.

The initial project would have never gotten off the ground without the help and encouragement of Barry Merkin, and this second edition was made possible by the creative talents of Frank Derato.

I owe a special debt to Emily Green whose help in the preparation of the revised manuscript was important and whose good humor throughout the process was invaluable.

Again, my thanks to the literally thousands of students who elected to study with me—who accepted the challenge and opted to read the difficult books, engaged the complex ideas, struggled with the difficulties of serious discussion and made the hard decisions about their own values—and to those special ones whose questions, insights and analysis continue to broaden my understanding and appreciation of our western heritage.

Trumbull, Connecticut
1992

FOREWORD

In *Alice's Adventures in Wonderland* there is a scene in which Alice, walking along, comes to a fork in the road. Pausing, she asks the Cheshire Cat, "Would you tell me please, which way I ought to walk from here?" The Cheshire Cat answers, "That depends a good deal on where you want to get to." "I don't much care where—" says Alice. "Then it doesn't much matter which way you walk," says the cat.

Which road to take, in this journey of life, is a problem which confronts all of us. In one sense all teaching rests on the premise that what path one takes is important, and the making of judgments as to which path is best can be even more important.

In this text we shall undertake the study of some political, moral, and economic theories. These basic ideas, as put forth by some of the great thinkers of western civilization provide signposts to the many and varied roads which can be taken in forming opinions on some very important questions. What is the proper relationship between the citizen and the state? How can we best judge right from wrong? Does every man have a price? If we accept the concept of majority rule, how do we deal with the desires of those in the minority? If we reject the concept of majority rule, what do we choose as the alternative? Capital punishment, abortion, war and peace, love and sex, free enterprise, communism, socialism—the issues are endless.

Since the issues are endless, the questions unlimited, and the ideas complex, this study shall be a presentation of the *basic* ideas and concepts put forward by some well known philosophers. We shall not attempt an in-depth study of philosophy; rather the goal is to make the reader aware of the important ideas of western philosophy, to undertake an analysis of the validity of the thoughts encountered, and to expand the number of options available in the making of intellectual choices.

In terms of the subject matter the goals of this study are modest. The major objective will not be met—we will fall short of the goal. But that too is part of the process which must be recognized. We often fall short of our goals—but if we know where we are going, at least we will know what road to take—and in that regard we are one step ahead of Alice.

We are about to embark on a study, a study of ideas. Many of the greatest thinkers from the ancient Greeks to the present day are going to help us in this study by challenging us with their thoughts about many questions. The general focus will be on political, moral and economic ideas, but in the process we will move in and out of topics which relate, sometimes directly, sometimes obliquely, to the major thrust of the course.

We could call this a study of the History of Ideas, or we could simply say we are going to discuss philosophy. Regardless of the title, the subject is the same.

What is philosophy? Why should we study it? What good will come of our efforts?

Philosophy, defined, means "love of wisdom." Please note, not love of knowledge, although knowledge is important, but love of wisdom. Philosophy has been said to be the art of making the complex simple, or a way of thinking, or a search for truth, or a search for meaning, or a way to live the good life. On a multiple choice question sheet the correct answer would be "All of the above" — and more. Socrates once said, "The unexamined life is not worth living." Life is important; if this is so, then we are obliged to try to learn how to live it well.

This text will present a very basic introduction to the subject. It will be long on politics, ethics, and logic; short on esthetics and metaphysics. This presentation is intentional; the purpose is to stimulate the reader to discuss these ideas and in the exchange, expand their understanding of issues of importance to them. We certainly will not cover it all. But we will be introduced to much, and much of what we learn will be confusing. But confusion is the beginning of wisdom—and that brings us back to the definition of philosophy.

PART 1

AN INTRODUCTION TO CLEARER THINKING

CHAPTER 1

Attitudes:
How They Affect our Thinking

One of the great debates centers on the question of faith or reason. How do we judge—on the basis of faith or reason? Man is, among other things, a thinking being. Thus, the thrust of this study is based upon the premise that reason is the best means of ascertaining truth, or, at least, some truths.

In a paradoxical but real way, however, everything begins with an article of faith. To consider reason as the best route to understanding requires that one accept the premise that reason is sufficient to the end desired. We trust our reason. Granted, there is much evidence gathered through experience that tends to justify our faith in reason, but in the final analysis the word faith is the operative term.

One can imagine all manner of possible answers to yet unanswered questions. Did we come into being by a conscious act of God? Or did the solar system begin with a big bang? Did that dust cloud some scientists talk about really explode into a universe of which we are a part? Or is it any less possible that, as one commentator speculated, once upon a time many years ago a space ship from a far off galaxy flew over planet earth and dumped its garbage—and that's how life began. Can we, should we accept any explanation to difficult questions that our imagination can conjure, or should we develop a system of critical thinking, careful analysis, and the development of our practical reason? The answer seems clear.

Before we attempt to learn how to think better about the problems which confront us, we should know that we bring to the study certain attitudes and prejudices that hinder the process. Where do these attitudes come from?

Our attitudes are formed in large measure by our experiences in five critical areas: the family, the culture, the school, peer groups, and the media.

Our first and most profound experiences take place in the family, which has been the most dominant force in all societies to date. The effect that our earliest experiences have on our attitudes is hard to shake. There is an old saw, probably apocryphal, which claims that the Jesuits say "Give me the child, and I'll give you the man." Whether or not the saying is true or false is unimportant. The implication is clear. During those most impressionable years at the beginning of the life process, children learn the most basic attitudes, many of which they carry with them forever. Certainly attitudes change over a lifetime as other affecters of attitudes come into play, but clearly the family is the first and most important element in the process.

It is in the family that children first learn the language; the words which transmit attitudes come first from the mother and father. Perhaps even more important than the words used, are the nuances of tone and emphasis and context which begin the process of bias long before there is any understanding of the meaning of that word. In the conversations at the dinner table, intonations of anger, pride, disparagement, joy, love, and hate - all enter into the dialogue. Children discover not only words but their deeper meaning.

Some of the most important attitudes of all are also cultivated, carefully and formally, in the family. Religious views, concepts of right and wrong, economic views, patterns of behavior, manners and tastes are taught in the home. Older siblings who were taught these concepts earlier reinforce the attitudes of the younger children.

Second to the family, but of great importance in transmitting attitudes, is the culture. Culture, simply stated, is the sum total of all the social forces in the environment which affect us. In this society, for example, we are in constant contact with others who generally act in accordance with certain standards of conduct. We observe then what is considered "socially acceptable" behavior and tend to pattern our behavior according to what our observations have determined to be "good." We learn what kinds of actions will allow us to move freely and comfortably in this society. The feeling of security we experience in knowing that our actions will be accepted by those with whom we come in contact reinforces the seeming correctness of those actions.

In one sense it might be better to say that we are limited by our

Getting out in of the case in a way

culture. We become aware very early in life that there are a great many activities which are different yet socially acceptable, but there are other actions we dare not take. Even in America where individualism is a cherished ideal and many people express themselves in many different ways, that expression, generally, is always within some very specific limits.

For example, American women adorn themselves with necklaces, earrings, makeup, hairstyles, all of which vary in style and color. The differences in taste between individuals vary greatly, and one person's extreme is another's commonplace. However, you can be assured that the cashier at the grocery store or the clerk at the mall will not be wearing a bone through her nose. While other societies may permit, even encourage, bones through the nose, this society says an emphatic no! The culture limits the mode of behavior by dictating the limits of permissible dress through the use of sanctions. Wear a bone through your nose and you will find a job hard to come by. You will also find yourself the object of unkind remarks and derisive comments about your appearance. Ostracism and ridicule will soon convince you of the "error" of your ways. The culture will "teach" you right from wrong in the matter of appearance and limit your actions.

break free from the cave if you can handle it.

Men are in one sense even more limited in dress. The code of dress for the American businessman is rigid. Early some morning spend the rush hour at Grand Central Station in New York City and you will be treated to a lesson in cultural motivation. The men leaving the trains, carrying briefcases, will be uniformly similar in appearance. Blue and grey will be the dominant color of their suits, their ties will be a subdued stripe or an even more subdued paisley. Shoes will be either wingtips or plain with tassels, and hair length will demonstrate the wearer's close relationship with his barber. Employment, promotion, success with clients and one's colleagues require a particular uniform—and serious departures from the standard spell failure.

Modes of dress and appearance are simple examples of the force of culture. The force of culture permeates every aspect of our daily lives: art, literature, entertainment, food, music, car styles, architecture, manners, language, are all shaped in some part by the society of which we are a part. Whether or not the standards of a culture are good or bad, right or wrong, better or worse than another culture is not the issue; the fact is that we are

osnt matter good / Bad here all oves to reak free from

affected by those cultural guideposts and they tend to affect our attitudes.

The importance of the school as a transmitter of attitudes can not be overstated. Obviously some of the most basic values are learned in the classroom as a part of the curriculum. In addition, the school inculcates values and thus creates attitudes as a result of the lessons taught by the organization of the school, the structure of the system, and the attitudes of the teachers.

The organization of the public schools in America is based, generally, on a September to June school year, with the better part of a youngster's day spent in the school. The system is so organized that virtually every child spends thirteen years of his life from age five to eighteen in this environment. Holidays are structured around traditional celebrations: Thanksgiving, Christmas, Easter and other assorted religious, political, and ethnic holidays. At a very early age children learn that not all days are the same, some are special. The repetition of these celebrations year after year affects how students define the values of society.

In school students are exposed to a life style different from the one they experienced in the home. The school has rules, lots of rules, formal rules; and through this system, in which the rights and wrongs of behavior are spelled out and systems of punishment for violations are in place, students soon learn the meaning of authority. They learn how formal authority operates, that there are different levels of authority, and that the outside world works more like the school than the home.

Many other values are encouraged simply by the mission of the institution. Intellectual values are encouraged by teachers, competition is encouraged by grading systems, excellence is honored by organizations such as the National Honor Society, and athletics are encouraged by coaches, parent groups and newspaper coverage. And in America today, the public school has assumed a wide range of responsibilities, from providing sex education to testing students' eyesight, all of which affect students' value systems.

Generally, in the public school there is a homogeneity of the student population. The students come from areas close to the school, certainly no farther away than a bus ride. This results in a general cultural homogeneity of race, ethnic background, parental occupation, and social status. Yet the homogeneity of the student population is nothing when compared to the homogeneous nature of the teaching staff. Historically, teaching has been a profession of "first entry," that is, many teachers are among the first of their family to graduate from college—most of them coming from lower middle class backgrounds. The "best" and the "brightest" who graduate from America's most prestigious colleges have not been attracted to the traditionally low-paying occupation of public school teacher. Thus, the attitudes most public school teachers transmit by example, by inference, by virtue of their own commitment, are the values of the broad middle class.

Peer influence on individuals affects everyone to varying degrees. Adolescents are generally conceded to be the most affected by peer pressure. Aristotle says that adolescence is an age of extremes. As one develops into a social being, when puberty and the recognition of sexual awareness come upon young people, the desire and need for acceptance is great. Life is an all or nothing event. Therefore, peer acceptance which is important to everyone, is terribly important to teenagers.

Young people tend to travel in groups, and want to have many friends. They ape their peers in style of dress, language, and most importantly, attitudes. A strong personality attracts and influences others in the group, and teenage groups tend to have unelected natural leaders. Often leaders tend to be members from outside the group and the object of adulation by the members of the group. Rock group stars, celebrities, sports heroes, all guide the thinking of large groups of people.

At times the pressure from peers causes people to violate values that they hold. Often a normal consequence of such behavior is a change in the attitude towards the value involved. No one wants to consider himself evil or wrong. We all tend to want to act in conformity with our beliefs and values. We don't want to act contrary to what we hold to be "good." So, when pressured into acting for peer approval we not only act, but begin the process of changing our values, and our attitude towards the value and like values.

Peer pressure affects all people of all ages—we all want to be liked. But the critical age for peer pressure and its importance in the development of values is adolescence. The complexity of the problems faced by those who are no longer children, yet not quite adult is often difficult to cope with. Adolescence is an age of powerful needs; if those needs are not filled by family, church, school, or society, the small peer group becomes disproportionately important in a young person's life—and the young lead the young.

Finally, the mass media are powerful affecters of attitudes. Newspapers, magazines, radio, movies, and, most importantly, television provide huge amounts of information, all of which affects our attitudes about the issues they discuss. Today, mass media provides information instantly to everyone about incidents that happen in the farthest reaches of the globe.

One of the problems inherent in the very concept of mass media is the idea of "mass." How does a magazine provide weekly information for a mass audience? At what level is the language used, how deeply can the complexity of the issues be discussed, how controversial can an article be to appeal to a mass audience? It seems fairly apparent that the larger the circulation of a magazine becomes, the more bland the content must also become. Most large circulation magazines have a reading level that appeals to a sixth-grader.

Radio and movies are basically entertainment media, and therefore their contribution to knowledge is less dependent upon fact than it is upon impact. The impact of such entertainment vehicles can and does affect attitudes. The problem posed here is that there is a minimum of factual information presented with a maximum of content for effect. To develop attitudes on the basis of information gathered from these two mediums is to make judgments based on an emotional response. Radio and movies are mediums whose very success rest on their ability to manipulate emotions.

The problems with newspapers is that newspapers try to present information as soon as the event happens. Speed and efficiency are the goals of most newspapers. Get the news "out while it's hot." Unhappily, speed and accuracy are often mutually exclusive. On June 29, 1985, the Associated Press reported "39 U.S. hostages leaving for Syria." Good news but simply not true. The hostages were not released for another two days. Probably one of the most famous pictures in the world is of Harry S. Truman smiling broadly, holding a newspaper with the premature headline, "Dewey Defeats Truman." Obviously, errors of such national importance are quickly corrected, and everyone soon becomes aware of the real story. Corrections or retractions of errors on local issues simply do not have the same impact as the initial error.

The problem of television is probably the greatest of all those posed by the mass media. The first and most obvious problem with television is the need of the medium to condense and edit due to the constraints of time. Think for a moment about the idea of the "news of the world in half an hour," commercials included. The necessity to condense often results in the simplification of complex problems, the problem of editing, by definition, results in the viewer seeing one of the few stories someone else thinks is important. Finally the most important problem that television presents is the problem that it misleads by the visual nature of the medium.

When we read, we can reread. We can read a variety of sources almost instantly. And we tend to be skeptical of what we read knowing that writers have a point of view. But with television we see what is happening, and therefore we are all the more convinced of its authenticity. But in fact we do not see everything—we see what the camera sees. Cameras do not have peripheral vision—we see only what is within the focus of the camera lens. Coupled with the editing process, we are viewing as real that which is unreal in the truest sense. And we are convinced by the illusion even if we are from Missouri.

Certainly beyond the five areas mentioned here there are others which profoundly affect our attitudes: churches, politicians, neighbors, certain happy or sad experiences. Also the interplay of the home, culture, school, peer groups, and mass media creates a totality of experience which helps us form our attitudes. Understanding these influences is important because during the course of this study one of the important goals will be to test these attitudes, values, and/or prejudices against conflicting ideas. Some attitudes will be strengthened by this investigation, others weakened, new ones accepted, old ones discarded—all, we hope, in the calm light of reasoned judgments.

Beyond those values which we learn from our home, culture, media, peer groups, and school, are two phenomena which can and do affect our attitudes towards others. "Ethnocentrism" and "xenophobia" are two words which are important to understand.

If you read a dictionary you will find xenophobia defined as "fear, distrust, or hatred of foreigners." Ethnocentrism is defined as a feeling of "superiority of one's own ethnic group." A fuller understanding of these two terms could very well prevent a person from becoming a xenophobe or ethnocentric according to the dictionary definition.

Ethnocentrism begins with a feeling of comfort or security that one gets, quite naturally, in familiar surroundings or with people like oneself. Xenophobia begins with a fear of the unfamiliar, a very natural feeling. These feelings however, can be the beginning of some deep-seated prejudices.

If one is comfortable and secure with those like himself, it is easy to assume that the feeling of well-being is the product of superior surroundings (nationalism) or people (ethnic or racial superiority). If one is uncomfortable with strange surroundings or people it is easy to assume that the feeling is based on some valid premise. Thus, the strange surrounding becomes the habitat of an enemy and the strange person somehow seems inferior. Two examples should help to illustrate this point.

Consider a young man out for a walk in the city late one afternoon. He starts out whistling a tune; with a spirited gait he walks along enjoying the scenery. As it begins to grow dark, he finds himself in a part of town which is unfamiliar to him and very different from his own neighborhood. His step slows, his whistle stops, and he begins to notice more and more differences in the makeup of this part of town. He notices, directly ahead of him, a large group of men standing on the sidewalk in front of a store. They are dressed in a very different style, they are of a different color, and they are speaking a language he cannot understand. As he approaches they pause in their animated conversation, and as he passes, they break out into hysterical laughter. The hair on the back of his neck bristles, he becomes nervous and wonders, "Oh my God! Why are they laughing... at me?" If he puts aside this very natural reaction and continues his walk—fine. If, however, he begins to swear under his breath about those "no good foreigners, those peons, how dare those animals laugh at me—they should be shipped back to where they came from," then he's a xenophobe.

Similarly, ethnocentrism begins as a feeling of comfort or security with those like oneself. Consider a young lady who is invited to a party by a friend of a friend. As she enters the hotel where the party is being held, she begins to have some feelings of trepidation (xenophobic feelings—strange place). But as she enters the ballroom she sees a laughing, animated group of people, dressed as she is, speaking in a very familiar accent. She immediately feels at ease and begins an evening of fun and enjoyment with some of the best people she has ever met. During the course of the evening she notices in an adjacent ballroom a group of people playing unfamiliar music, speaking in a strange accent. As the party progresses she hears loud noises and screams from the next ballroom. If her reaction is, "Why can't they act the way we do?—in a civilized manner," that's ethnocentrism. That ethnocentric thought would cause her to be very embarrassed when she finds out the hotel is on fire and that's the reason for the noise in the next room, and that the people in the next room were there to honor Mother Theresa.

Attitudes—we learn them from the home, culture, school, peer groups, and media. Ethnocentrism and xenophobia can result from misreading some very natural feelings. Now we know where attitudes come from, and although the emphasis has been on the negative effects of the sources, these sources can and do enrich us by providing diverse, new, exciting and interesting contrasts which can be the basis for understanding.

CHAPTER 2

Classifying Viewpoints:
Conservative and Liberal

Liberal and conservative are two terms that are often used to describe people, or people's political views. In fact each of us has hundreds, if not thousands, of attitudes and opinions on all sorts of issues. Since we shall be studying basic political, moral and economic ideas, and to a lesser extent the educational and social implications of those ideas, we should understand the meaning of the terms conservative and liberal in a larger and more complete sense.

First, let us understand that no one is a liberal and no one is a conservative. We are categorizing attitudes, not people. It would be foolish, indeed dangerous, to categorize people as one or the other. We all have attitudes and opinions which can be described as liberal and conservative, but those views can be different depending on the issue one is dealing with. It is quite frequently the case that a person can be basically conservative in a moral sense, and liberal in his educational views. Or one can be socially liberal and politically conservative. However, certain basic attitudes people hold, especially concerning the nature of man, often become the cornerstone of their philosophy. It then seems to be very reasonable and desirable to develop attitudes which are consistent. Before we begin the study of philosophical distinctions we will examine these two broad views of the world.

There are actually five broad visions of the existing institutions. Those visions affect our judgments about how those institutions will function best. A *reactionary* is one who would have things as they once were. He yearns for an olden time and a simpler way. He has a vision of the world which idealizes the past; he remembers the "good old days." The *conservative* is relatively satisfied with the way things are. If change is in the offing he tends to be skeptical and favors tried and true methods of advancement. He would rather live with the "devil he knows, than the devil he doesn't." The *liberal* sees change as a necessary and positive good. He is optimistic about the future and is willing to chance the results of progress. He lives by the maxim "things can be better than they are now." A *radical* wants to destroy the existing institution he is dissatisfied with, and create a new world, usually without institutions. He usually envisions a utopian world once the existing institution is destroyed. He wants to start all over again, and this time get it right. Finally, there is the *middle of the road* view of the world. The middle of the roader has no opinion, or more probably, cannot decide which position to take on an issue, so takes none. Often he lacks information or concern about the issue, so he chooses not to choose.

At this point let us be clear about the middle of the road position. Often it is confused with the idea of "moderate." The two terms are, in many cases, used interchangeably. In particular, as a political designation, the two terms are properly interchangeable and similar. But for our purposes, the middle of the road is the failure or inability to make a value judgment, and therefore, not a moderate position. As a matter of fact, the conservative and liberal are moderates, the reactionary and radical are at the extremes, while the middle of the road is simply not making a judgment and therefore, not expressing an attitudinal choice.

For our purposes we are going to eliminate consideration of the three positions other than liberal and conservative. The reactionary wants us to go back to a better time. In fact we can never go back; time, technology, population, scientific discoveries all change the world—in a real sense. We cannot go back to buggy rides in New York City, except in Central Park; we cannot expect a thriving steamship business transporting people across the Atlantic, now that we have airplanes. The reactionary who grew up in a small New England town with the town meeting form of government may remember it fondly, but will fight a losing battle if he attempts to reinstate it in Stamford, Connecticut.

The *radical* wants to destroy existing institutions; he blames them for our problems. Somehow the very institution is corrupt and without redemption, and his "new world" requires we begin

[handwritten marginal notes:]

that would change the failures that experienced the ignorant

makes the middle of the road seem lazy when they could just not have the same view/strategy for every situation.

isn't it possible to be in the middle and still have an opinion not just an extreme one or one that agrees with a side

a more ignorant person is the past because they have not experienced to go back then today then want to make them

understand that always our story and start a new.

reactionarys are people who would not leave the cave they'd rather not understand what evers simple is for them.

anew Edmund Burke, many years ago, noted that to destroy an institution—and it takes a revolution to do that—is to create a vacuum into which no one knows what will come. He would claim that man is an institution-creating animal, and that the destruction of the offending institution is only going to result in its replacement with another, maybe better, probably worse. In any case, to destroy what exists, in the hopes of gaining Utopia, is dangerous stuff. To reform the institution in need of repair seems a more reasoned approach.

The middle of the roader is not making judgments about the issues, and therefore, for our purposes is not important. We shall be studying a process of making judgments, reasoned judgments, about some important issues; the middle of the roader is not interested, he doesn't care. He would rather not know the issue, not join the debate, not make a judgment about the question. However, when one says, "I cannot choose because I do not have enough facts to make a judgment," that is a deferred judgment and laudable in fact as well as in relation to this study.

So let us briefly examine some of the general tenets of conservatism and liberalism. The extreme liberal is usually radical and the extreme conservative is often reactionary. The farther the two move away from their extremes the closer they become to one another, and at times the distinctions blur. And yet there are some basic tenets of each which have been fairly consistent over the years. We shall examine how both look at the nature of man, morality, society, politics, economics, education, and the world in general.

THE NATURE OF MAN

Conservatives view man as a very complex and intricate being, imperfect and imperfectable, a mixture of good and evil, but because of his flawed nature, with a propensity towards evil. Christian conservatives refer to this condition as "Original Sin." This view of man's nature has great implications for the way conservatives view man's relations with one another and the institutions he creates.

The conservative sees man as a dualism, a combination of mind and body. The mind is the knowing aspect, the body the

sensing and feeling aspect of his nature. Since Aristotle pro-
claimed reason as the element in which man has his essence,
conservatives obviously believe in the primacy of reason over
the feelings and emotions. The problems men have are a product
of their defective human nature, rather than of a defective social
order. Problems will always be with us. At best, through reason,
authority, tradition, self discipline, and a faith in God, man
should be able to prosper in this life—as Aristotle said, "through
good work and good fortune."

The liberal views man as basically good. He sees man as an
integrated whole, mind and body acting with and in response to
his environment. With man naturally inclined to do good, and
with an unlimited ability to control his own destiny, liberals tend
to be optimistic about man, the future, and the eventual perfect-
ibility of the social order. They see man, unfettered, as being able
to control the environment, which they hold responsible for
man's faults, and able to correct both personal and social ills.

Liberals tend to see the emotions, as at least the equal to
reason, and tend not to separate the two. Some consider feelings
as superior to cold reason, and believe that if man is naturally
inclined toward good, to go with those feelings is to go in the
right direction. The implications of the basic liberal view of the
nature of man will produce different approaches to man's
problems and the problems of his institutions.

MORALITY

Conservatives tend to believe in God, free will, absolutes,
prudence and self-discipline. Faith in God is the touchstone of
the conservative position. God is the perfect being from whom
absolutes flow and who has endowed man with free will to either
accept or reject those absolutes. Since the conservative recognizes the power of the emotions, prudent behavior is the balance
among the extremes to which our emotions carry us. Self-
discipline, in a way, is the demonstration of the primacy of
reason over the emotions, and therefore is high on the conservatives list of virtues.

The liberal tends to believe in man. This is not to say that the
liberal is an atheist, but in general, liberals prefer to attend to the
perfection of man, rather than to dwell on the perfection of God.

Liberals tend to believe in freedom, relativity, and self-expression. The freedom to experiment allows for the hoped-for progress, while the self-expression allows for a fuller life. Values are relative, since values are no different from anything else on earth, and everything on earth is subject to change. Liberals who believe in God would probably view God as an understanding God, while conservatives would see God as a forgiving God.

SOCIETY

To the conservative, society is like a living organism. It exists today as the sum total of the contributions of countless generations of individuals whose wisdom we would do well to contemplate. The conservative stands for order, tradition, evolutionary change, and a social structure based on the concept of a natural aristocracy. When societies experience violent upheaval they lose their continuity with the past and thereby jeopardize their future. Order and tradition provide the stability from which progress springs. No nation in turmoil can progress and improve. Since all men are equal only before God and the law, the conservative notes that all men are unequal in their talent and ambition. Given the freedom to exercise their talents, social diversity is a demonstration of a free society.

The liberal sees society as an institution which inhibits individuals, and therefore, places a premium on the need to experiment, change, reform, and progress. The liberal, looking to the future rather than the past, is willing to discard tradition easily. Social change is encouraged, especially when it results in equality, a virtue high on the liberal's list of priorities. Science and discovery are the vehicles liberals use to bring people into a better future, and the future is where they place their hopes. In short, liberals have an optimistic view of change, while conservatives are more pessimistic in their outlook.

POLITICS

The conservative view of politics is that the purpose of the state is to promote the good life. They believe in limited government, order, the rule of law, and enlightened representative leadership. Conservatives believe that ruling is a special skill which is learned by practice and example. While they don't subscribe to a fixed aristocracy, they do assert that the best rule is the rule of the best. The importance of good government requires that the good govern.

Law, to the conservative, is the result of centuries of imperceptible growth, not the work of one generation of constitution makers, or court decisions based on some current trends. Law, and the order that results from its enforcement, is necessary to provide for the stability which allows government to carry out its necessary functions. Conservatives generally support constitutionalism; limited government safeguards the people from the abuses of the power-hungry, and safeguards the government from the tyranny of the majority.

Liberals believe that government exists for the welfare of the people. Basic liberal postulates about the state and the role of government, are egalitarianism, the greatest good for the greatest number, democracy, and freedom. They see the state as a servant to the common well-being, equalizing opportunity and the benefits that the state provides. Democracy is the best means to accomplish the goals of the state, since a majority decision, by definition, provides the greatest good for the greatest number.

Freedom and free expression are the best means to effect the reforms that the liberal sees as necessary. Participation in the process, and the faith in democracy as the best means to achieve the ideal state, are major liberal assumptions. Through participation, freedom, and democracy, the liberal is eager to change any rules, written or unwritten, to equalize opportunity for all. While committed to change through existing institutions, in the final analysis, if all else fails, the liberal would accept a revolution to effect the required change.

ECONOMICS

The conservative views man as a competitive animal. The government should not regulate the economy, but should not allow a purely *laissez-faire* system either. The ideal would be a system where free competition would be encouraged, but laws would be in place to ensure justice. Due to man's innate inequalities, any attempt by government to distribute wealth equally would be unnatural and bound to fail. Private property is the economic foundation upon which all economic advancement is based. To tamper with the individual's right to private property would be to court economic disaster.

The liberal initially based his economic theory on the concept of freedom, and favored *laissez-faire* capitalism. As the inequities of wealth that resulted from unfettered *laissez-faire* capitalism became apparent the liberal view changed somewhat. The role of government became greater in order to limit the economic power of big businesses and safeguard the "life, liberty, and property" of the citizenry. Since the liberal sees man as basically cooperative, the government must restrain the abuses of the few, to free the majority to cooperate and progress economically. The concept of the greatest good for the greatest number is operative in liberal economics as well as in politics.

EDUCATION

Given the conservative's view of the nature of man, certain educational premises are forthcoming. The conservative believes in discipline, the primacy of the mind, the need to be a civilizing influence, and to transmit the cultural heritage. Since students would choose fun rather than work, discipline is necessary in the conservative educational environment. All people have rationality in varying degrees; reason is essential to human nature and therefore, all students should be taught to develop their minds. Students should be prepared to think, work, and become productive links in the unbroken chain of society.

The liberal believes that a child will choose good over bad and will not have to be forced to be productive if he is properly motivated. Also, since there is no mind-body dichotomy, there can be no primacy of the mind; thus physical, technical, and skill training exist on an equal footing with activities of the mind. Any problems which children manifest in the classroom are not willful acts but can be traced back to the environmental forces of the home, society, and school. Freedom of expression, experimentation, and creativity are encouraged in the liberal educational environment.

THE WORLD VIEW

There are many terms which describe how the conservative looks at the world. Caution—these are general terms which apply only to attitudes about issues. The conservative tends to be pessimistic about change, sees man as imperfect and imperfectable, but with a free will, seeks order and stability, cherishes tradition, ritual, the rule of law, authority, religion; believes man is competitive, is elitist, and supports limited government. He is a dualist, with a belief of the primacy of the mind, but with a faith in God.

The liberal on the other hand, sees man as good, society as the culprit. He favors change, experimentation, creativity; he believes in democracy, the greatest good for the greatest number, majority rule, egalitarianism, and redistribution of wealth. Man is cooperative, perfectible, and in control of his own political destiny; he is a humanist, with emotions which are natural and equal to the mind.

Of course one basic problem in defining these conservative and liberal terms is that historic development has brought about many flip-flops; i.e., ideas held by liberals were appropriated by conservatives, and vice versa. There is, then, a historic dimension which renders the definitions somewhat tenuous. Perhaps a good word to use in describing the attitudes of each would be "propensity." We could say that both conservatives and liberals, based on their premises, have a propensity to gravitate to the positions enumerated above.

Conservatives and liberals are both committed to achieving the "good life" for humankind. They both seek to improve the political, moral, social, economic and educational institutions which play such an important role in the daily lives of all of us. Both, however, begin with different premises. Thus they both have different solutions to the same problems. Both views of the world are continually changing as well; to be sure conservatives tend to change more slowly, while liberals tend to change more quickly—but that's the nature of the beast.

CHAPTER 3

Epistemology and Logic

Over two thousand years ago Pontius Pilate uttered one of the most profound questions ever asked, "What is Truth?" Epistemology seeks to answer that question and several other related questions. Epistemology is the study of knowledge: How do we know? Can we know? What can we know? What are the limits of our understanding? Questions about truth, knowledge, the uses of knowledge, have yielded several theories, some of which we will discuss in this chapter.

There are two broad theories about truth: one, that truth is objective; the other, that truth is subjective. Those who accept the objective theory of truth contend that there are certain truths, and those truths are absolute, eternal, immutable. The subjective view asserts that everything is relative; there are no absolutes.

The *absolutist* believes that there are truths that exist despite our opinion. Some absolutists believe that these truths can be known, others believe that some can and some cannot be known. All agree, however, that truth does exist. When many people believed that the world was flat, the objective fact was that the world is round, and regardless of the opinions of all those people who thought otherwise, the absolute is and was true. Later we will discuss the many ways we use to discern the truth, but for now, the point is that this theory states that the truth is objective, absolute, and often knowable.

The *relativist* believes that truth is relative and subjective. All of us apprehend knowledge, basically, through our senses. It is obvious that the senses can deceive, and therefore, all of us perceive things differently. The very different ways we make our judgments prove that truth is simply a matter of opinion. "Mary is a very beautiful girl" says John. Bill responds, "Yuk!" Same girl, two different opinions, how come? We shall spend a good deal of time investigating these two positions.

There is a third concept of truth, which is called *skepticism*.

This view contends that we cannot know truth, it is unknowable. Probably the most extreme Skeptic was a Greek named Gorgias. Essentially his contention was, "There is nothing. If there were something I wouldn't be able to explain it to you. If I were able to explain it to you, you wouldn't be able to understand it." For our purposes, skepticism is an unacceptable view of the world. If we were to accept skepticism as valid, this inquiry into the great ideas would be foolish. And in a larger sense, we would close all the books, shut all the schools, cease all study. To act in accordance with the philosophy of skepticism is to act in accordance with a philosophy which rejects the very basis for all action. (This is not to say that we should not be skeptical, or question, or challenge—the skepticism referred to here is the philosophical contention that we cannot know.)

We will discuss briefly some of the theories about the nature of truth and how we come to know it.

Idealism is a theory which contends that truth exists independent of man, as universal ideals. Those ideals are perceived by the mind and are understood perfectly in the mind, and in the mind only. Take for example, the concept of a circle. A circle exists as a universal, a perfect one dimensional figure of three hundred and sixty degrees, each point of which is equidistant from the center. One might see an automobile tire and say, "That's a circle." The idealist would contend that the tire is but a poor imitation of a circle, a material manifestation of the idea of a circle, but *not* a circle. A circle exists as an absolute (Plato called these ideals, forms), to be known only by the mind, and only the mind is capable of perceiving truth.

The *realist* sees truth as a reality which exists not simply in the mind, but in the relationship between mind and matter. Take the idea of a wall. The idealist would say that the cinder blocks piled in a room, which will eventually be the wall, are nothing more than a pile of cinder blocks. The mind of the mason conceives the idea of the wall. The blocks become the means to his realization of the idea. The realist, however, would contend that the idea of a wall is simply that, an idea—a wall is an integral combination of the idea and the blocks. Or as Aristotle would say, "No form without matter, no matter without form." Truth is discoverable by the senses as well as the mind.

A theory called the *correspondence theory of truth* is, in a sense, a realistic theory of truth. The correspondence theory contends that if an idea squares with the reality, then that idea is true. For example, if one has an idea that Boston is north of Providence, that idea is true if the idea corresponds to the physical reality of the relationship of those two cities. If a person talks of Shangri-La, an ideal place, a perfect land, the inability to make that idea correspond to the reality requires that we acknowledge Shangri-La to be a myth, a utopian dream—not a reality. Whenever an idea can be validated by the fact the idea presumes, we have truth.

The *pragmatic theory of truth* asserts that if it works, it's true. The way we determine truth is by the efficacy of action proven by results. It is true for example, that aspirin relieves headache pain. One has a headache, takes two aspirin, and the headache pain subsides. It follows pragmatically that the contention that aspirin relieves headache pain is true. This simple example may convince people of the validity of the pragmatic theory. In more complex areas, however, the concept of negative pragmatism is advanced; that is, if it doesn't work it can't be true. If one has a headache, takes aspirin, and the pain subsides, it could be because the pain was subsiding of its own accord, that the act of taking the aspirin triggered a psychological response which relieved the pain, or some other factor. Thus, one might assume pragmatically an erroneous conclusion. If, however, you have a headache, take aspirin, and the pain continues, you can be certain, according to negative pragmatism, that it is true the aspirin did not work.

The *existential theory of truth* contends that individuals create truth by choosing it. There are no truths independent of man; man is, in fact, the measure. Truth is subjective; each person chooses those truths which are important to him. And each man is free to choose, and in one sense, that freedom is the essence of truth. The basic tenet of existentialism, existence precedes essence, implies that there are no essential truths except within the particular existence of individuals. Obviously, existentialists do not reject the idea of physical reality, they do not bang their heads against stone walls—but—the essential nature of things is determined by the individual. Only the individual can determine the essential worth (value) of banging one's head against a wall.

The preceding theories are some of the more common approaches to understanding the answer to the question, what is truth? Obviously there are others, some worthy of consideration, others fallacious. What criteria one uses in determining truth is essential to what one comes to believe.

To use criteria such as majority rule, emotions, customs, and various other approaches can be valid. However, a reasoned understanding will help overcome the dangers of the subjective nature of these methods. Most people tend to determine truth and to act on the basis of personal, particular, and emotional responses to stimuli. Hopefully we can learn to determine truth and to act upon general, universal, and rational principles. It is important to note that the discovery of truth based upon sound methods of making the determination is nothing if one does not have the will to act upon those discoveries.

One of the means to better understanding is through clear thinking. Logic teaches us how to think clearly, reason properly, and in the process, discover truths. There are many kinds of logic; common sense is a type of logic called natural logic. Induction is a type of logic wherein we gather information and come to tentative conclusions. Deduction requires we argue from the universal to the particular. The study of logic is a major task; to understand the basics of logic could easily require a semester or two. Obviously we will not have the time in this introduction to basic philosophical ideas to learn formal logic, despite its importance. Hopefully, however, a short explanation of the syllogism, the classic deductive method, will whet the appetite for more inquiry into the study of logic. Also, we will examine some other methods, less formal, but of real value in the development of critical thinking skills. None of what follows will guarantee that we will perfect our thinking skills, but an awareness of the need to improve those skills should become apparent.

One of the best brief explanations of the syllogism appears in the National Council of Teachers of English publication, *A Glossary of Literature and Composition* by Arnold Lazarus and H. Wendell Smith.

Syllogism - A formal argument, chiefly in deductive reasoning, couched in rigid form, and observing rules that insure the validity of the conclusion. A typical syllogism

consists of three statements, as follows:
   a) Major premise: All cows are females.
   b) Minor premise: Bessie is a cow.
   c) Conclusion: Bessie is a female.
   ...The following kinds of syllogism will be discussed: (1) categorical, (2) conditional, (3) alternative, and (4) disjunctive.

   1. *The categorical syllogism* is so called because each of its statements is categorical, or absolute, with no "ifs" or other limitations. Understanding the principles of valid reasoning in the categorical syllogism requires a knowledge of the parts of the syllogism—their names, their aspects, and their functions.

   (a) *Term:* Each of the things named in the syllogism. In the syllogism about Bessie the cow, the terms are cows, females, and Bessie. Every categorical syllogism has three terms: the major term (the term in the predicate of the conclusion), the minor term (the term in the subject of the conclusion), and the middle term (the term that appears in both premises but not in the conclusion).

   (b) *Class:* Each term refers to (or names) a group whose members share certain characteristics. Cows are a class; females are a class; Bessie is a class—this time a class with but one member, or "a class of one."

   (c) *Statement:* A subject-predicate assertion; every syllogism contains three. Each statement contains two terms: one the subject of the statement, the other the predicate-complement of the statement. The two terms are linked by a verb, usually a state-of-being verb like is or are. When some other verb appears, the statement usually can be translated into an is or are statement; for example, if we assert that "All cows give milk," we must understand that milk is not a term in the statement, but milk-giving animals is the correct term, and we translate the statement as, "All cows are milk-giving animals." Statements in the syllogism do not imply equality. "All cows are females" does not assert that cows equal females; it asserts, rather, that the class called cows is included in the class called females. Syllogistic statements include or exclude; they do not equate.

(d) *Premises:* The first two statements in a syllogism, the major premise containing the major term, the minor premise containing the minor term.

(e) *Conclusion:* The final statement in the syllogism. It draws an inference based upon the two premises—and, when valid, justified by them.

(f) *Four forms of statement:* To understand how statements work in the categorical syllogism, we must consider two special aspects: quality and quantity.

In the context of deductive logic, quality concerns whether a statement is affirmative or negative. The statement "Bessie is a cow" is affirmative; it affirms that Bessie is a cow. The statement "No cats are cows" is negative; it denies that cats are cows.

In the context of deductive logic, quantity concerns whether a statement is universal or particular. The statement "All cows are females" is universal; it refers to all of its subject class—all cows. The statement "Some birds are robins" is particular; it refers to only part of its subject class—some birds.

These aspects make possible four forms of statement, designated by the symbols as A, E, I, O:

"A" form: the universal-affirmative (All x is y)
"E" form: the universal-negative (No x is y)
"I" form: the particular-affirmative (Some x is y)
"O" form: the particular-negative (Some x is not y)

These four forms of statement may be combined in several patterns to produce a syllogism - as long as their combination does not produce any violation of the rules of validity.

(g) *Distribution:* The "all" or "some" aspect of a term. Terms refer to classes of things; but when a term appears in a statement, it may refer to all members of a class or only to some members of the class. A term that refers to all members of its class is a distributed term; a term that refers only to some members of its class is an undistributed term. It is helpful to know the pattern of distribution of terms in the four forms of categorical statement:

Forms of Categorical Statement
in Deductive Syllogisms

<u>Statement</u>   <u>Distribution</u>

<u>Subject</u>   <u>Predicate</u>

"A" form: D   U

"E" form: D   D

"I" form: U   U

"O" form: U   D

Reference to the diagrams will show that a term whose circle is entirely shaded or entirely unshaded is a distributed term; a term whose circle is partly shaded is an undistributed term.

In the statement "All cows are females" we are discussing all cows; cows is a distributed term. But we are not discussing all females—only a few of them, the females that are also cows; therefore, females is an undistributed term. A few moments of study with the diagrams as aid will clarify the matter of distribution of terms.

(h) *Fallacy:* An error in the form or process of a syllogism. The most common fallacies in the categorical syllogism are these:

(1) *Undistributed middle:* The middle term in a categorical syllogism must be distributed once—and only once. Consider:

> All x is y.
> All z is y.
> Therefore ...?

No valid conclusion is possible, since the middle term, y, is undistributed in both of its appearances; it never refers to all members of its class. Also consider:

> All p is q.
> No r is p.
> Therefore ...?

Again, no valid conclusion is possible, since the middle term, p, is distributed both times it appears.

(2) *Four terms:* Every syllogism must have three terms, and only three. Consider:

> All c is d.
> All e is f.
> Therefore ...?

No conclusion is possible, since the minor premise is entirely irrelevant to the major premise.

(3) *Two particulars:* Every syllogism must have at least one universal premise. Consider these:

> Some Americans are men.
> Some girls are Americans.
> Therefore ...?

It is invalid to conclude that some girls are men, since girls may be among the Americans not mentioned in the first premise. Neither premise is a universal statement.

(4) *Two negatives:* Every syllogism must have at least one affirmative premise. Consider these:

No mothers are men.

Some grandparents are not men.

Therefore ...?

It would be invalid to conclude any relationship between grandparents and mothers. Neither premise is an affirmative statement.

(5) *Particular switched to universal:* If either premise is a particular, the conclusion must also be a particular. Consider:

All natives are citizens at birth.

Some natives are of foreign parentage.

Therefore, all who have foreign parentage are citizens at birth.

The conclusion is invalid, for it is an "all" statement when one of the premises was a "some" statement.

(6) *Negative switched to affirmative:* If either premise is negative, the conclusion must also be negative. Consider:

No voters are aliens.

Some citizens are voters.

Therefore, some citizens are aliens.

The conclusion is invalid, for it is affirmative although one of the premises was negative. The conclusion becomes valid if we convert it to negative: "Some citizens are not aliens."

(7) *Undistributed switched to distributed:* Any term that is undistributed in a premise must also be undistributed if it appears in the conclusion. Consider:

Some Texans are Democrats.

No Democrats are Republicans.

Therefore, some Republicans are not Texans.

The conclusion is invalid, for the term Texans is distributed in the conclusion although it was undistributed in the major premise. The conclusion becomes valid if we convert it to "some Texans are not Republicans," leaving the term Texans in undistributed form.

(i) *Enthymeme:* An elliptical syllogism. A valid conclusion may be drawn although not all the stages of syllogistic reasoning have been made explicit. Consider:

All lazy students are underproducers.

Therefore, Tim is an underproducer.

(j) *Sorites:* A series of interlaced syllogisms in which the conclusion of one syllogism becomes a premise of another, so that the chain leads to a conclusion connecting the subject of the first statement to the predicate of the last.

2. *The conditional syllogism* is so called because its initial premise is introduced by an "if" clause—a conditional clause. This "if" clause (called the antecedent) is followed by a "then" clause (called the consequent):

If he goes to the game, then he cannot study.
(antecedent)   (consequent)

Conditional arguments depend for their validity upon the proper application of a second premise, which must be in one of two modes:

(a) *Affirming the antecedent (modus ponens)*, in which the second premise affirms that the "if" clause, the condition, is true: "He goes to the game."

(b) *Denying the consequent (modus tollens)*, in which the second premise denies that the "then" clause is true: "He can study."

If he goes to the game, then he cannot study.
He goes to the game (modus ponens).
Therefore, he cannot study.
If he goes to the game, then he cannot study.
He can study (modus tollens).
Therefore, he does not go to the game.

Fallacies of the conditional syllogism occur when either of these modes is violated. The fallacies are affirming the consequent and denying the antecedent. For example, a second premise saying "He cannot study" would not permit a conclusion that "he does not go to the game"—because it is possible that he cannot study for other reasons. And a second premise saying "He does not go to the game" would not permit a conclusion that "he can study"—because the initial premise did not say anything about what might happen if he does not go to the game...

3. *The alternative syllogism* offers in its major premise an alternative in the "either-or" form: "Either we eat, or we starve." One of the alternatives must be true: therefore, if we show that one of them is false, we prove that the other is true. A valid argument reads:

Either we eat, or we starve.

We do not starve.

Therefore, we eat.

The major premise is an alternative (either-or) statement. The minor premise and the conclusion are both categorical statements, the minor premise denying one of the alternatives and the conclusion affirming the other. If the minor premise affirms an alternative ("we eat"), a fallacy appears:

Either we eat, or we starve.

We eat.

Therefore, we do not starve.

Odd as it may seem in the given context, the conclusion is not valid, for there is nothing in the premises to assure us that we cannot eat and also starve. The second premise commits the fallacy of affirming an alternative.

4. *The disjunctive syllogism* has a major premise in the "not both ...and ..." form: "Men are not both dishonest and happy." One of the two conditions must be false; therefore, if we show that one of them is true, we show that the other must be false. A valid argument reads:

We cannot both eat our cake and have it.

We have eaten our cake.

Therefore, we cannot have it.

The major premise is disjunctive; the minor premise and the conclusion are both categorical—the minor premise affirming one of the two disjunctive conditions. If the minor premise denies one of those conditions, the argument commits the fallacy of denying a disjunctive.

When one is familiar with the basic concept of syllogistic logic, an awareness of the problems of clear thinking should be apparent. This awareness, hopefully, will translate into some action—further reading in sources that deal with logic and related subjects. Recently, materials on logic, critical thinking, problem solving, and writing skills have become abundantly available for students at every level.

Beyond the ability to think clearly is a need to put those thoughts into writing. Often, writing itself is an excellent means to develop thinking skills. A very simple device which can help develop some ability in putting one's thoughts on paper in an organized manner is called the "resolve." This method is especially good in writing expositions. It employs the classical dictum "Define Your Terms." Take any assertion and apply the following outline.

I —Statement
II —Define any vague or ambiguous terms in the statement
III —Restate the proposition according to the redefinition
IV — A) State one fact to defend the statement
        1) Give evidence to support the fact A
        2) Give more evidence to support the fact A
    B) State another fact to defend the statement
        1) Give evidence to support the fact B
        2) Give more evidence to support the fact B
V —Conclude by affirming the proposition in III

The evidence in the body of the resolve—IV, A, 1, 2; B, 1, 2—can negate the statement that appears in III, allowing for the conclusion not to affirm but to deny the proposition.

Like the syllogism, the resolve is a rigid form and not particularly given to inspire the creative impulses. It is, however, a dialectical process; thus if we employ the "walk before we run" philosophy, within this concept, creativity can begin and hopefully develop along with the ability to think clearly and write well.

Thinking skills and writing ability can be greatly improved if one has an understanding of the syllogism and the resolve. There are, as stated before, several valuable methods which can be used to help develop critical thinking skills. But the most valuable asset a person can have is the disposition to meet problems with a critical, systematic, reasonable approach to the solution. In Chapter Four we will discuss fallacies, many of which will be easy to discern as erroneous contentions. The "why" of those errors should challenge your critical thinking skills.

CHAPTER 4

Fallacies:
Errors of Language and Logic

If indeed, the search for truth is difficult, as we have seen in the discussion of epistemology and logic, then an understanding of fallacies is an indispensable help in the process. A fallacy is an unintentional misuse of words or the reasoning process which causes misunderstanding, confusion, or false conclusions. We will not, in fact, study all the fallacies that it is necessary to recognize in order to reason correctly; rather we will study some of the more common errors, learn to recognize them, and hopefully develop an attitude toward listening which is more thoughtful, perceptive and helpful to understanding.

Linguistic fallacies are errors in the use of words. They are more common in the spoken word in the English language due to the nature of the language itself. *Red* or *read?*—the past tense of *r-e-a-d* is pronounced *r-e-d*. In context it should not pose too many problems, but this is a simple example of some more complex problems that arise when words are misunderstood because of misuse. We shall study six linguistic fallacies, all dealing with the misuse of words.

Non-linguistic fallacies are errors in the use of logic. Errone-ous reasoning causes these fallacies. If a person reasons, "Every time it rains the grass gets wet," and one day sees that the grass is wet and says, "the grass is wet, it must have rained," he has just committed a logical fallacy, a nonlinguistic fallacy, an error in reasoning. This, too, is a simple example of a logical fallacy, but most fallacies are more subtle and occur often in argumentation. We shall study eight nonlinguistic fallacies.

A sophism is an intentional fallacy, a deliberate misuse of words or logic with the intention of deceiving the listener. Aristotle called the Sophist one who "gives the semblance of wisdom without the reality." The purpose of studying fallacies is to recognize them, not use them. As with all knowledge, how it is used is critical. Happily, after the study of fallacies, morality will be the topic to be discussed; the juxtaposition of the two is not without reason.

LINGUISTIC FALLACIES

EQUIVOCATION Whenever a word is used more than once in a particular discussion or argument with more than one meaning assigned to that word, that is the fallacy of equivocation. This problem occurs when one assumes that the connotation is the same throughout the discussion. Often vaguely defined words cause this problem. It is interesting to note that one of the first principles of philosophical inquiry is "Define your terms." To do so is to guard against the fallacy of equivocation. Some examples of this fallacy follow.

> Every teacher is an academician.
> Every mother is a teacher.
> Therefore, every mother is an academician.

It is easy to see that the problem here deals with the word *teacher*. In the major premise it is used in a technical sense, while in the minor premise it is used in a general sense. Thus, the conclusion is false.

> Johnny is tall.
> Tall is an adjective
> Therefore, Johnny is an adjective.

This example shows how another false conclusion, as well as a foolish one, is the result of the use of one word which has been assigned two different meanings. Once again, the examples here are simple and would not cause problems in most discussions, but the subtle use of this fallacy can often confuse.

AMPHIBOLY This occurs when a sentence allows for two interpretations. Unlike equivocation, which is limited to a single word, amphiboly is ambiguity in a phrase or in the grammatical construction of a sentence. The most common cause of this fallacy is with dangling modifiers or misplaced modifiers. Often amphibolies can be the source of humor —"While driving to work one morning the dog was hit by the car." Or, "While standing on his hind legs the little boy played with his dog." But, sometimes an amphiboly, by allowing two interpretations, can pose a serious problem, as in Shakespeare's *MacBeth* —Act IV Scene I, where MacBeth is told, "Be bloody, bold, and resolute ...for none of woman born shall harm MacBeth."

COMPOSITION AND DIVISION   This problem occurs when in the course of a discussion a concept is taken collectively in one part and divisively in another, or vice versa. Errors due to the fallacy of composition and division are commonplace. For example, statements like, "Amherst College is a great school. John Jones, who teaches there, must be a great teacher." Or, "John Jones must be a great teacher. He teaches at Amherst College, a great school." Either way, however sound those statements seem, they are nothing more than fallacies of composition and division.

We come in contact with this fallacy daily when we hear about a particular teacher who is considered good; thus the school he teaches at is also "good." We hear about all the "big" games, and usually the media hype tries to equate the talents of the individual players with the forecast of who will win the "great" game. When a teacher describes his class as "great," the student who takes that comment personally, shouldn't. We simply cannot take comments that refer to groups, teams, organizations, and particularize them. Nor can we take evaluations about individuals or parts of a whole and generalize about them.

ACCENT (VICIOUS ABSTRACTION) This fallacy is least evident in the form its title suggests. The problem of misplaced emphasis on a word or syllable is usually easily detected and no great cause for concern. Sarcasm is usually easily discerned, so when some says, "You're a real winner," it is usually evident whether it's a compliment or an insult. When your mother says, "I hope you know what you're doing," you usually can tell whether she means, "I hope you know what you're doing," or "Don't do it, you'll mess up."

The more common form of the fallacy of accent is called

"vicious abstraction." Whenever a statement is taken out of context, it is, in effect, misplacing emphasis. This fallacy also occurs when a statement is taken out of the context of time. When you hear the axiom, "Money is the root of all evil," you have just been victimized by the vicious abstraction. Saint Paul really said, "Love of money is the root of all evil." There is a profound difference in the two statements. To accuse a person of recklessness for urging the use of the atomic bomb in 1945 without mentioning 1945 is an example of taking a statement out of the context of time. Politicians often accuse one another of the use of the vicious abstraction, both in terms of taking quotes out of context and out of the context of time.

PARALLEL WORD CONSTRUCTION   This fallacy (Fallacy of Form of Expression) consists of misconstruing the form of a word for its meaning. Usually this fallacy results from misunderstandings brought about by confusion over suffixes and prefixes. The most famous example of this fallacy occurs in John Stuart Mill's *Utilitarianism,* in which he states, "The only proof capable of being given that an object is visible, is that people actually see it. The only proof that a sound is audible, is that people hear it; and so of the other sources of our experience. In like manner, I apprehend, the sole evidence it is possible to produce that anything is desirable, is that people do actually desire it."

Mill's serious error lies in his confusion with suffixes. That which is visible is that which can actually be seen, that which is audible is that which can actually be heard, but that which is desirable is not so much what can actually *be* desired, but rather, that which is *worthy* of desire. We cannot help but see that which is visible, we will hear sounds within our hearing, but we can choose to reject that which we should desire.

Less important than Mill's problem with suffixes, but more relevant to our daily experiences, are the simple confusions which take place when we have problems with words like "inflammable," which used to be painted on the sides of gasoline trucks. Probably cigarette-smoking people who knew that the prefix "in" stands for "not" blew up a few of these valuable vehicles, not to mention themselves. Now we have a picture of a lighted cigarette surrounded by a bright red circle with a bright red line through it—all because of that misunderstood prefix. Words like "impatient," which means "not patient," and words like "impassioned," which means "full of passion," are typical of the types of problems that the fallacy of parallel word construction generates.

EMOTIVE LANGUAGE   When terms are used to arouse an emotional response rather that convey definitive meaning, the user commits the fallacy of emotive language. Of all the linguistic fallacies, this one is perhaps the most frequently used. Terms like Fascist, Communist, racist, chauvinist, are often used, not to convey understanding of what a person stands for, or believes in, but rather to disparage, insult, or undermine credibility.

Often the term Fascist is not used to describe a person who believes in irrationalism, the corporate state, or the organismic theory of the state, but is used simply to smear. If one has a serious disagreement on a question of policy, it is easier to call a person a racist than to convince him of the "error" of his judgment. And so it goes with words like Communist, extremist, chauvinist, feminist, ultra-conservative, knee-jerk liberal, bleeding-heart, fanatic, etc., *ad nauseam*. Some of the terms described here can be used to illuminate, some are pejorative and are used to denigrate. We should always be on our guard to know the difference.

It is important to note that all the fallacies discussed here have been due to the misuse of words:

Equivocation—using the same word with two different meanings.

Amphiboly—ambiguity in a phrase or sentence.

Composition and division—confusing collective and divisive terms.

Accent—misplacing emphasis, especially taking words out of context.

Parallel word construction—assuming that words which look alike have like meaning.

Emotive language—using words which evoke an emotional response.

NONLINGUISTIC FALLACIES

ACCIDENT   This fallacy occurs when one assumes that a

general rule (moral universal) can be rigidly applied in all cases that seem to fall under the extension of that rule. Whenever we take a general rule and apply it to a specific case we can create the problem of this fallacy. When we argue from the truth of the general to the supposed truth of the particular, we commit the fallacy of accident. For example:

> Youth is inexperienced.
> Joe is a youth.
> Therefore, Joe is inexperienced.

The major premise is a moral universal—by definition, youth is inexperienced when compared to older people. The minor premise is fine. The conclusion is valid. To conclude however, that Joe is inexperienced in particular activities, or a specific activity, would not necessarily be true. Joe might be young, but an exceptionally experienced sailor compared to most older men.

This fallacy also occurs when one confuses an accidental predicate with an essential predicate. White, for instance, is accidental to the essential nature of man; so is religion, nationality, or any color. To use any one of these accidental predicates to comment on the essential nature of any human being is to commit this fallacy. The concept of accidental predicates and the relationship to essential predicates extends beyond humans. Any confusion that arises when one attacks the essential nature of a thing, because of some accidental quality that in no way diminishes the thing itself, is an example of this fallacy.

SPECIAL CASE   This is the opposite of accident. If one presumes that what is true in one or more special cases is true in all cases without exception, he commits the fallacy of special case. Usually any leap from the truth of one or a few particular instances, to assuming a universal truth without exception, causes this fallacy. The two most common forms this fallacy takes in mistaken logic are 1) citing examples of an abuse of a thing to call for its abolition; or 2) noting the efficacy of a particular remedy in a few special cases, then claiming that it is universally effective. Consider one of the great fallacies of the sixties: "Everyone I know over thirty is untrustworthy, so, never trust anyone over thirty." Or a more mundane comment often heard about remedies: "Whenever I have a headache, I take _____(fill in the blank); take two of them and your headache will disappear."

Because of our lack of understanding of this fallacy, we continually recommend remedies, doctors, lawyers, stock brokers, only because our limited experience has been successful. Also, and perhaps worse, we seek to abolish all manner of things, not because of their intrinsic evil but because of abuses we know or hear about. Thus, prohibition of liquor was enacted because of drunkenness, and recently some have called for the abolition of Halloween trick-or-treating because of doctored candy and fruit being offered to children.

BEGGING THE QUESTION   Also called the circular argument, this fallacy arises when one tries to use his initial premise as proof of the conclusion reached. It is circular in that the argument continually refers back to the initial contention, which has not been proven, but is offered as proof. Consider the following dialogues:

> "Why do you drink?"
> "I drink to forget my problem."
> "What is your problem?"
> "I drink."

Or probably more familiar to many young people:

> "It's time to go to bed - go."
> "Why do I have to go to bed?"
> "Because I said to."
> "Why are you saying it?"
> "Because it's time to go to bed."

FALSE CAUSE   This fallacy assumes a cause and effect relationship when in fact there is none. We commit this fallacy when we assume that because something follows, it follows due to some causal relationship. This fallacy is often called *post hoc, ergo propter hoc* (after this, therefore because of this). When we see things in some juxtaposition, we conclude a necessary relationship which is not necessarily the case. To assume that since day follows night, night causes day, is an example of this fallacy. Also, this fallacy often gives rise to superstitions: find a four leaf clover, have good luck; or knock on wood, ward off bad luck.

A variation of this fallacy is called the inductive fallacy. In this instance we actually create in our mind the causal relationship. Most of us have probably had an experience with the inductive fallacy, or one similar to the following scenario. You are sitting in a room alone, reading. A young man enters the room, sits down, quietly begins to read. You finish your reading, get up, leave the room, and begin to walk out of the building. You notice you don't have your pocketbook with you. You run back to the room. It's empty, and there is no pocketbook in sight. So you say to yourself, "Son of a gun, that guy took my pocketbook." You call for help, help arrives, and as you search the room you find that the pocketbook had slipped behind the chair where you were sitting. The feeling of embarrassment that comes over you is the penalty you pay for committing the inductive fallacy.

FALLACY OF THE CONSEQUENT   This fallacy occurs when one assumes that, because one thing necessarily follows another, the reverse must also be true. If a person reasons that in order to have a baby one must be a woman, then concludes that to be a woman one must have a baby, that person has just committed this fallacy. Also, although we may have observed an authentic cause/effect relationship, we may not assume, when we see a similar effect, that the cause was the same. Earlier in this chapter an example of the fallacy of the consequent was used to show how some errors of logic occur. To conclude, because when it rains the grass gets wet, that it must be so that if the grass is wet it must have rained, is to be guilty of this fallacy, for in fact the grass may be wet for one of several other reasons.

COMPLEX QUESTION   This fallacy puts questions into a complex form which precludes all possible answers, either by asking more than one question in a sentence, or by phrasing the question in such a way that the answer must incriminate the respondent. The classic example is, "When did you stop beating your wife?" Or, "Do you always cheat on your tests?" Probably the less apparent, but equally frustrating, are questions like this, "Was Alger Hiss an intelligent and honest man?" The *fallacy of the complex question* often arises in debates or in movie court-room scenes.

TU QUOQUE   This means you yourself do it. When one says that a statement by an individual is false because the individual does not act in accordance with that statement, a *tu quoque* fallacy exists. For example, a teacher tells his students that they shouldn't smoke, it's bad for their health. The students respond, "Don't tell us that we shouldn't smoke. You do." The teacher's bad habit, or lack of will power, has nothing to do with the accuracy and veracity of his statement. Children are always questioning their parents about bed time, "R" rated movies, drinking liquor, and many other things that parents do while forbidding their children to do the same things. The mere fact that an adult does that which he forbids his children to do does not make the adult a hypocrite. Adults need less sleep, thus the child should be in bed earlier. "R" rated movies are rated for adults and not for children, because the content is at a more mature level. Drinking liquor in moderation is legitimate for adults. Young children, because of body weight alone, can and should be put off from such activity.

IGNORING THE ISSUE   This is also called the fallacy of irrelevant evidence. This fallacy consists in either disproving what has not been stated or proving a point other than the one at issue. This fallacy is very difficult to deal with because when a person is committing the fallacy his argument can and often does sound perfect. That's because the argument often *is* perfect—it just doesn't relate to the issue under discussion. This fallacy takes many forms, all of which divert attention from the critical issue. The most common examples are:

a) *Argumentum ad hominem:* Instead of dealing with the issue on its merits, this fallacy consists of attacking the man himself, his reputation, his honesty, his personal life, or any other shortcomings he may have. If one says, "Don't believe what he says, he's a convicted felon," that statement might have some merit if it relates to the felon's comments on his guilt or innocence. But, if a felon speaks on an unrelated issue, that issue must be refuted on the basis of it validity according to the facts.

b) *Argumentum ad miseracordium:* This fallacy ignores the evidence and attempts to divert attention from the facts to another issue which will evoke sympathy, pity, or any other emotion which will enhance the position of the arguer. When a student asks a teacher to change his grade to an "A" because if he doesn't get the "A" he will be rejected by the college his parents want him to attend, that's an appeal to pity and never addresses the question of why the student got the lower grade in the first place. Or, perhaps more important, the student's appeal does not address the question of why he should get the "A" when in fact he hasn't earned an "A". There are some very valid arguments a student can make which would justify the change, but those arguments must have merit in substance, not emotion.

c) *Argumentum ad baculum:* When the threat of force, coercion, intimidation, or other strong words are used in place of a reasoned argument, then the fallacy of *ad baculum* is operative. When a parent tells his child that he'd better clean his room or he'll be spanked—*ad baculum.* Or a more subtle example occurs when an employer mentions to an employee that the road to promotion is open to those who do not belong to the union, or when an employee mentions to an employer that the next pay raise had better be large or there just might be a strike.

d) *Argumentum ad vericundium:* This is an appeal to prestige. This fallacy occurs, when to gain acceptance of an idea, a product, or a position, one tries by association to link up with a prestigious person or institution. One sees this fallacy in operation most frequently when celebrities endorse products and the public is asked to purchase the product, not because there has been any demonstrated superiority of the product, but simply because the celebrity has commented favorably on it. Celebrities who campaign for political candidates are using public recognition and acceptance to convince others to vote for a particular person. If the celebrity says, "Vote for this man. I know him. He's a good person, and I intend to vote for him for the good of the country," that's an *ad vericundium* argument. If the celebrity makes a cogent argument, speaks to the issues, and presents the facts, and on that basis, convinces - then the argument that is advanced is not tainted by the *ad vericundium* fallacy.

e) *Argumentum ad populum:* This fallacy is an appeal to the masses, their emotions, their prejudices, their feelings. This fallacy contends that quantity is quality - we see it in advertisements: "Three out of four people interviewed chose _____(fill in the blank)." The most familiar form of this fallacy occurs whenever we hear the phrase, "Everybody's doing it, so it must be OK." Or "Billions of hamburgers sold." The idea that everybody's doing it, everyone is reading it, everybody is dressing this way, everybody likes so and so, is a meaningless comment. The issue is—everyone is reading it, but is it worth reading, is it good reading, and why?

f) *Argumentum ad ingnorantium:* The appeal to ignorance. In this fallacy there are three forms which constitute the appeal to ignorance: 1) it is assumed that what might possibly be true is actually true; 2) it is assumed that a statement is correct simply because an opponent cannot prove it false; 3) it is assumed a complete argument is false because some non essential element in the argument is proven false. Examples of each of these fallacies follows:

Form 1—President Eisenhower once warned us about the power of the "military/industrial complex." To say there is some sort of collusion between the military and industry is easy, since both work closely together. But to say it is not to prove it, and prove it you must.

Form 2—When a person proposes a thesis it is his obligation to prove it, not to challenge another to disprove it. So, to say "Life on Mars does exist, prove me wrong," is an example of form 2.

Form 3—Often called "nit picking," this form takes a minor, non essential part of a statement, proves it wrong and concludes that the whole statement is false. For example, "On December 7, 1941, at 9 a.m., the Japanese attacked Pearl Harbor, which effectively brought the United States into World War II." "Ha!" says the nit-picker, "the attack took place at 8 a.m.—You are wrong." The statement is essentially correct. The time is incidental to the truth of the statement .

These are just some of the nonlinguistic fallacies that get in the way of the accuracy needed to reason well. It is not so important that we know all of them, but that we are aware of what they are and how they hinder our approach to thinking, and therefore, our understanding. All the following nonlinguistic fallacies are errors in reasoning:

Accident—applying general rules to specific cases.

Special Case—creating an absolute general rule from a few examples.

Begging the question—stating your conclusion in your premise then proving your premise, going round and round.

False cause—assuming a cause and effect relationship where there is none.

Fallacy of the consequent—assuming that if A causes B, then B must cause A.

Complex question—asking more than one question at a time or stating the question in such a way so as to preclude a correct answer.

Tu Quoque—invalidating a premise because the poser cannot live up to it.

Ignoring the issue—side-stepping the issue and making a cogent argument about another matter.

PART 2

MORAL PHILOSOPHY: IDEAS OF GOOD AND EVIL, RIGHT AND WRONG

CHAPTER 5

Moral Philosophy:
A Brief Introduction

It seems that man is by nature a value setting animal. We speak of the good life, and ask how best to go about achieving it. Aristotle begins his *Nichomachean Ethics* with the statement, "Every art and every inquiry, and similarly every action and pursuit, is thought to aim at some good; and for that reason the good has rightly been declared to be that at which all things aim." So, we begin the study of ethics, the study of the right and wrong of human conduct. We shall examine some traditional views and some contemporary views as to how we go about determining some of the rights and wrongs of human conduct. Finally, we will learn about twelve moral philosophies and discuss the unique contribution of each to this most important subject.

The terms ethics and morality are often, and properly, used interchangeably. However, there is a technical difference between the two terms. Ethics is the study of human conduct, and attempts to determine the norms which are considered to be good, as well as those which are considered to be bad. Morality attempts not so much to decide first principles, but to decide how to act upon them. Ethics deals with the study of right and wrong, morality deals with the doing of right and wrong.

Immanuel Kant put forward three postulates which he determined to be necessary to the study of ethics:

1) *Free Will.* Kant maintains that one must accept the concept of free will if there is to be any value in the study of ethics. If man is a determined being, has been shaped by his environment, and simply responds to stimuli, then there is no reason to study ethics—we do what we are programed to do and cannot assess value for acts over which we have no control. Free will is the basis for our human acts which have moral worth—to choose or not to choose, that is the great moral question. Kant contends that

we have that ability. Indeed, we must have that ability. He grants that the environment has an effect on us, but in the final analysis we have the will to choose freely, right or wrong.

2) *The immortality of the soul.* The idea of the soul which transcends our brief existence on this earth is also one of Kant's premises. He maintains that some of the choices we are faced with must be seen in a context larger than the immediate results that a particular choice will produce. The concept of a spirit, an everlasting aspect of our being, must necessarily be taken into account in making moral choices. Moral choices are too important to be made simply on the basis of whether or not we will be pleased with the results for the moment.

3) *The existence of God.* There is a standard which exists for all men, set by the Author of the Universe, which we are duty bound to try to meet. The idea of a standard, set by ourselves, changing whenever we feel the mood or inclination to change, evolving as we grow older, determined by accidents of birth, birthplace, nationality, and culture would render ethics useless—sociology would be more important.

Obviously there are contrary opinions about these three requirements set by Kant. Is it necessary to believe in God in order to be good or to be able to tell good from evil? Must one look to eternity in order to be good, or can one see the value of good conduct in this life, for this life? And if, indeed, we are conditioned to be one thing or another, does that render us incompetent to make valid judgments about the acts we witness or perform? We will be looking for answers to these questions, from existentialists, hedonists, pragmatists, and others. We will however, begin with the traditional view, and use it as a starting point, to be developed or challenged.

Ethical inquiry employs two methods from which determinations as to the rightness or wrongness of human conduct are made. *A priori*—which means "before experience"—deals with postulates which are considered to be self-evident, and deduces moral judgments from the premise. Some a priori postulates— One should do good and avoid evil; all men are equal before God, or before the law. *A posteriori*—"after experience"—deals with judgments which we make on the basis of our experiences, from which we determine the rights and wrongs of human conduct inductively. Some a posteriori examples—we see how drunkenness ruins lives, thus conclude drunkenness is bad; we see how lying disrupts family, friends, and neighbors, thus determine lying to be bad.

When we say that a person has acted morally, we have made a judgment about the act as being right. When we say that a person has acted immorally, we have made a judgment about the act as being wrong. When we say that a person has acted amorally, contemporary usage notwithstanding, we are are making a judgment about the *act* as being neither right nor wrong. Most acts are amoral acts. How do we determine the difference between moral acts and amoral acts? How do we know when an act is immoral or simply undignified, or unpleasant?

Traditionally, moral acts have been considered to be a) serious, b) affecting the basic direction of our life, the life of others, or society, c) willful acts. Aristotle and St. Thomas Aquinas have proposed that a moral act has three main qualities:

1) *Knowledge.* A moral act must be one which engages the use of the intellect. One must focus upon the act to be performed, have knowledge of the ends desired, the means employed, and finally, must reflect upon whether or not the act should be performed.

2) *Voluntarism.* A moral act must be an act of the will; it must be a willed act. Earlier we spoke of knowledge of the truth as important, but acting on the fact is even more important. To know, and with that knowledge and after the deliberation, to act, is the essential nature of a moral act. A willed act is not necessarily a willing act. One can willingly accept an invitation to the movies, one can also unwillingly accept an invitation to the movies—and in both cases have employed an act of the will. In both cases the element of voluntarism could, and would, be present.

3) *Freedom.* This presupposes that there are moral choices; it is similar to voluntarism but with some differences. If one is faced with a situation where in fact there is no moral choice, one can voluntarily act even though he was not really *free* to do so. In the previous example dealing with movie invitations, you are free to choose to go or not to go. But if while in that movie your companion faints, you are not really free to leave him lying there; you are, in a sense, obliged to help. Thus, freedom is lessened in that situation. Or, if you become emotionally involved in an

issue, freedom can be lessened because your emotions obscure the issue of choice. Interestingly, your emotional involvement will increase voluntarism.

Of the three criteria of a moral act, knowledge, voluntarism, and freedom, voluntarism is most important in that there are consequences that follow voluntary acts. The consequences are—simply put—responsibility. There is responsibility in the actor, imputability in the act, and merit in both. That is, the actor is responsible, in a positive or negative sense, for his action. The act cannot be recalled; it produces a positive or negative result. There is merit in both the actor and the act, but of major significance is the concept of *intent*. Intent is the primary determiner of whether the actor and the act has merit. Any good act, performed with knowledge, voluntarism, and freedom, can have a bad result. The result cannot be changed—but if the intent was good, the moral worth of the actor is not diminished.

There are, however, modifiers of responsibility. Ignorance, passion, fear, force, and habit can alter an individual's responsibility for his moral acts.

There can be no voluntarism where there is complete ignorance. Also, there are two kinds of ignorance, vincible and invincible. Invincible ignorance is that ignorance which cannot be overcome, either because the person involved does not know he's ignorant, or if he does know, cannot find the information to correct the problem. Vincible ignorance is ignorance which can be overcome by obtaining the requisite information. The amount of effort in proportion to the person's ability to overcome his ignorance is the determining factor of responsibility.

A person who is truly ignorant, is invincibly ignorant, has no responsibility. A person who buys a stolen piece of property from a reputable store cannot be held morally culpable. Invincible ignorance destroys responsibility.

Vincible ignorance does not destroy responsibility, but it can lessen responsibility. If, for example, a person is ignorant and does not make sufficient efforts to educate himself, the consequences of his action are, in effect, his responsibility. Certainly he is not responsible to the extent of one who has full knowledge, but is responsible to the extent that the consequences of ignorance could have been avoided. If a person who is not prepared to fly an airplane takes a rider up with him before he is in full command, crashes the plane, and the rider dies, the pilot is not fully responsible for the death, but is responsible for the crash which caused the death.

The less knowledge, the less responsibility. But always remember that the less effort exerted to overcome ignorance, the more responsibility—while the more effort exerted, the less responsibility.   but

There is another category called "affected ignorance," which can either lessen (only in the sense that all ignorance affects knowledge), or usually, increase responsibility. If one purposely remains ignorant in order to have an excuse if his actions turn out wrong, he can actually increase responsibility because, in fact, he has willed to be ignorant. If a person who is offered a Rolex watch for fifty dollars is asked by the seller, "Don't you want to know how I can sell this so cheaply?" and replies, "No, I don't want to know anything about it," the buyer is using ignorance to facilitate the act. The bartender who doesn't want to see an ID, for fear of what he will learn by seeing it, is responsible for serving the teenager. The bartender who doesn't ask for an ID because a person truly seems to be of age is less responsible.

Succinctly, then, invincible ignorance destroys responsibility; if there was no way to know, lack of knowledge absolves the actor of responsibility. Vincible ignorance lessens responsibility; there was a way to know, and to the extent the actor tried to know, his responsibility is lessened. Affected ignorance in no way lessens responsibility; the actor purposely chose to be ignorant in order to have a ready excuse for an act he was about to commit. Affected ignorance can actually increase responsibility.

Passion is that strong emotion which engulfs us; anger, pity, disgust, lust, grief, joy, all affect us, often in a spontaneous way, due to circumstances. If these feelings overwhelm us in a spontaneous incident, it is called "antecedent passion," and it lessens responsibility. If, however, these feelings are fostered, nurtured, even conjured up by ourselves for our own purposes, it is called "consequent passion," and it can increase responsibility.

Antecedent passion can destroy responsibility. If a person is totally overcome by an emotion and performs an act over which he has no control, responsibility is destroyed. This is probably a rare occurrence, but it is possible to be so spontaneously overcome as to be rendered incapable of voluntary action. If a person is so overcome by grief after witnessing a terrible tragedy that he rushes recklessly into the street and causes a serious accident, he is, in fact, morally not responsible. Usually, however, passion is not the controlling factor in our actions. Most of the time passion affects us, drives us, often tempts us, but hardly ever controls us. To the extent that passion lessens our freedom to act, to that extent it lessens our responsibility.

Consequent passion can actually increase responsibility. It certainly doesn't lessen responsibility. The person who knows that X rated movies arouse him to the point of performing sexual acts on unwilling partners, and chooses to enter that X rated movie house, is fully responsible for any immoral act resulting from the consequent passion. A person who daydreams about the pleasure of money, jewels, and riches to the extent that he commits robberies to fulfill his daydreams is also responsible.

Fear can lessen responsibility; it does not destroy responsibility. If the fear is so overwhelming that one is out of control, it would be more akin to passion. Fear is a modifier of responsibility when it enters into a considered judgement. A person cheats because he is afraid of failing, lies on his college application because he is afraid of rejection—this is the type of fear we are discussing here. Each person has a greater or lesser tolerance for fear than every other person. To the extent that a person resists the fear and attempts to face possible negative consequences, to that extent he has modified his responsibility.

Threats, duress, intimidation, all can cause us to act in an immoral way, but they do not force us to act in an immoral way. When we choose to act one way because we are afraid of the consequences of acting another way, we are responsible. However, to the extent that the fear is real, to the extent we fight it, to the extent we wish we did not have to act—to that extent responsibility is modified.

Force is the actual perpetration of violence upon a person, and to the extent that we resist, physically and/or by internal resistance, to that extent we are not morally responsible. Internal resistance is simply non compliance with the aggressor; external resistance is actual physical resistance. If, indeed, a person knows that physical resistance is useless, he need not resist physically. One may never voluntarily comply, however, with the aggressor. A woman being raped is bound to resist physically. If, however, a gun is put to her head and death is imminent, she need not resist physically, but simply not comply with her aggressor, mentally or physically.

Habit is a way of acting learned from constant repetition, to the point where the action becomes second nature to us. How often have you seen a person light up a cigarette when he still has one burning in the ashtray? The lighting of the cigarette was more from the force of habit than an intellectual choice to smoke. If he were thinking, he would have reached for the one in the ashtray.

Some habits are deliberately acquired. People who automatically say, "yes, sir, no, ma'am," have acquired a habit, and could have acquired it purposely. Habits acquired purposely, if good or bad, are our responsibility. Other habits we acquire knowing that the action can become habit-forming, but with no intention of forming a habit, are our responsibility also—like smoking or drinking. Most smokers begin to smoke knowing smoking is habit forming, but convinced that they will not become addicted.

Other habits are unintentionally acquired, and we are responsible to the extent we accept the habit without efforts to change. A person who unintentionally becomes addicted to a drug, and begins to destroy himself through the use of this drug, is obliged, once he knows he is addicted, to try to break the habit. He is responsible to the extent he makes the effort: great effort, less responsibility; little effort, greater responsibility.

The foregoing are some of the most basic traditional, rationalist concepts about how we determine moral actions. These ideas come under the general heading of "traditional morality." Other concepts will be introduced in depth as we examine philosophers who challenge the ideas of Aristotle and St. Thomas. For now, some of the philosophical ideas contrary to the traditional are:

Pragmatism: The philosophy which contends that the truth and validity of an idea, and its moral worth, are in the result when the idea is tested. John Dewey's brand of pragmatism is called Instrumentalism; Dewey considers ideas as instruments used in the scientific method of solving problems.

Hedonism: The philosophical idea which maintains that pleasure is good, pain is bad, and that is the basis upon which we make our moral judgments—and ought to.

Utilitarianism: This philosophy maintains that actions should be judged in a moral sense according to their utility in providing the greatest good for the greatest number. There is a hedonistic aspect to Utilitarianism, defined differently by Bentham and Mill, but with pleasure as the central theme.

Existentialism: The idea that existence precedes essence, and that man's only essential characteristic is that he is free and what he is or becomes is the product of his free choices. Existentialism is very contrary to rationalism, in that existentialists believe that a man becomes what he chooses to be, rather than chooses because of what he is.

Philosophical positions such as Naturalism, Skepticism, and Pessimism will all be examined in the following chapters. We have begun with definitions of ethics and morality, examined some traditional postulates about reason in ethics, and with a premise of free choice and the individual's responsibility for his actions, referred to those modifiers of human responsibility. Now we will examine what individual philosophers have to say about ethics and morality. Obviously there will be great diversity of opinion, mainly because each begins with a different postulate. Each has his *"summum bonum,"* his greatest good, and based upon what each sees as the highest good, he will develop his idea of right and wrong, good and evil.

As we work our way through the next six chapters there are certain key questions to aid understanding that should be asked when reading about the philosopher's views. What is his position about the nature of man? How does he think we know, so that we can make the judgments about how to act? What is his concept of the highest good *(summum bonum)*? How should we go about achieving the *summum bonum*? What are his views on good and evil? What is virtue and how does one become virtuous? Finally, what constitutes the good life?

CHAPTER 6

Plato and Aristotle:
Idealism and Realism

Plato (427-347 B.C.)

From the time of Plato's death to the early Middle Ages, his thought dominated the Western world. He was the first Greek philosopher who sought to elevate the idea of knowledge, from means to ends, to a valuable end in itself. Plato's idealism is the philosophy which became the cornerstone of the temple of western thought.

Plato was born in Athens in 427 B.C., one year after the death of Pericles. His father, Ariston, who died when Plato was a child, belonged to a prominent family of the Periclean Age that could be traced to the last king of Athens. Perictione, Plato's mother, was descended from Dropides, a relative of Solon, the great Athenian lawmaker. After her husband's death, she married her uncle Pyrilampes, an intimate friend and supporter of Pericles. Wealth and position in high Athenian society enabled Plato to obtain the best education offered at that time. He was brought up in a household committed to the traditions of public service and imbued with ideas of Periclean democracy.

Although Plato's home life was secure and stable, he was born into and lived through a period of moral degeneration and political turmoil. From his seventh letter (epistle), the chief source of biographical information we have about Plato, we learn that he was always interested in political affairs. He reveals his ambition to have a political career, but also tells of many youthful disappointments with politics, perhaps the most profound of which was his witness of the fall of Athens.

At the age of twenty Plato met Socrates, who was to become his teacher and good friend. This relationship intensified Plato's interest in politics. However, the new revolutionary government horrified him, yet with the return of democracy came the execution of Socrates, which shattered Plato's faith in politics and in democracy. After the death of Socrates, Plato withdrew from politics and devoted himself to philosophy. He used the Socratic method and continued to investigate the nature of ideas.

For about ten years after Socrates' death, Plato traveled; he also began to write. The attempt to put his writings into a sequential order has been made by many authorities, and it is generally accepted that in his "Socratic" period he wrote *Apology, Euthyphro, Crito, Charmides, Laches, Protagoras, Meno, Euthydemus, Gorgias,* and *Lysis*. During the "Platonic" period he wrote *Cratylus, Symposium,* the *Phaedo,* the first part of the *Republic,* then the *Phaedrus, Theaetetus,* and *Parmenides* and the rest of the *Republic,* and finally the *Sophist, Politicus, Philebus, Timaeus, Critias,* and the *Laws*.

At about the age of forty Plato settled down in Athens and established a school to teach and explore the ideas learned from Socrates. In his works, *Protagoras* and *Meno,* he questioned whether it is possible to teach such ideas, and determined that it was possible. Thus was born the Academy.

Plato devoted the latter part of his life to teaching and lecturing at the Academy, where his most famous pupil, Aristotle, studied. His *Dialogues,* of which the *Republic* is the most famous, is the earliest masterpiece of philosophy. He began his life believing that politics was the means to the good life, and ended his life looking to philosophy as the answer to life's most crucial issues.

Before we begin the study of Plato's moral philosophy, we should examine his concept of the nature of ideas. To Plato all sense experience is faulty and transient. For example, the straw in a half-filled glass of water looks crooked due to the illusion caused by refraction. Our sense of sight, then, deceives. If we touch dry ice, it feels hot, when, in fact, it is cold. We cannot hear the high pitch of a dog whistle, yet dogs react immediately. Our senses often deceive us. If this is so, then the experiences to which we give so much credence are flawed. Certainly, true knowledge cannot be obtained from the actual world. Note that he uses the word "actual," not "real." The material substances which make up the phenomenal world are less real to Plato than the idea (form) of the thing itself. What are these ideas, and how does Plato explain them? Before we undertake to understand this concept, it is necessary to know that to Plato the term "idea" and the term "form" are interchangeable, one and the same.

Take for example, horses. Horses come in many different sizes and colors. Some can run fast, others can pull heavy loads. They are, while all alike, different. Yet there are certain characteristics which are central to, and constant in, horses. All horses have hooved feet, particular facial features, particular type of hair, generally similar legs and torsos. All have four legs, tails, and can easily bear the weight of a man. We can, in fact, describe a horse generally, and compare the similarities and differences of a horse with a mule and a zebra. There is, says Plato, the ideal horse, the pattern of which, though immaterial, is the real horse. The reality of the ideal (form) is eternal, immutable, and perfect. The actual horse is material, sensual, and transient. The essential nature of a horse does not exist in the person of Man o' War, but rather in the form which Man o' War approximates.

Since reality exists as an idea, immaterial and eternal, one cannot expect to obtain knowledge through sense experience. Surely, the physical world is a reflection of reality, but not reality itself. Logically, it follows that the mind is the means to understanding and truth. And the method, learned from Socrates, is the dialectic. The dialectic is simply the critical examination of ideas, pushing each to its logical conclusion, to find the truth. Or pushing an idea to its logical conclusion, to show the error.

An example of how Plato sought to teach an understanding of his doctrine of ideas is the "Allegory of the Cave." This is a story, in parable form, about a group of prisoners in a cave, chained in such a way that they can only look at the wall in front of them. The light from the cave's entrance casts shadows of the people, cattle, and wagons that pass by the entrance, onto the wall of the cave. Thus, the prisoners see only shadows, and those shadows are their only reality.

One of the prisoners frees himself from the chains, and escapes from the cave. As he enters into the sunlight, he is blinded by the brightness of the sun. Slowly, his eyes adjust to the light, and he begins to see the people, cattle, and wagons as they really are. Eventually, he is able to see the sun itself. Thrilled by the discovery, not only of the "light," but the source of the light, he returns to the cave to tell his former prison mates of his new-found knowledge.

[handwritten margin note: horse example]

When he explains to those still chained that what they understand to be reality is nothing more than a world of shadows, and that outside the cave there exists the real world of light and color and three dimensions, they not only refuse to believe, they laugh and revile him. The moral, then, of the "Allegory of the Cave" is that no one can be taught to understand reality; one must discover it for himself. And it is a difficult task; one must understand that the senses deceive, the familiar is difficult to discard, and one must be willing to venture forth into a strange and foreign world in order to know.

In addition to his theory of ideas, Plato believed in the doctrine of Teleology. A teleological view of the universe maintains that every thing has a purpose. Nothing comes into being for no purpose, and conversely, everything has a purpose, including man. What is man's purpose, then, and how does Plato come to determine what the end is? Plato contended that there are scientific ideals, and ethical ideals. The scientific ideals are found in math, numbers and proportion. The ethical ideals are found, less precisely, in the concepts of justice, temperance, and courage. It is in these ethical ideals that Plato sees the teleological end of man. Plato concludes that the teleological end of man is virtue. But why should a man be virtuous, and how does one become virtuous?

Each of us, says Plato, is composed of three basic elements— reason, spirit, and appetite. Based upon what we already know about Plato, it should be easy to discern the hierarchy that he assigns to each. How each individual develops each of these three elements in their proper proportion and relation determines his character. The teleological end of reason is wisdom. The teleological end of spirit is courage. And the teleological end of appetite is temperance. The man who develops wisdom, courage, and temperance in their proper proportions is a just man, and the just man is morally virtuous. Later, when we discuss Plato's political philosophy, we will see how this concept of justice applies to the state. But for now, we will try to understand how justice, properly proportioned, is architectonic.

An analogy will help to understand the idea of architectonic justice. A man wants to build a magnificent home and to that end hires the best craftsmen he can find. The best framer, roofer, painter, door-maker, window-maker, cabinet-maker, etc., etc.

One might mistakenly assume that the home will be a masterpiece, with all the best men available working on it. Not so. There is one major factor that is missing, without which the home might easily be a disaster. Without an architect to see to it that all these excellent components are put into a proper relationship, one with the other, the necessary symmetry of the whole will be askew.

Likewise, a man must not only perfect his mind, spirit, and appetite, he must do so in proper proportions. If one is basically intellectual, wisdom should dominate. If one is basically appetitive, he must develop a greater temperance; that virtue will be most necessary since he lacks intellect and spirit. A man whose basic disposition it to be spirited, must harness that attribute and develop courage. Each man must develop to the fullest those attributes with which God has endowed him, and in doing so will create the house which the architect has designed. Plato applies this theory to the state, which we will see in his political theory, and develops a pyramidal organization which he conceives as the ideal state.

Since knowledge, the means to wisdom sits atop this pyramid, it is the supreme good. In many of his dialogues some of the characters challenge Plato's contentions. Some of the characters in his scenarios argue that men would forsake knowledge for pleasure while others contend that they might choose power. Plato rejects both in his dialogues with the sophists Glaucon, Thrasymachus, and Callicles. The sophists contend that injustice is better than justice, since it provides the greatest pleasure, i.e., happiness. The person who can be unjust on a grand scale and achieve power over others will be much happier than those over whom he exercises power. It is better to dominate than to be dominated.

Thus, there arises the issue of knowledge or pleasure, which is the highest good? Plato maintains that knowledge is the highest good, and that when men act in pursuit of pleasure, they are simply acting in ignorance. Plato believes that no man knowingly does evil, but that when one is overcome by pleasure, knowledge is blurred, and evil occurs. If one knew for certain that a particular act was wrong, he would not perform it. Because some acts are so obviously wrong, most men do not murder, steal, rape, plunder, and pillage. Plato would contend that it is the knowledge of the evil of those acts which restrains us. Most evil comes from the lack of understanding of the nature of the act. When we are faced with decisions that we have to ponder, should I, shouldn't I, we can, and often do, choose evil over good. But, says Plato, if we knew, *truly knew,* what we were doing, we would choose the good.

When one understands Plato's concept of the physical world—that it is imperfect, temporary, deceptive, and in that sense, evil—one can begin to understand his view of knowledge. Knowledge is the understanding of the *good,* and the *good* can only be known through the mind. This world we know through the eyes; the real world we know through the mind. That eternal, perfect, immutable world of forms which exists outside the material world is where we must look to find the *good,* and we can, if we seek knowledge and obtain wisdom.

Aristotle (384-322 B.C.)

Aristotle was born in Stagira in 384 B.C. His father, Nichomacus, was a doctor and the personal physician of King Amyntas II of Macedonia, father of Philip the Great. After his parents' death, Aristotle was brought up by a relative in Atarnea.

At the age of eighteen Aristotle went to study at Plato's Academy. He remained there as a student, and probably in part as a teacher, for twenty years, until the death of Plato. Then, unhappy with the program of the Academy without Plato, Aristotle left with a group of students and continued his studies. He developed a close relationship with Hermias, a fellow student who was a political ally of the King of Macedonia. Through this connection Aristotle got a job as tutor of the King's son, Alexander. At the age of forty-nine, Aristotle left Macedonia and returned to Athens, where he founded the Lyceum. It was at the Lyceum that he taught, wrote, researched, and developed the greatest library in the ancient world.

When Alexander the Great died in 323 B.C., Aristotle left Athens in the wake of anti-Macedonian sentiments, which some say threatened Aristotle's security. Rather than fall victim to Socrates' fate, Aristotle left, not allowing Athens to "sin against philosophy twice." He died a year later on the island of Euboea.

Aristotle considered himself a Platonist, but developed, nevertheless, new and opposing directions of his own. During his

early writings after leaving the Academy, he worked out interpretations of Plato that he felt were more in keeping with reality,
which he saw as a combination of mind and matter. The
Aristotlean dictum, "no form without matter, no matter without
form," is the basis for his philosophy, called *realism.* When
challenged as one who had been Plato's favorite and seemed to
have turned on his teacher, Aristotle is reported to have said,
"Plato is dear, but truth is dearer still."

Aristotle was a prolific writer, who wrote on virtually every
subject known to man. It has been said that he knew all there was
to know at his time in history. His *Nichomachean Ethics* is the
first systematic treatment of ethics. In it he outlines his idea of
happiness as self-realization. This rests on a concept of natural
law which requires a "thing fulfill the essence of it's being," i.
e., achieve it's potential.

The Lyceum, founded in Athens by Aristotle, was dedicated
not only to teaching, but to independent study, research, scientific investigation, and to the preservation of the existing academic knowledge of the ancient world. The Lyceum, like
Aristotle, was the repository of the most comprehensive accu-
mulation of intellectual achievements of his time.

The first and important difference between Aristotle and
Plato in their metaphysics is in the problem of ideals. Plato
contended that they were real in and of themselves. Aristotle
maintained that they were real only as they were actualized in
material objects. Aristotle believed that everything sought to
fulfill the essence of its being, to become what the combination
of form and matter was meant to be in its final form.

Plato's ideals were eternal and immutable, so he maintained
that change was really one's senses deceived. Aristotle, finding
this explanation wanting, concluded that while matter remains
the same, the form changes. Thus, Plato's idea of form becomes
Aristotle's essence of a thing, and the concept of matter becomes
Aristotle's substance, the combination of which is reality.
Aristotle saw change as a manifestation of a thing moving
toward it's essence. He used the term "entelechy," which means
the final purpose, to describe the process. Nature makes nothing
in vain, so every thing is designed to reach its natural end. The
goal of every thing is to achieve the end for which it was made,
to move from its potential to its actual.

The Four Causes which Aristotle describes are principles by which every thing moves from potential to actual, to the perfection that their end requires. They are 1) material cause, 2) formal cause, 3) efficient cause, and 4) final cause. It works like this. A piece of clay (material cause) is determined by the potter to become a pot (formal cause), is molded by a pottery maker's hands (efficient cause), so that it can be used for the purpose it was intended (final cause). The piece of clay is simply formless matter. The pottery maker provides the energy, the force to change the clay into something else. But that change has to be directed according to some plan (shall we make a pot or a plate?), and finally, the pot must be put to the use for which it was intended, to perfect the process by which unformed matter reaches its full realization.

Since God and nature do nothing in vain, the implications for ethics according to Aristotle are clear. What is man's end, what is the highest good? Aristotle chooses that which he claims is self-sufficient, that which needs nothing else, but is complete unto itself. The highest good, then, is Happiness. That is the goal each man seeks. Many of the things which we confuse with happiness are often just means to happiness. For example, pleasure, wealth, good health, may all be a part of happiness but are not self sufficient, as is happiness, and therefore are not adequate to make one happy. Happiness, according to Aristotle is an activity of the soul (mind) in pursuit of virtue.

Virtue, then must be defined. Aristotle does so, as follows. What is the obvious essence of man's nature? Answer—reason. Man is the rational animal, reason is the one thing that distinguishes man from all other living things. Thus, for man to fulfill the essence of his being, as all things must, he must live a life of reason. And to live a life in accordance with reason is to lead a virtuous life. This then, is intellectual virtue. Moral virtue is developing the habit or predisposition to do good. The person who can control those desires which could lead him into immoral choices is morally good. As noted earlier, his *Nichomachean Ethics,* begins by stating, "...the good has rightly been declared to be that at which all things aim...."

Since we all have desires and passions, they are not in and of themselves evil. How we deal with them is the issue, and

Aristotle maintains that one must choose the "Golden Mean," the virtue itself, not it's excess or deficiency. Courage is a virtue. A deficiency of courage would be cowardice, an excess of courage would be foolhardiness. Courage is the mean, the virtue to be chosen, and one must develop the character, through habit, necessary to choose the virtue at all times. He lists many virtues along with their excesses and deficiencies, such as modesty, the virtue; timidity, the excess; shamelessness, the deficiency. Other virtues that he lists are temperance, liberality, gentleness, truthfulness, friendliness, magnificence, wittiness, magnanimity, and ambition. Justice is the sum of all the virtues, and the just man not only understands but acts according to them.

Aristotle has often been called the philosopher of "common sense." One reason may be that beyond his concept of moderation, he is wise enough to see that it is not enough for man's intellect to gain philosophical wisdom without the ability to translate that wisdom into human action. We must pursue truth to gain philosophical wisdom, but we must also have practical wisdom, which is wise conduct. Plato had asserted that to know the good was to do it; Aristotle disagreed. Knowledge of the good does not automatically bring with it the desire to act upon that knowledge. In addition to knowing the good, we must develop the habit and attitude which impels us to do the good, since often we may know what is right, but if we have not developed the habit of making our reason dominate our emotions, we might yield to temptations.

According to Aristotle, God, perfect and eternal, exists as pure reason, contemplating Himself. Thus, the reason within us is in a sense, divine. And the exercise of that reason, the life of contemplation, would be the way to happiness. But, Aristotle concludes that this type of existence is "too high for man," and that "eudaemonia" (happiness) cannot be achieved by man through pure thought. The good life for man on earth consists in activity with moral choices, in accordance with moral virtue, living the Golden Mean. As he said, through philosophical and practical wisdom we achieve happiness, "the activity of the soul (mind), in pursuit of virtue."

Thus man too is form and matter. He can contemplate, and when he does he is at his best, closest to God. But he also lives in a material world, and needs those material goods: friends, food, clothing, shelter, leisure time, and even good luck. The rational man then, filled with philosophical wisdom, through good work and habit, develops practical wisdom, lives according to the Golden Mean, and if he doesn't get run over by a truck, lives a happy life.

CHAPTER 7

Epicurus and Epictetus:
Pleasure and Apathy

Epicurus (342-270 B.C.)

Epicurus was born of Athenian parents on the island of Samos in the Aegean Sea. He was educated on the island and remained there until after the death of Alexander the Great, when the Athenians were driven out of Samos. Epicurus then moved to the island of Lesbos off the coast of Asia Minor and established himself as a teacher. With the growth of his school, Epicurus moved in about 306 B.C. to Athens, where he purchased some property (a part of which became the famed "Garden of Epicurus") and established a society of men and women who became his friends and disciples.

His school was very popular, particularly after the death of Alexander, since it provided a source of relief from the social disorganization of the time. With the decline of the city state and the security and loyalty it fostered, people began to turn inward to a more personal view of the world. Epicurian philosophy associated good with pleasure and evil with pain; its goal was not to attain the greatest pleasure, but rather to maximize equilibrium or absence of pain. Epicurus personally lived a very simple life, was frugal with material goods, and generous to a fault with his friendship and concern for others. It is ironic that the word "epicurian" today is often used in conjunction with the word "delights" and conjures a vision of gourmet food, fast living with the "beautiful people," champagne, and shallow cocktail-party talk.

He was a prolific writer, but little of what he wrote survives. Most of what we know of his philosophy comes from his disciples. The Roman, Lucretius, wrote *On the Nature of Things,* from which we learn most of the doctrines that Epicurus taught. Epicurus died after a painful illness in Athens in 270 B.C. His school prospered long after his death, and remained a vital force in the teaching of his philosophy until the third century after Christ.

The moral philosophy of Epicurus, most simply stated, revolves around one major principle: achieve a life free of pain and filled only with pleasure. There are, however, several other premises from which Epicurus builds his particular brand of Hedonism.

The world, he says, is composed of atoms. These atoms are infinite in number, residing in an infinite amount of space. Since, Epicurus states, "Nothing is created from nothing and nothing is resolved into nothing," the world then was not "created" but exists in an infinite amount of time. All matter exists in two basic forms, that infinite matter which exists as bodies recognized by the senses, and that infinite space in which matter exists. Thus the universe exists eternal and unchanging, and this concept is critical to one of his two very important postulates necessary to living a life of pleasure.

Epicurus maintains that there are two main problems which worry man and cause the anxieties which get in the way of leading the tranquil life that each man seeks. Men fear two things, "the gods" and death. These fears overshadow every waking moment and in varying degrees upset the search for pleasure. They are nagging fears that intrude upon our best moments. In the case of the gods, Epicurus says, since the universe was not created, exists eternally, and cannot change, then the gods do not watch over us, punish us for transgressions, or become in any way involved in our affairs.

Similarly, one need not fear death. Man exists as body and soul, both composed of atoms, each necessary to the other. The soul receives sensations through the body which is necessary to transmit them to the soul. Thus, the body and soul are dependent upon one another, and it is that union which causes life. While the soul remains in the body there is sensation; when at death the soul leaves the body, there is no longer a way to experience sensation. Therefore, there is no need to fear death. Death is the end of sensation, the end of pain, and with that understanding, an end of fear. There is an even more positive aspect of this theory; not only is there nothing to fear—no pain, no sensation, no punishment after death—there is a kind of immortality in death, since those atoms of the soul set free in space are indestructible and live on eternally.

With these two major problems out of the way, Epicurus begins to prescribe how one can live the good life. Happiness is the "highest good, the beginning and end of which is pleasure." There are two kinds of pleasures, *kinetic* and *katastematic*. Kinetic pleasures are the pleasures that comes from satisfying urges and desires. They are active pleasures, both mental and physical, and require an active pursuit. Katastematic pleasures are pleasures of the mind. One does not actively pursue these pleasures; rather, one is open to them and enjoys them as they come. The katastematic pleasures are purer, longer lasting, have no negative side effects, and are in all ways superior to the kinetic. Happiness is achieved when one is free of pain and fear, and a balanced tranquility of mind and body exists. The happiness that results from this passive view of pleasure is called *ataraxia*. Ataraxia is similar to the concept of nirvana, a peaceful, pleasurable contentment which is not sought after, but absorbed and assumed.

While Epicurus is committed to the value of the pleasures of the mind, he is not against physical pleasures, yet he is skeptical of them and enjoins his followers to exercise great prudence in their pursuit. Physical pleasures are short-lived and usually futile, and often have future consequences more harmful than the enjoyment was pleasurable. One should be satisfied with little rather than much. If one learns to control his physical desires so that he is satisfied with a few, he will be better able to pursue those intellectual pleasures which will provide him with true happiness.

Prudence is the key. The prudent man understands the difference between fleeting physical pleasures and enduring intellectual ones. The prudent man also knows that the only two realities in the pursuit of happiness are pain and pleasure. Also, one must never simply pursue pleasure. Often one must endure some, even great, pain in order to achieve a future pleasure. And while one cannot be happy if one is starving, being overstuffed with food is intemperate and wrong. Prudence, according to Epicurus, is the means to achieve that delicate balance of physical well-being and intellectual bliss; the latter, the means to true happiness; the former, simply an aid to the greater good.

Prudence also is required because man is in control of his own destiny. Man, according to Epicurus, not the gods, nor the fates, nor the stars, determines what will happen in this life. If man is in control of his life, he would do well to be in control of himself. Then the outcome of his judgments and acts will enhance his own well-being. The rash man may act imprudently, then curse the gods, his bad luck, etc. The prudent man knows he is in control, and by acting well can bask in the good that happens, since he is its cause.

One of the greatest means to the attainment of true happiness is the pleasure that comes from the enjoyment of good friends. Friendship is one of the great relationships man can have on this earth. In his garden, Epicurus had not just a school of philosophy, but an association of friends. Women as well as men were admitted to his school, and that extended his circle of friends, as well as provided a revolutionary example of equality in Greek society. Friends were his family, and in a sense were better than a family, since families require that one assume responsibilities that are imposed upon, rather than chosen by, the person involved. While Epicurianism is a self-oriented philosophy, this concept of friendship is not contradictory, since Epicurus maintains that the friend who extends himself for others will get, in return, the pleasure others can give.

Epictetus (A.D. 55-130)

Epictetus was born in Hieropolis in Asia Minor. He was born into slavery and spent his youth in Rome. Like many slaves with a disposition for study, he was allowed to become educated. (Actually, many Roman slaves were intelligent men of other nations who had been captured in battle.) He studied under the Stoic philosopher Musonius Rufus, and after completing his education he became a freedman. In A.D. 90, Epictetus, along with most philosophers, was expelled from Rome. He spent the rest of his life in Nicopolis, Greece, where he taught until his death.

Like most Stoics, Epictetus believed that what is in our power, that which resides in the will, is what man must be concerned with. The world, outside forces, and other people must never be mistaken for things as valuable as the individual's unconquerable will. To most people, the term "stoic" conjures up the idea of a person bearing pain and suffering without complaint. To Epictetus, a Stoic is one who is acutely aware of those things which he can change and those things which he can not change. The wise man expends his energies on the former and not the latter. Often, shops sell decorative signs which bear the aphorism, "God grant me the courage to change the things I can, the serenity to accept the things I cannot change, and the wisdom to know the difference." If Epictetus didn't say it first, he certainly would have liked to.

An example of his view of the world is evidenced by a story about his youthful experience with his angry master. His master, while administering a beating, began to twist Epictetus' leg. "If you continue to twist my leg, you will break it." The angry slave-owner twisted even harder. "You are going to break the leg," said Epictetus. At that point the leg broke, and Epictetus said, "You see, I told you, you were going to break it."

Epictetus wrote nothing, but his lectures were preserved by a student, Arrian, and are entitled *Discourses* and *Enchiridion*.

Stoicism became the dominant philosophy in Rome, in keeping with the character of an earthy people in response to the excesses they saw about them in society. Soldiers in particular could relate to it as a philosophy which seemed to mirror a soldier's view of the world. A soldier does not decide whether or not a particular battle should be fought. He simply does the best he can when the battle begins. He is not in control of the decision, so he learns to act stoically when the decision is made. All segments of Roman society were influenced by Stoicism. It is interesting to note that the two great Roman Stoics were Marcus Aurelius, an Emperor, and Epictetus, a slave.

The key word to know in trying to understand the Stoics is apathy. They mean apathy in quite the literal sense: "Want of feeling; lack of passion, emotion, or excitement." The Stoic believes that one should be apathetic to the world and the world forces around him. Early Stoics were ascetics who remained detached from most social and political activities. Apathy and resignation are both terms which Epictetus subscribes to, but in a moderate sense, as we shall see.

Epictetus has as a basic premise the idea that we live in a rational universe. God, the supreme intelligence, is responsible for the laws which govern the universe, and we are responsible for trying to understand the universe of which we are a part. Beyond that, man with his ability to reason, has a spark of the divine within him. Epictetus has said that man, being rational, is a "fragment torn from God." The ethical implications of these premises are profound, not only for morality but for politics as well. Reason and a rational understanding of the world are the basis for morality.

This purpose and intelligence which permeates the universe imply that there is purpose in all things. The individual is duty-bound to attempt to find his place in the scheme of things, find out how to please the God who put him here by accomplishing those things which God intended for him. (Obviously, only those things which are within one's power should be of concern, since what is beyond one's power was meant to be so.) Such a person is virtuous—and virtue is its own reward. There are no material goods to be acquired, no fame and glory to be achieved, no end of any kind, except to do one's duty.

What then should one do? Learn self control, learn how to relate to outside forces, and most of all develop the attitude of dealing with the world as a neutral entity. Everything that happens in nature is neutral. Only our attitude towards the happening makes it good or bad. There is no such thing as an "evil" storm, earthquake, or tornado; neither is there such a thing as a "good" day, sunny, warm, and breezy. Nature is morally neutral; we assign values and, in most cases, shouldn't. If, indeed, a picnic is planned for a particular day, and on that day it rains, to become angry because of the rain is foolhardy, since that only doubles the problem. The rain is a reality, and requires that plans in some way be changed—that's an inconvenience. Now, to get angry, as well, is to compound an existing problem, and the anger has absolutely no chance of solving the problem. And to assign a value to that day is the supreme foolishness— only the attitudes of the picnickers have value.

While it is evident that the major thrust of Epictetus' philosophy is based on a personal exercise of the will to control oneself, there is a social ethic which evolves from his philosophy. If each of us has the "divine spark" of reason, then each of us is equal to and has an obligation to his fellow man. While the Stoic philosophy begins with a moral premise, it has profound implications for political and social philosophy. One of the great statements of the social aspect of stoic philosophy comes from the *Meditations* of Marcus Aurelius, who said, "The reason, in respect of which we are rational beings, is common; if this is so, common also is the reason which commands us what to do, and what not to do; if this is so, there is a common law also; if this is so, we are fellow citizens; if this is so, we are members of some political community; if this is so, the world is in a manner a state... My nature is rational and social; and my city and country so far as I am Antonius, is Rome; but so far as I am a man, it is the world."

Epictetus attacked the Epicurian philosophy of pleasure, sensation, and matter. Every assertion is an act of the will; therefore, the will is vital, not pleasure, sensation, or even matter. What happens is less important than is our response to what happens. What happens, happens according to a divine plan, intelligent and purposeful, and is to be viewed from a distance. If we get involved, we get involved by reacting to events and become upset not by the event, but by our reaction to the event. It is not because of our lack of things that we are miserable. It is because we give in to our wants and desires that we become miserable.

Epictetus believed that his philosophy of reason is simple to understand and difficult to refute, that there are a multitude of Stoic principles that most men would agree to, e.g., that it is better to be in control of our emotions, rather than have them manipulated by outside forces. The problem, in reality, is the putting into practice these ideas which people recognize as valid. What, then, do people do? Obviously, they become in a sense their own worst enemies, bringing sorrow, upset, and distress into their lives—upsetting the tranquility that stoicism bestows on those who understand and practice rational behavior.

CHAPTER 8

Aquinas and Descartes: Faith and Reason

St. Thomas Aquinas (1225-1274)

St. Thomas Aquinas was born in Roccasecca, Italy in 1225. He was taught by Benedictines at Monte Casino, but because of unsettled political conditions returned home and in 1239 studied for a while at the University of Naples. Then, in 1244, in spite of strong opposition from his family, members of the Italian nobility, he entered the Dominicans, a religious order of preachers. From 1245 to 1252 he studied philosophy and theology in Paris and Cologne under Albertus Magnus.

In 1252 he returned to the Dominican convent of St. James in Paris where he lectured, now as a priest. In 1256 he was appointed to one of the chairs of philosophy for the Dominicans at the University of Paris. In 1259 he returned to Italy and remained there for nine years.

By this time in his life he had written much, including commentaries on the works of other important philosophers. In 1258 he wrote *Summa Contra Gentiles,* in which he tried to convince non-Christians that the doctrines of Christianity were reasonable. In 1265 he began his most mature and most celebrated work, *Summa Theologica,* in which he systematically explained Christian theology. During this period he used his understanding of Aristotle to begin the process of reconciling Aristotelean philosophy with Christian theology.

From 1268 to 1274 he taught alternately at Paris and the University of Naples. While in Naples he revised the curriculum and continued writing. He was called to Lyons to consult with Pope Gregory and, on the way, became ill and died in a Cistercian Monastery on March 7, 1274.

Aquinas is considered an Aristotelian. He combined Aristotle's teachings about reason with the Christian concept of faith. He argued that there is no conflict between reason and faith. Philosophy, he contended, is based on reason, and reason can support faith. Aquinas accepted on faith that God exists, but he formulated proofs of His existence to support that belief. Aquinas' five proofs for the existence of God are rational explanations of an article of faith.

There are two main concepts in Aquinas' moral doctrines: the Aristotelean ideas of eudaemonism, i.e., happiness as a result of the activity of the soul (reason) in pursuit of virtue, and teleology, i.e., that everything has a purpose and naturally moves toward the fulfillment of that purpose. Aquinas agrees with Aristotle that happiness is the proper end of human action and that it is natural that men seek happiness, since the will cannot help but desire it. Thus men should act, with their free will, to achieve happiness, and their actions can be determined to be good or bad depending on how their freely willed acts conform to the end desired. The critical question for Aquinas was to determine what constitutes the ultimate happiness.

Ultimate happiness must include God, so Aquinas outlines a path for man to follow on the road to God. First Aquinas describes the relation between our appetites and desires and the human intellect. Intelligence is the essence of man, a gift from God, the divine spark within us. In all cases our intellect must have primacy over our appetites and desires. Man also has free will. While the intellect tells us what we ought or ought not to do, it is the will which causes us to act. Thus, when we act in accordance with reason we act well, when we act against reason we act poorly. Man's greatest good is to act in accordance with reason. Whatever is contrary to reason is considered evil.

A self-evident axiom is, "One should do good and avoid evil." The person who lives according to this axiom is virtuous. Virtue, then, according to Aquinas, is the permanent disposition to act in conformity with reason. He who acts in conformity with reason is intellectually virtuous. Since man has free will and since all men are also imperfect, man must be morally virtuous as well as intellectually virtuous. Moral virtues consist of those personal habits and qualities which control the appetites and desires, such as temperance and fortitude. The intellectual virtues, knowledge, wisdom, and prudence, inform the will of the right path to take toward virtue. If man were perfect, he would only have to know the good to do it (remember Plato?), but man is imperfect, flawed by original sin, and needs to develop and perfect moral and intellectual virtues in order to do good.

Aquinas contends that a good act has four criteria:

1) the intrinsic value of the act;
2) the intention of the actor;
3) circumstances which affect the actor and/or the act;
4) the end result of the act. For an act to be perfect (in a moral sense) all four of these criteria must be met.

For example:

1) A person wishes to give food to the poor
2) because his intention is to do good and help others less fortunate than himself.
3) He proceeds to buy the food and delivers it to the local soup kitchen
4) where the poor are fed. Thus, it is a perfect act in intrinsic value, intent, circumstance, and result. We can also write many scenarios in which most of the conditions are present and *some* good results. A perfect act, however, must meet all the criteria.

For example:

1) A person wishes to give food to the poor
2) because his intention is to do good and help others less fortunate than himself.
3) He proceeds to buy the food and delivers it to the local soup kitchen where it is destroyed by a fire,
4) so the poor are not fed.

There is great merit in many aspects of the act described, and much moral good, but it is obviously not a perfect act—the good result was lacking.

The perfect and the less than perfect acts described above seem fairly easy to distinguish. There are, however, some acts that are more difficult to judge. For example:

1) A person wishes to give food to the poor
2) because his intention is to win the next political election.
3) He proceeds to buy the food and delivers it to the local soup kitchen,
4) where the poor are fed.

A perfect moral act? Not according to Aquinas. A perfect moral act must satisfy the demands of reason both in intention and ends. We could get into some really fine-line arguments here; what if the politician was fighting a criminal opposition regime and needed the votes from the soup kitchen's neighborhood in order to win and throw the rascals out? Aquinas would want each criteria examined on its own merit. Thus our politician would have committed an act with good results, but not a perfect moral act.

Man should strive, through the development of his intellectual and moral virtues, to act in accordance with reason. This will bring him closer to God. God is absolute truth and wisdom, and man, with the reason which separates him from all other creatures should seek to cultivate that "God-like" quality. By developing one's intellect one is fulfilling his part in the natural order of things. Through reason and contemplation one can, in a sense, approach God, since "when human reason fails, we must have recourse to eternal reason." Aquinas contends that, since there is a part of God's absolute goodness in him, man wants to do good, despite his flaws. If he works at developing the intellect he will come into contact with God's laws, all of which can be discovered by the intellect. Aquinas lists four types of law: eternal, natural, human, and divine.

4 typos of law

1) Eternal law is that law of the universe which is discernable through reason. We can see that there are certain laws of nature which affect nature, all to some purpose and therefore, in accordance with "God's will."

2) Natural law is a reflection of eternal law. It is the dictate of man's practical reason concerning the good which is to be sought and the evil to be avoided. Since the natural law, albeit an extension of the eternal, is discovered through the use of human reason, man is a responsible being. He has moral autonomy. The constancy of human nature testifies to the constancy of natural law, and thus the validity of an absolute eternal law.

3) Human law. Aquinas agrees with Aristotle that the state is natural and necessary to man, that man is by nature a political animal and the state is the means to fulfill life in society. Therefore, human law is as necessary in God's plan as is eternal, natural, and divine. Human law is meant to be obeyed as is all law, in order to bring man closer to God.

4) Divine law is the written word of God as found in the Commandments, the Bible, and in particular, in the books of Matthew, Mark, Luke, and John. Divine law should be the basis

for human law, signposts that human reason can see are in harmony with the eternal and natural, therefore in harmony with God's will.

Predictably, Aquinas sees religion as the means to achieve the highest level of human existence. The same way Aristotle sought to contemplate God to achieve happiness, Aquinas seeks through religious contemplation to have a "vision of God," which is the supreme happiness. Aquinas distinguishes between *superior reason* and *inferior reason*. Through a spiritual, religious life, one can achieve superior reason, an understanding of good, truth, beauty, and other non-temporal concepts. Inferior reason deals with the temporal world: science, materialism, and mundane human affairs. Dealing with the material world brings pleasure, which is not bad; dealing with the spiritual world brings joy, which is much better.

This union with God comes through God's grace. We cannot, in a real sense, earn the vision of God. It is a gift of God's grace. With free will, however, we can reject God. Thus, through grace, with the development of intellectual and moral virtues, through reason, and with an understanding of eternal, natural, divine, and human law, we can gain the happiness this world has to offer and also the ultimate happiness that the next world offers—when the vision of God becomes actual.

One of Aquinas' major contentions was that faith and reason are not contradictory. If, indeed, they were contradictory, he contended that reason would prove faith false. Thus, if reason could prove faith false there would be no way to have faith. When one discusses faith in God's existence, one must be able to put forward some reasonable explanation to justify that faith. Aquinas would also contend that faith comes first, that everything begins with an act of faith. This is not to say that one can prove God's existence, just as one cannot disprove it. But rational explanations are required. Aquinas has put forth five rational proofs for the existence of God:

1) *The argument from motion:* We observe that there is motion in the world. Everything that moves must be put into motion by something else. A thing cannot be both mover and moved, it cannot move itself. If everything is moved by something, one must admit to an infinity of moved and movers, and there would be no first mover. If this were so there would be no

movement, since the second mover depends on the first, the third on the second, etc. There must be then a first mover of the universe. This first mover we call God.

2) *The argument from efficient cause:* No being can be its own efficient cause. Since the cause is necessarily anterior to its effect, a being would have to be anterior to itself in order to be its own efficient cause. This, of course, is impossible. The material world is contingent, it is an intermediate cause in a series of causes, thus requires a necessary uncreated being, a first efficient cause. This first efficient cause, the cause of being, we call God.

3) *The argument from necessity:* This proof begins by distinguishing between possible and necessary. Possible is that which is contingent, it can either be or not-be. It is not necessary. Also, a possible thing has its existence from outside itself, from an efficient cause. If all things were merely possible, everything could not-be, and thus there would have been a moment when nothing existed. If this were so, it would have been impossible for anything to have begun to exist. Thus not all beings are possible, something must be a necessary being, something which exists independently. This necessary being, we call God.

4) *The argument from degrees of being:* Some things are good, bad, better, best. They are measured to be more or less good as they approach something which is considered the highest. If there are degrees of perfection, there must be a perfect being whose existence makes it possible for things of relative perfection to exist. This perfect being we call God.

5) *The argument from design:* It is obvious that there is order in the universe. This order must be to some purpose. It cannot be ordered by chance since chance means out of order and to no purpose. This orderly situation could not have occurred by chance, since then there would be an effect without a cause, which is impossible. This order must be the product of an intelligent being. "There cannot be a watch without a watchmaker." The designer of the universe, this intelligent being, we call God.

Thus the pagan philosophy of Aristotle was taken by Aquinas and reconciled to Christian theology. Aristotle's view of reason, eudaemonism, teleology, intellectual and moral virtue, the state, and countless other philosophical concepts were used by

Aquinas to show that Aristotle did not threaten the Christian's faith but complemented it. The greatest mind of antiquity met with the greatest mind of the middle ages, and the result was the Neo-Aristotelean Christian philosophy that dominated the western world for over five hundred years.

René Descartes (1596-1650)

René Descartes was born in 1596 in the village of La Haye, France. He was educated by Jesuits and was well trained in Scholastic philosophy. His forte was mathematics, at which he excelled, especially in the area of analytical geometry. As a matter of fact, Descartes is credited with creating analytical geometry.

In addition to an excellent education, his background included extensive travel throughout Europe. He settled in Holland for about twenty years. The liberal philosophical climate there was suitable for an energetic mathematician/philosopher. His *Meditations* and *Principals of Philosophy* were published in French, contrary to the tradition of publishing major works in Latin. His *Discourse on Method,* also published in Holland, completed a trilogy of his most important philosophical works.

He later traveled to Sweden and in 1649 moved to Stockholm where he became tutor to Queen Christiana. He developed pneumonia and died in 1650, the victim of an inhospitable climate.

Descartes believed that the only reliable knowledge existed within mathematics. Instead of separating mathematics and philosophy, he attempted to combine the two, thinking that mathematical principles underlie all other areas of investigation. His basic approach to all areas of study rested on a skeptical predisposition to doubt everything except "self-evident" truths. He was not a skeptic, however; his doubt was a suspension of judgment, not a denial of judgment.

The moral philosophy of René Descartes is based primarily on his method of logic. He had four basic precepts which he employed:

1) Accept nothing as true which is not clearly and recognizably so.

2) Divide complex problems into as many simpler parts as

possible in order to judge the truth or falsehood of each part.

3) Deduce from those few truths the implications that follow in an orderly and logical fashion, moving from the simple to the more complex.

4) Finally, keep records that are accurate and review the logical order carefully so that the accuracy of the result will be unquestionable.

This logical process must begin with self-evident truths, premises which cannot be denied. The mental operation by which these truths are established is referred to by Descartes as "intuition." Descartes defines intuitions as innate ideas perceived by the mind without any sense-involvement whatever. These innate ideas are in man at birth. Mathematical axioms are examples, as well as the idea of the soul, the idea of God, the concept that nothing comes from nothing *(ex nihilo nihil fit),* and the Aristotlean idea that a thing cannot both exist and not exist at the same time. The careful application of the mind's intuitive knowledge followed by steps two, three, and four will enable one to seek and find truth.

The mental process which led Descartes to his first and most important premise, however, is that of *methodical doubt.* Everything must be looked upon with doubt, at first, in order to make the operations of intuition possible. When one doubts everything in the universe, no matter how obviously true it may seem, the only reality which is accepted initially is the reality of the act of doubting. Doubting, reasons Descartes, implies a doubter, an entity which is giving the act existence. Since he defines doubting and all other mental processes as "thinking," he accepts as his initial and guiding self-evident truth, "Cogito Ergo Sum"— I think, therefore, I am.

This concept gives his entire philosophy its justification. He proves, not only his own existence, but the existence of God, and in turn uses the existence of God to prove the reality of the material world. Of three basic proofs for the existence of God, one deals with innate ideas. He claims that a finite being could not create the innate idea of an infinite being, thus the infinite being, God, must exist. "I should not, however, have the idea of an infinite substance, seeing I am a finite being, unless it were given me by some substance in reality, infinite."

This infinite substance, God, is "A thing which exists in such a way as to stand in need of nothing beyond itself." God is the only absolute substance. All other substances are His creation. Since the substance called God, and the substance called the universe cannot be the same, he concludes that the universe is composed of two finite substances, mind and matter. Each substance has a primary attribute. The mind's principal attribute is thinking, the body's principal attribute is extension—it occupies space. A thing must be one or the other. The mind (soul) cannot occupy space; the body (corporeal) cannot think.

Body, matter, or material (Descartes used the terms inter-changeably) is that which has extension, which is his term for length, breadth, and thickness. It has motion, the force which causes bodies to move from one place to another. All laws of nature are laws of motion, therefore all knowledge of the laws of motion would enable one to understand the universe. He assumes the reality of the physical universe because an infinite, omniscient, omnipotent God would not deceive his creation—man.

Mind, the other substance, is the thinking substance he thought of as independent of matter. The mind of man, the soul, is what makes man different from animals. Animals live according to the laws of motion, man has free will. When the body dies, the soul lives on.

The problem, of course, is how does one reconcile this dualism of mind and matter, this mechanistic idea of a physical universe and the idea of a soul which is free and independent. At first Descartes avoided the problem. But with the soul free to move the body as well as to think, and the body which clearly seems to affect the mind at times, the problem called for an answer. He developed the theory that the extended substance and the thinking substance affect each other through the "animal fluids" which surround the pineal gland, an organ at the base of the brain. This weak explanation caused him, later in life, to claim that the interaction was caused by "constant intervention of God."

Although he tried to avoid it, Descartes eventually had to admit that the body is not completely commanded by the mind. Although he continued to believe that the goal of man should be to free the mind from the influence of the body and other outside forces, he realized that this ideal could probably not be fully achieved. Therefore, he said that moral decisions should be made on the basis of the application of the reason and will of the mind to the appetites of the body. He derived a code of maxims for dealing with the practical world,

1) Obey the laws and customs of your country, your family, your religion, and avoid excesses, which have a tendency to be bad. When in doubt as to the relative merit of two courses of action, the more moderate is to be chosen, and the results evaluated.

2) Be firm and stand by your convictions once they have been well thought out. He uses an analogy of travellers lost in the woods. If they wander from place to place, or stay in one place, they will not get out. But if they walk as straight as possible in one direction, they will get out. He believes one should stick to a premise, testing its virtues rather than wavering from opinion to opinion.

3) His third maxim was "to try always to conquer myself rather than fortune, and to alter my desires rather than change the order of the world, and generally to accustom myself to believe that there is nothing entirely within our power but our own thoughts."

4) Finally, choose a life's work which is best suited to you. And "cultivate (your) reason, and in advancing (yourself) as much as possible in the knowledge of the truth."

The influence of Aristotle and Epictitus is evident in Descartes' maxims for a moral life. Like Aristotle, he conceives the intellectual love of God as the highest happiness one can achieve. Finally, we are moral to the extent that we can control our passions by our reason.

Descartes' contribution to philosophy has caused him, because of his introduction of the scientific method, to be called the "Father of Modern Philosophy."

CHAPTER 9

Hume, Bentham and Mill: Subjectivism and Utilitarianism

David Hume (1711-1776)

David Hume was born in Edinburgh, Scotland in 1711. His father died soon after his birth, and he was raised by his mother. He was an exceptional student, and his mother, noting his brilliance, hoped he would pursue a career in the law. Hume, however, was interested only in philosophy and "general learning."

Hume did most of his early writing at a country retreat in France. It was in France that he wrote his most famous work, *Treatise of Human Nature,* which was published in 1739. Although this book failed miserably, Hume continued writing. His other major works, *History of England, History of the House of Tudor,* and *Inquiry Concerning the Principles of Morals,* which he considered his best, were either unnoticed or criticized. *Political Discourse,* written in 1752, was his only book to receive any attention and success.

As he grew older, his literary reputation grew, and an acceptance of his ideas grew also. He was invited to accept various political posts in France and England, which drew him away from the the reclusive life he led early in his career. His influence in the areas of skepticism and empiricism was great, and his historical writings are considered among the first significant works of their kind.

David Hume was a skeptic, who believed that certainty could not be known. This skepticism was the product of his basic premise, which states that all knowledge consists of perceptions from which we obtain impressions and ideas. Impressions, says Hume, are all the sensations which the mind acquires through sense experience. Ideas he calls the "faint images" of these impressions in thinking and reasoning. Impressions are of two

e.m./k?

kinds, original and secondary: the first are sense impressions, while the second class belong to the passions, or feelings and emotions, excluding bodily pleasure and pain, which are original impressions. This is how simple ideas are formed.

Hume expands this concept by further explaining the union of simple ideas to form complex ones by means of association. There are three forms of association: resemblance, contiguity in time or place, and cause and effect. Resemblance is the impulse to think about things which look alike. A picture of a tree reminds us of an actual tree. Contiguity results from relationships that exist in proximity, e.g., mention one hotel and other hotels come to mind. Cause and effect is evident when we think of a plane crash and associate it with a loss of life. These are the means by which ideas are connected in the imagination and then are united with other associated ideas in the memory.

Hume contends that moral distinctions are derived not from reasoning, but from the moral sentiment. The basis for moral judgment is neither reason nor response to contemporary events. Moral judgment occurs when the sentiment of approval or disapproval is applied. If something pleases a person, the person considers it "good," conversely when a person is displeased, he cites the source of his displeasure as "bad." All moral judgments, then, are the product of a personal response to a personal sensory experience. Morality is not discovered through reason. It is based upon the actions of people in response to emotional stimuli. As a matter of fact, Hume contends that, "reason is, and ought to be the slave of the passions." This is not to say that reason does not exist, but rather, it exists as an instrument of passion, not as a sole sufficient cause to action. A person does not rationally decide on a course of action. He uses reason to justify an action that he considers to be "good" on the basis of his personal sensory experience.

"Morality, therefore, is more properly felt than judged of." Virtue also consists of approval and disapproval. A virtuous act, or person, gives the feeling of pleasure and approval. Acts which cause a feeling of displeasure or disapproval are considered unvirtuous. When, however, we do not feel personally, we still can understand the feelings through what Hume calls "sympathy."

By sympathy Hume means, not the specific feeling or emotion of compassion, but a general tendency to feel whatever emotions or passion we observe in others. Our perception of what another person is feeling is turned into a corresponding impression of what we observe. We can feel moral approval for a quality according to its usefulness or pleasantness, or moral disapproval for a disagreeable or unpleasant quality we observe in others. We can do this as disinterested spectators. Thus, we can evaluate acts from two different standpoints, as interested actors, and as impartial spectators. As participants, we evaluate our acts and the acts of others as good or bad as they cause us pleasure or pain. But we also feel pleasure and pain through sympathy, and thus are able to evaluate acts as impartial spectators.

It is also through sympathy that social ethics evolve. We not only can feel through sympathy, approval or disapproval, but we can see the utility of certain virtues. Hume maintains that justice is the result of its utility value. Actually, "Public utility is the sole origin of Justice." If everyone were able to have all the goods he needed, if everyone were good to one another, and if there were no selfishness in man, justice would be quite unnecessary. Justice, then, is an artificial device created by man to prevent men from interfering with another's property, or another's well being, and thereby serves as a remedy for human selfishness.

Justice depends on the utility which people feel. Men establish the laws of justice out of a concern for their own and the public good. This concern is derived not from reasoning about the eternal and necessary relation of ideas, but from our impressions and feelings. Men feel it is in their interest to establish a scheme of justice, and they approve of customary conventions which remedy the inconveniences that accompany human life. Reason enters the issue when particular rules are needed, but those rules are designed to produce good feelings. Once again, "reason is the slave of passion."

Hume's skepticism, mentioned earlier, was based on his concept of sense experience, the limitations of reason, and his belief in *metaphysical nihilism*. He was a skeptic in metaphysics because he believed that man could not know ultimate reality because he could not have knowledge beyond sense experience. This belief in sense experience alone made him a skeptic about the use of reason in ethics. Also, he was a skeptic about the existence of God. Reason is too weak to prove the existence of God, he believed. Hume does not say that there is no God, just that there is not enough evidence to prove that there is.

Hume, along with other British philosophers, attacked the long history of rationalism and the concept of innate ideas. His contribution to the philosophy of skepticism and subjectivism made him Scotland's most important philosopher. He died in 1776.

Jeremy Bentham (1748-1832)

Jeremy Bentham was born on February 15, 1748 in London, England. In 1783 he graduated from Queen's College at Oxford. Although trained for the law, he never practiced, but instead decided to devote his life to the study and correction of the abuses he saw in the the social, legal, and political system.

Bentham's philosophy, called Utilitarianism, which he learned in part from the writings of David Hume, means that ideas are judged on their basic utility, and utility is defined as the object's ability to produce happiness. Also, happiness and pleasure are thought to be synonymous. Utilitarianism, according to Bentham, has three major points. First, all pleasure can be accurately measured; this is his concept of *hedonistic calculus.* Next, he defines *psychological hedonism,* which maintains that individuals care only about increasing pleasure and decreasing pain. Finally, he believes that a person should always do that which produces the greatest good for the greatest number, which is called *ethical hedonism.*

Because of Bentham's criticisms and suggestions many reforms were completed in Great Britain. For example, the law courts were reformed, health, prison, and insurance laws were passed, and the poor laws were changed.

In 1776, Bentham wrote *Fragment on Government,* a political criticism. His greatest work, however, which contains a clear statement of the principles of Utilitarianism, is *Introduction to the Principles of Morals and Legislation.*

Jeremy Bentham died June 6, 1832. At his request, his body was dissected in front of his friends, and then stuffed. A wax facsimile of his head placed on the body, which is seated in a chair, encased in glass, and to this day, is on display at the British Museum.

Jeremy Bentham believed that man by nature was a pleasure seeking animal. Man has two sovereign masters, pleasure and pain, and the sum total of all our actions is directed to the seeking of the one and the avoidance of the other. The very nature of man, then, leads to the only ethical principle, the principle of utility. He reasons that since pleasure and pain, our "sovereign masters" must determine our actions, good becomes synonymous with pleasure and evil with pain. Man by nature pursues pleasure. Therefore, in seeking pleasure one must pursue the greatest possible amount of it.

The principle of utility dictates, as an ethical principle, that every man is morally obligated to promote the greatest good for the greatest number. The greatest happiness principle, since there is no ultimate principle of good or bad in the universe, is a relative moral position. Good and bad, not being absolutes, are determined by social factors. The measure of good and evil is the effect of an act upon people now, or the bearing of an act upon the future. Also, to act under the principle of utility will bring the greatest good to the one acting.

Bentham created a system called "hedonistic calculus," a method of measuring pleasure and pain in an accurate manner in order to make those judgments which will insure the greatest amount of pleasure be derived from an act. So that each act will produce pleasure and minimize pain, there are seven quantitative areas which are to be taken into account before acting:

1) *Intensity:* How intense will the pleasure resulting from this act be?

2) *Duration:* How long will the pleasure last?

3) *Certainty:* How sure can we be that a particular action will produce the expected pleasure?

4) *Propinquity:* How close, in time and space, is the pleasure to realization?

5) *Fecundity:* What are the prospects for future pleasures resulting from the immediate ones received?

6) *Purity:* How free from painful elements will the pleasure be?

7) *Extent:* How many others will be able to share in the pleasure produced?

While it is obvious that this philosophy is concerned with physical pleasure, is subjective, and in large measure egoistic, the concept of extent deals with the social aspects of utilitarianism. The implication that we all share in pleasures produced by our actions imposes an obligation to act for the group as well as the individual. Also, to head off the criticism that this philosophy could easily result in run-amuck greed, selfish excess, concern with self, even malevolence towards others, Bentham cites four social sanctions which he believes will prevent excesses of behavior.

1) *The physical sanction:* If one overdoes a physical activity, including eating and drinking, the physical pain that results will restrain such actions.

2) *The political sanction:* If one violates the laws of society for his own personal pleasure, the law will penalize him, and the pain should outweigh the pleasure gained.

3) *The moral sanction:* If one violates the laws of propriety and accepted behavior, he will be ostracized, censured, and suffer the pain of social disapproval.

4) *The religious sanction:* If one engages in immoral or forbidden behavior, the fear of punishment by God or in the afterlife will restrain the unacceptable behavior.

Thus, while the philosophy is personal, sensual, and subjective, it functions in close interrelationship with society. In fact, the most moral man is concerned with society, the moral man with personal pleasure and helping others, and the least moral man is asocial. The immoral man is one who purposely harms others.

According to Bentham, the value of an act resides in its consequences. An intention is good or evil only in so far as it considers the consequences from the beginning. However, there is no such thing as a good or bad motive for an intentional act. One man's desire for pleasure is as legitimate as another. One's motives cannot be selfless or disinterested, since that would be a contradiction in terms. Each person seeks pleasure, and that is at the root of all motive; thus morality must be determined by the only measurable criteria—results.

Finally, his hedonistic calculus, which he felt could be developed to a mathematical certainty, is also called "quantitative hedonism." He believed that there is only one kind of pleasure, and it varies only in quantity, not in quality. There can be no difference between a spiritual and physical pleasure. All pleasures are physical, and physical pleasures are the highest pleasures attainable. Perhaps some of the feelings that result from certain physical pleasure could be called "spiritual," but the source of those feelings must be sensual.

Because of no good or bad in the universe.

John Stuart Mill (1806-1873)

learned through the good and bad days

John Stuart Mill's father, James Mill, began an educational experiment when John was three years old, and John was the subject of the experiment. The father taught the son Greek, Latin, logic, philosophy, economics, and mathematics. By the time John was fourteen he was not only well versed in these subjects, but had developed the mental faculties necessary to deal with the complexity of the ideas he had learned. In addition, because of James' close friendship with Jeremy Bentham, John at an early age became the intellectual heir to Bentham's utilitarian philosophy.

After suffering a nervous breakdown at the age of twenty one, he married, took a job with the East India Company, and began writing. Late in life he was elected to Parliament, and he continued writing. It is interesting that much of his influence, based on his ethical theory, is in the field of political philosophy. *Utilitarianism* is his most important essay on ethics, and his essays *On Liberty* and *Considerations on Representative Government* are important political statements, while his *Systems of Logic* is considered to be his best work.

John Stuart Mill inherited a philosophy from his father and Jeremy Bentham, and he remained a utilitarian throughout his life, but he did make a major break from the theory he had learned. While Bentham was a quantitative hedonistic Mill became a *qualitative* hedonist. That is, Mill believed that while the basic utilitarian premise is absolutely correct, there are two kinds of pleasures, physical and intellectual. Each is different, and one is better. Intellectual pleasures are superior to physical pleasures because they are the ones that make man the superior being. Mill contradicted Bentham's view of sensual pleasure by stating, "It is better to be a man dissatisfied, than a pig satisfied;

better to be Socrates dissatisfied, than a fool satisfied."

This statement not only makes clear the belief in the superiority of intellectual pleasures, but also indicates who can make the determination. If we have a fool who can enjoy all the physical pleasures but is too ignorant to enjoy those intellectual pleasures, the fool only knows part of the experience. An intelligent person, however, can experience both, and therefore can be the judge of which is better. A fool and a wise man can enjoy a good meal, but only the wise man can enjoy the intellectual pleasures of art, literature, music, dance, poetry, and the like. The implications of this concept for Mill's political philosophy are as interesting as they are profound.

Mill also differs with Bentham's view that one's nature requires that he seek happiness/pleasure as an individual and similarly seek happiness/pleasure as a socially aware being. Not so, says Mill. True, we seek happiness/pleasure for ourselves. It is our nature. But the fulfilling of our social obligations Mill sees as something we *ought* to do, i.e., it is a moral imperative, not a natural drive. This concept leads Mill to what he calls the "internal sanction."

While Bentham had four sanctions to insure acceptable behavior in the social sense, Mill sees but two. The first, which is simply "hope of favor, fear of displeasure," is the external sanction. But even the external sanction is in a real sense, self imposed—we choose what will bring favor or displeasure. So, the second, the internal sanction is the more important one. Mill claims that all men have a "feeling for humanity," and this feeling becomes the basis for the internal sanction. The intelligent man knows that however different the opinions of others might be in contrast to his own, all our basic aims and desires are the same. This is what "makes any mind of well-developed feelings, work with, and not against, the outward motives to care for others..."

Thus John Stuart Mill developed, expanded, and completed the task of explaining the utilitarian philosophy he learned at his father's knee.

CHAPTER 10

Kant and Schopenhauer: Idealism and Pessimism

Immanuel Kant (1724-1804)

Immanuel Kant was born in Königsburg, East Prussia. His parents were deeply religious and hoped for a career in the ministry for their very talented son. He had a sound education as a youth and entered the University of Königsberg, ostensibly to study for the ministry. Instead, he studied mostly mathematics and science.

After the death of his parents, he had to discontinue his studies because of lack of funds. He worked as a tutor for many prominent local families, then resumed his studies and eventually became a professor of logic and metaphysics at the University of Königsburg. He was an extremely popular teacher and writer and although his reputation grew throughout Europe, Kant never left the immediate environs of his hometown.

While personally a man of rigid habits and careful routine (it was said that neighbors would set their clocks according to his comings and goings), Kant had a liberated mind which actively pursued interests in religion, the French and American Revolutions, as well as philosophy. Eventually, his religious views which were at odds with the government, were censored and he was forbidden to write on the subject.

His major work, *Critique of Pure Reason,* was published in 1781, followed by other works dealing with morality, *The Fundamental Principles of the Metaphysics of Morals* and *The Critique of Practical Reason.* He also wrote *Perpetual Peace,* an expression of his social and political views, in which he suggests a "League of Nations" to solve international disputes.

Immanuel Kant's old age was marred by serious mental and physical deterioration, and he died ten years after the onset of his illness, in 1804.

E/M Immanuel Kant approaches moral philosophy from a position which places the concept of the "ought" above all other considerations. He contends that empirical evidence muddles what is, with what ought to be and thereby confuses the study of ethics. If ethics deals with the "ought," moral judgments must deal with universal and binding rules regardless of personal opinions or preferences. Thus, the concept of a priori knowledge becomes the cornerstone of his philosophy. (A priori means prior to experience.) Kant seeks to discover those principles which are valid and universal regardless of personal experiences.

The question of good, then, is important, and Kant immediately claims, "It is impossible to conceive of anything at all in the world, or even out of it, which can be taken as good without qualification, except a *good will*." Thus, if one wills to be good, then the good is in the willing, and circumstances, consequences, and other conditionally good things do not diminish a good will. Kant maintains that reason has a practical function, to produce a good will. He contends that reason does not make us happy. To the contrary, instincts are better at doing that. But since all things exist to some purpose (note the teleological premise), reason must exist not to make us happy but to produce a good will, which is a greater end than happiness.

This, then, leads to Kant's concept of duty. He identifies three possible motives for any human action: inclination, self-interest, and duty. The first two may be done in accordance with duty, while the last is done for the sake of duty. Kant insists that a good will acts for the sake of duty. "Duty is the obligation to act in reverence for the moral law." Three examples should show how Kant distinguishes the differences.

If a person does not cheat his customers, he is acting in accordance with the moral law. If he chooses not to cheat those customers because he knows cheating is a bad business practice, and in the long run it will hurt him (self interest), he is acting in accordance with duty. If a person is upset with the condition of his life, contemplates suicide, and then out of fear (inclination), decides not to end it all, he too is acting in accordance with duty. But in neither example is the person acting for the sake of duty. Acting for the sake of duty is acting in response to the command, "Do not cheat," or "Do not take your life," with total disregard for your own self interest, inclination, or any other external condition.

Kant then introduces the concept of maxims. A maxim is a subjective principle for action. There are two kinds of maxims, material and formal. A material maxim is one in which the actor has a motive and seeks some particular result. Since a good will cannot be concerned with results, since moral acts are good (or bad) regardless of results, the material maxim is insufficient to produce moral worth. Therefore, Kant introduces the formal maxim. The formal maxim is a principle for acting regardless of desire, self interest, results, or consequences. If one acts on the formal maxim for the sake of duty, then the act has moral worth.

Kant's supreme law of morality is the *categorical imperative*, which is the product of applying the formal maxim according to this principle: "I ought never to act except in such a way that I can will that my maxim should become a universal law." If one is about to act on a subjective principle, which he has free will to do or not to do, Kant requires that one simply ask, "what would happen if this act, which I am about to choose to do, were to become a universal law, which all others in my circumstance would have to do?" If, indeed, one were to apply this categorical imperative, knowing what should or should not be done would be obvious.

There are, according to Kant, three kinds of imperatives—*problematic hypothetical imperatives* (rules of skill), *assertoric hypothetical imperatives* (counsels of prudence), *apodeitic categorical imperatives* (laws of morality). Problematic hypothetical imperatives involve actions that are good only as a means to something else. They are used simply because of the desirability of the end, whatever that end might be. Assertoric hypothetical imperatives are also geared to the attainment of some end, but a natural end such as happiness. An example of a rule of skill would be, "If you wish to learn to play the piano, you must practice." An example of a counsel of prudence would be, "If you wish to be healthy, you should eat wisely." Neither of these hypothetical imperatives deals with the moral law. Only the categorical imperative can serve as moral law.

The categorical imperative is an unconditional moral command. It holds true in all circumstances, on all occasions, regardless of consequences, desires, or qualifications. If it holds in one instance, it holds in all. It is universal. If, for example, one is faced with the opportunity to lie for convenience' sake, by applying the maxim, "I shall choose to lie to avoid an unpleasantness" to the concept of the categorical imperative one would have to add, "Now everyone in my circumstance will, as a universal law, have to lie to avoid an unpleasantness." Our practical reason will tell us immediately that the result of that willed action becoming a universal law would be chaos. Thus, the moral law requires that we do not lie, not for profit, convenience, to fulfill desires, to help others, not for any reason whatever. And the reason for not lying is not fear of being caught, nor punishment, nor any other thing save the reverence for the moral law.

One should understand that the hypothetical imperatives can be and often are worthy goals. Kant's contention is that hypothetical imperatives have great value, simply not any moral value. Moral value emanates only from the will, a good will, and cannot have other factors of an a posteriori (after experience) nature involved. In fact, any factors of an experiential nature which affect our judgments mitigate against the purity that moral judgments require.

Finally Kant deals with what he calls the "postulates of practical reason," ideas of freedom, immortality, and God. Freedom, Kant says, is simply an extension of the autonomy of the will. Since morality deals with the "ought," the clear implication is one "might not." Thus, morality is contingent upon choice. If we had no choice we could have no morality. If, indeed, we were beings programmed by forces outside ourselves, our actions would be the result of the programming, not our choice. Moral acts are the direct result of our choices. The categorical imperative requires the concept of freedom. One must be free to will to act, or will that his maxim become a universal law. This Kant says is not a theory; it is a practical necessity. If morality is to be considered binding, practically we must be free to choose.

The second postulate is that of immortality. Kant maintains: 1) that the *summum bonum* is the supreme and unconditioned good—the good will; and 2) that the *bonum consummatum* is the complete, the whole good. Kant recognizes that happiness is a part of man's teleological end, and thus the perfect good would be virtue and happiness. However, he also understands that virtue does not necessarily lead to happiness; more often than not virtue can and does lead to unhappiness. If, then, it is correct to pursue virtue and happiness, but there is no necessary connection between the two, then the dictates of practical reason require that immortality, the continued existence of our spirit after death, is a practical necessity in order to achieve the perfect good, i.e., virtue and happiness.

Finally, God is also a postulate of practical reason. Since there will be no just distribution of happiness in relation to virtue in this life, God must exist if one accepts the possibility of the goal of the *summum bonum* and moral goodness. Kant contends that since we are not completely rational, and thus not completely good, the concept of an absolute good demands the existence of a fully rational and good being. This being is called God. The belief in morality and the search for perfection require their attainment somewhere. That requirement is met by the existence of God.

To sum up, Kant sought to establish an a priori basis of morality. His concept of the good will as being unconditioned good focuses attention on the intent, not the consequences, of moral acts. Duty and respect for the law follow, and through the use of the categorical imperative one achieves the essence of all moral laws. Through the categorical imperative the concept of universality is made clear, and the importance of universality to morality is made necessary. Through the investigation of the various imperatives, the idea that man is an end in himself, and not a means is crucial to his concept called "intuitionism." Finally, his ideas about freedom, immortality, and God as necessary conditions to the study of morality have had great impact on how men study ethics. In fact, it has been said that the study of ethics, while it can be approached without accepting Kant's postulates, cannot be approached without taking Kant's postulates into serious consideration.

Arthur Schopenhauer (1788-1860)

Arthur Schopenhauer was born in Danzig, Germany into a prosperous and cosmopolitan family. His entrance into the world of academia began early and continued in several countries as he studied and traveled in France, Germany, England, Switzerland, and Austria. He began writing with an intense desire to earn fame, but most of his early attempts to publish were rebuked, and even his most important work, *The World as Will and Idea,* published in 1819, was received coldly by the critics.

In 1820, he began lecturing at the University of Berlin, but there, too, he encountered rejection. At the time, Hegel was one of the University's most popular teachers, and it is said that Schopenhauer purposely scheduled his classes opposite Hegel's. In this competition for students, Schopenhauer lost badly. He wrote several more works, with the same result, until he published *Essays from the Parerga and Paralipomena.* This collection of essays began a period of gradual acceptance of his ideas, and led eventually to the fame he yearned to achieve.

Plato and Kant greatly influenced his thought. Kant's concepts of *phenomenon* and *noumenon* were crucial to his theory of knowledge. Kant believed that that there is a real distinction between the appearance of a thing to the perceiving mind (phenomenon) and the thing itself (noumenon), which exists outside of experience and therefore is unknowable. Schopenhauer's philosophy turns on the concept of reality and how it is known. His approach to the concept of "will" and "idea" becomes the basis for his ethical philosophy.

It is ironic that his philosophy, called Pessimism, became exceptionally popular after his death, while during most of his life his pessimism was validated by his experience. Throughout his life his desire for popularity was always thwarted.

Schopenhauer begins his most famous work with the statement, "The world is my idea." What he is in fact saying is that he believes that we know only by way of our sensations and ideas. The world is object for subject; its reality consists in being perceived by a subject. Presentations can be intuitive or abstract—intuitive ideas are possessed by both men and animals, while abstract presentations can only be possessed by man. If we are to know, he says, we must know from within ourselves. The material world can only be identified and described with words. To know it is to perceive it in our own mind and then, through our mind, know it.

This is not to say that the intellect is the force which leads man to understanding. To the contrary, Schopenhauer claims that the underlying force in the universe is the Will. The Will (later referred to as the Will to Live) is an all encompassing force which exists within every living thing. The Will exists in man, in animals, in plants, in every living being. All other attributes are at the command of the Will. Men think that the intellect guides the Will. Not so, says Schopenhauer. The Will commands the intellect. The Will decides; the intellect rationalizes the desire into some logical explanation.

Abstract concepts are formed by reason, not in order to understand the real nature of things—reason is incompetent to do that—but rather to facilitate the Will to Live. Abstract concepts are necessary for communication and to pass on information. They are instruments for satisfying the needs of an organism more highly developed and complicated than an animal. In animals, mere instinct is sufficient to satisfy the needs of the Will. In man both instinct and reason are necessary.

Let us for a moment try to understand this concept of the Will. In plants we see seeds take hold in the cracks in sidewalks, in animals we see birds build nests for the unborn, ants work tirelessly, and insects lay their eggs where the larvae will find food. None of these observable phenomena is the product of reason, but rather the product of the Will to Live, manifested in the instinct of every living thing. This Will is an endless striving, a blind urge which knows no cessation, and it can never find satisfaction. Knowing it is a world force is important, but knowing its implications for man is more important, because it explains the essence of man.

What then are the implications for man also subject to this primeval force? First, every living thing has the urge, the powerful urge, to reproduce. The Will to Live finds its most observable proof in this urge to reproduce. In the animal world it is a stark world of simple life, reproduction, death. Man follows the same pattern, but creates concepts to explain the instinct reasonably. Love, for example, is just another word for sexual attraction; sexual attraction is nature's way of perpetuating the species. The notions of love, marriage, romance, companionship, and living happily ever after, are merely by-products of the urge to reproduce.

In addition to sex, the Will is insatiable in all other things. The Will can never be satisfied; therefore life is a constant state of wanting. Life is pain, because life is desire, and desire cannot be satisfied. Even the attainment of greatly desired ends simply gives way to new desires. How many times has one said, "If I only can have this, I'll be happy forever," only to be soon bored by the possession. Or, "I'm so stuffed, I won't want to eat for a week," only to be hungry later that evening.

Life, then, is an evil we have to bear. It is evil because we are never sated. It is evil because we feel pain, and pain is the norm, not the exception. Short respites of pleasure or happiness are fleeting moments in a life filled with unfulfilled desires. Schopenhauer contends that the more highly developed the organism, the greater the suffering. A plant feels no pain; a man does. The more intelligent, sensitive, complex the man, the more he will suffer. The intelligent man knows with frightening certainty that he is doomed to strive, compete, desire—to live—and in the midst of the struggle—he will die. Perhaps ignorance is bliss. In addition to not being satisfied, in addition to the pain our very intelligence causes, we are then faced with a world of competition, conflict, and greed—in a word, war. What is to be done?

The obvious answer is, "If life is so terrible, end it." But suicide, Schopenhauer says, is not the answer. Suicide does not overcome the Will. It is simply an individual act which has no effect on the Will, which lives on in the species. There is a better way, and Schopenhauer explains how man can overcome, not succumb to, the Will.

There are two ways of escaping the slavery of the Will. The first is the way of aesthetic contemplation. If one can become a disinterested spectator and observe art, not as an object of desire, but as an object of aesthetic contemplation, he will be able to temporarily escape the servitude of the Will. Beyond this, one who can translate ideas into works of art rises above the subjugation of the Will. In particular, Schopenhauer thinks music is the highest art form, in which the Will itself is illustrated. In music, man receives a "direct revelation... And he intuits this reality, revealed in the form of art in an objective and disinterested manner, not as one caught in the grip of the Will's tyranny. Further, if it were possible to express accurately in concepts all that music expresses without concepts, we should have the true philosophy."

Schopenhauer offers a second, and lasting, way to be released from the Will. This is achieved by the renunciation of the Will to Live. The Will to Live manifests itself in egoism, self-assertion, striving, and conflict—morality requires a denial of the Will. He sees a four-step process which man can follow towards the only salvation available. First he must realize that he is acting from self-interest in relation to his desires, thus recognizing that he has a problem. Then he must understand that all other individuals are all on the same level that he is. Out of this realization will come a sympathy for all his fellow men. After all they are all like rats on a sinking ship. And finally his individual Will denies the Will to Live. He advances to a nirvana-like state, desirous of nothing phenomenal, contemplating only the noumenal, the object as it is in its essential form. He will have no need for others, for approval, for companionship, sex, or any of the desires of the will. Rather, he will simply contemplate beauty, especially art, and the intellect will have defeated the Will.

The process described here saves the individual. How can we save the species? Schopenhauer answers, "by overcoming the will to reproduce." If men can realize how women use their sexual devices to muddle men's thinking and thereby distract them from more worthy goals, the beginning will be at hand. Women, by nature, cannot overcome their desires, because the desires are too strong and the intellect too weak. Men can overcome those desires, but only through the intellect. The intellect must learn to distinguish sex from beauty. That which we call beautiful in women, is not beauty but sex. The only women we call beautiful are those of child bearing age. No love sonnets are written for female octogenarians. The pictures in *Playboy* are not art, not even artistic. They are sexual attractions, meant to stimulate men and render their intellects useless. So, he advises men to avoid women, develop the intellect, diminish the Will, and slowly the world will move towards the extinction of the race. When procreation ceases, the Will is overcome, and the peace that only death can bestow triumphs.

CHAPTER 11

Nietzsche and Sartre:
Naturalism and Existentialism

Friedrich Nietzsche (1844-1900)

Friedrich Nietzsche was born in Rocken, Saxony. After the death of his father, in 1849, the family moved to Naumburg. There he was educated in the best schools and attended Schulpforta, a famous Protestant boarding school, where he founded an artistic society called Germania. He studied at the Universities of Bonn and Leipzig, and at the age of twenty-four he became professor of classics at the University of Basel in Switzerland.

The Birth of Tragedy from the Spirit of Music, Nietzsche's first book, written in 1872, dealt with Greek tragedy. He explored the two basic desires in man, the conflict they produce, and how tragedy must be understood in the terms he called Apollonian and Dionysian. Apollo, the sun god, represented the force of order, while Dionysus, the god of wine, represented the irrational forces in the universe which drive man. Nietzsche saw the union of these two forces as a means to propel man into a new morality.

In Thus Spoke Zarathustra, Beyond Good and Evil, Genealogy of Morals, and The Antichrist, Nietzsche attacked the religious foundations of morals, the conduct of Europeans, and the Judeo-Christian heritage, and called for a re-evaluation of traditional morality. The Will to Power, his last work, also dealt with the philosophy that is clearly enunciated in the title.

In 1880 his mental and physical health began to deteriorate, and in 1888 he suffered a severe mental breakdown. It is ironic that Nietzsche, the creator of the "Superman," spent the last twelve years of his life in a childlike state, totally unable to communicate, fingering the keys of a piano, alone and docile.

Nietzsche's basic premise is based on a philosophy called

Naturalism. The concept is similar to Schopenhauer's view that instincts dominate reason, but rather than see that fact as a cause for pessimism, Nietzsche rejoices in it. While Schopenhauer sought to overcome instinct through reason and thus temper desire, Nietzsche saw instinct as natural and good. Anything which is validated by nature and by the basic natural principals of survival, striving, and life itself, is worthy. Since whatever conforms to nature is good, whatever hampers the natural instincts to power, assertion, and domination is wrong. This view is at odds with the Europe Nietzsche was born into. As a matter of fact, Nietzsche saw the whole of western civilization as the product of a process of rationalism and a liberal democratic tradition—in short decadent, deficient, and doomed.

Schopenhauer called the instinctive force in the world the Will to Live. Nietzsche called this natural law the Will to Power. The Will to Power is manifested throughout nature; each creature from high to low seeks to dominate within a natural order. Larger animals devour smaller ones, stronger ones dominate weaker ones, faster ones overtake slower ones. When we see the lion overcome a natural enemy in the forest, then roar to announce the victory, we do not refer to the lion's "evil" act. We understand the natural "valueless" reality of each creature seeking to assert that power that is within him. Self preservation of all species is a natural law, but not the first law. It is an outgrowth of the Will to Power. If this is so in nature, why should man be different? Nietzsche, of course, says man is not substantially different.

In a moral sense, there are no absolutes. What one chooses as best for himself is good; what one rejects as a hindrance is bad. Each man seeks to expand his world, and however he does it, it is good for him. Traditional morality hinders man in this process, so man must overcome it. In fact, Nietzsche says there are two types of morality, the "master morality" and the "slave morality." Master morality is the way the free spirits look at the world—their actions are "good" or "bad" as they affect themselves. The herd sees morality "good" and "evil," terms which describe absolutes. Nietzsche, a subjectivist, declares that only the individual can determine what is good for himself; he is the judge. Once the concept of "evil" is introduced, the judgement is taken out of the hands of the individual and put into a definition.

The herd associates power with "evil" and seeks to limit the power of their betters by linking the two terms. If, indeed, the herd can convince others that the linkage is valid, the result is a limitation of the powers of others. The superior man, however, is creative, courageous, and determines values according to his own lights. It is obvious that the superior man is an individual, and as such acts alone and is not afraid to choose what he requires. The herd, or slave, morality is in fact a morality of utility; they (the members of the herd) cannot act alone, are afraid of the superior individuals, and therefore create a morality meant to inhibit those superior to themselves. That morality is one that calls "evil" all those qualities of power, strength, courage, creativity, and individualism. Conversely, that morality calls "good" all those things which protect the herd.

Beyond his appeal to nature, Nietzsche traces the concept of the master morality back to the Romans. (The Roman word for virtue translates literally into "bravery" or "strength.") The concept of the herd, or slave, morality he traces first back to the Jews. He considers Jewish ethics a device created by a weak and oppressed people to inhibit their tormenters by threatening them with the retaliation of God. The Ten Commandments are not God's laws, says Nietzsche, but were the Jewish rules for self-preservation in a world in which they were unable to compete. Unable to compete according to the rules of strength, courage, and individual effort, they resorted to cunning, deception, and as a group, created the herd morality. The Christian ethic of humility, passivity, charity, and meekness is equally despicable to Nietzsche. Interestingly, Nietzsche admired Christ, whom he considered an anti-establishment man; it is Christianity, the established religion, that he despised.

There are several problems which emanate from this slave morality. In addition to making whole races of people docile and lifeless, the inhibitions imposed on individuals limit personal progress of an untold number of potential geniuses. Beyond the problems imposed on individuals is the social retardation that takes place. Progress is stifled, creativity is hindered, civilization's very growth is slowed. The master mentality, creative, passionate, and eager to risk everything, produces the art, music, beauty, that can only be born of cruelty, suffering, and the exhilaration of power.

master and slave morality.

Once the free spirits, the aristocrats of the world, free themselves from the chains that traditional morality has imposed upon them, they will begin a new race. This new race will be composed of men unfettered by standard morality, who will violate old values, choose new ones, and to whom nothing will be forbidden that contributes to growth, creativity, power, and life. The goal is not to achieve the betterment of mankind (mankind is a mass term), but the betterment of man. These "Lords of the Earth" will, through natural selection create better and better men to mate with better and better women and evolve into supermen. The Superman will be the legacy of Nietzsche's new morality. And while most moral philosophy seeks to provide norms for all, Nietzsche's supermen will stand apart from the mass, like the title of his book "Beyond Good and Evil."

The mass man, of course, would fear these aristocrats, full of power and strength. Certainly the strong would overpower and enslave the weak. Not so, says Nietzsche; these free spirits are not mean spirits. Understanding that good and bad are individual judgements, they would be tolerant of different views. Nietzsche's moral man has no need to impose his morality on anyone. He is self-sufficient, tolerant, wise, and free. And if the mass man holds on to outmoded, impotent concepts of "evil," that's not the problem of Nietzsche's hero—he's too busy living life to the fullest to care.

It will be the job of this new man to complete the task of bringing moral philosophy into harmony with the principles of Naturalism. This is called the transvaluation of values. Transvaluation of values requires that all the values of the Judeo-Christian ethic be exposed for the anti-life forces they represent. In their place he asks that the values of power, creativity, courage, and a subjective view of the world be instituted. These values are not meant to appeal to all, nor could the mass man accept them. These values are for the few, the strong, the men with the courage to grab and embrace them. In a sense, Nietzsche is simply calling for a return to the world he believed existed prior to the dominance of the Judeo-Christian ethic, with, however, an understanding of how and why the Judeo-Christian ethic took hold. Thus, the new man will not be inhibited by it, and the future will be dominated by the new race of men.

[Handwritten margin notes: "power directly", "Smother creativity is", "Power needed because of fear", "Sounds a lot like Hitler"]

Jean-Paul Sartre (1905-1980)

Jean-Paul Sartre was born in Paris, France on June 21, 1905. His father died when Jean-Paul was two years old and he and his mother moved in with his maternal grandparents who were closely related to Albert Schweitzer, the famous physician and African missionary. In his youth he was plagued by feelings of bitterness because of his lack of monetary and social status, his concern with his physical unattractiveness, and his general attitude toward what he considered to be a hostile society. At an early age he became a "loner" and decided to become a writer. Also, he was dominated by two strong religionists, his Roman Catholic grandmother and his Calvinist grandfather, so that at the age of twelve he made his final religious decision. He not only rejected their sectarian views, he rejected religion entirely and became a lifelong atheist.

He studied at the Lycée Henri IV in Paris and received his degree in philosophy from the École Normale Superieure. While studying for his degree in philosophy he met Simone de Beauvoir, who became his lifelong companion and collaborator. In 1933 he was awarded a fellowship at the Institut Francais in Berlin. There he was introduced to the existential philosophy of Martin Heidegger and the phenomenological philosophy of Edmund Husserl. The basis of his own philosophy was thus formed, and he expanded and developed an existential view of the world from that point on.

World War II had a profound effect on his thinking also. When the Germans occupied France and he was taken prisoner for a year, he changed from an iconoclastic viewer of the world into a politically active mover in the world. His anti-Fascist philosophy coupled with his earlier view of society, moved him to the left, where he moved in and out of socialist and communist political causes. He generally supported the "working class," cooperative economic systems, the leveling of the classes, and the political positions that advanced that point of view.

He was a prolific writer of novels, plays, and philosophical treatises. *Nausea, The Wall,* and *The Age of Reason* are three of his most important novels. His most famous play, *No Exit,* appeared in 1945 and was an important dramatic existential statement. His other plays include *The Flies, Dirty Hands,* and *The Condemned of Altona.* His most famous philosophical work, *Being and Nothingness,* explains his existential philosophy. He also continued developing his views in *Existentialism is a Humanism, Critique of Dialectical Reasoning,* and *Search for a Method.*

Jean-Paul Sartre was probably the most influential of the atheistic existentialists. He reached the height of his popularity during "the sixties," that decade between 1965—1975 when his brand of existentialism was very influential among the young. He died in 1980.

Almost all discussions of existentialism begin with the statement, "Existence precedes essence. There are several ways to approach that statement for understanding. In one sense it means that there are no absolutes, no eternal truths, no Platonic ideals or Aristotlean essences. Also, this concept maintains that everything exists only in our consciousness. There are no metaphysical realities, only descriptions of what exists as psychological realities. In another sense, not only does existence precede essence, there is never a real essence, since each occurrence has an effect on that which exists and thereby changes it. Thus, each individual gives meaning to things. There are no independent realities outside the individual.

There are two types of existential philosophies, theistic and atheistic. The early influences on Sartre, Kierkigaard and Heidegger, were theistic existentialists, as was Sartre's contemporary Martin Buber. But Sartre committed early to the atheistic position and his existentialism reflects that position. He disputes the existence of God on three levels. First, all existence is contingent on other factors, so if God exists, He exists as a dependent being, and the concept of an all-powerful God is nullified. Second, Sartre's concept of absolute freedom requires that man choose his own essence, his own nature. If God existed and created man, man would have a God-given nature and could not create his own; therefore, God cannot exist if Sartre's premise of freedom is true. Finally, if God is all-powerful, then limits on man's freedom are possible, and Sartre claims this cannot be so. Therefore, God cannot exist.

Two terms which are important to Sartre's concept of being are "being in-itself" and "being for-itself." The idea of in-itself deals with objects as they are. These are the objects of the phenomenal world, as in Kant's phenomenon. There is no such thing as noumenon. According to Sartre, what you see is what is, and there is no difference between what a thing seems and what a thing is. The idea of "for-itself," deals with man, who has no fixed nature and therefore is an absence of being or *nothingness*. Man is a subjective being. His human consciousness is not a thing in-itself, but a thing for-itself, therefore, incomplete, an absence of phenomenal qualities—therefore, nothingness.

Through this concept of nothingness, Sartre constructs his concept of the nature of man. If man's consciousness is nothingness, then there is no structure whatever. No structure whatever means that man is free, and thus man's essential nature is freedom. Man does not choose to be free; he is free by lack of design, because he is a subjective being, and therefore is constantly creating, by his choices, his own nature. Man, says Sartre, is "condemned to be free," which imposes a terrible responsibility. There are no excuses to be made, no forces outside oneself to blame, and no God to look to for forgiveness or mercy. Man is free, he is responsible for his actions, his choices make him what he is. In short, man is the sum total of his actions. This is a frightening concept: total freedom = total responsibility.

The realization that one is free, responsible, and alone, is a cause for great anguish and anxiety. The weight of the responsibility for creating, in effect oneself, is no small concern. The realization that one is alone in an absurd (undefined) world is frightening. The prospect of continually choosing and being responsible for those choices, with the simultaneous knowledge of certain death, is another difficult concept with which to deal. In addition to all the personal responsibility, there exists a social responsibility which only serves to exacerbate the problem. Sartre contends that one's actions affect not only oneself, but others. Therefore by a process similar to Kant's categorical imperative, Sartre claims that one realizes his responsibility not simply to himself, but to all mankind.

This concept requires some explanation. If man is the creator of his own values, if he rejects all claims of any objective values, and if there are no premises upon which one must rely in order to create his own values—what, then, prevents men from acting with total irresponsibility? Sartre asserts that it is the very fact that there can be no excuses for one's actions. This is why the moral responsibility which falls upon each individual will be met. In an existential world of no excuses, each man knows full well when he is wrong, and realizing that fact will act responsibly. He says, "nothing can be good for us without being good for all." Add to this the concept of Humanism, which Sartre equates with existentialism, and the idea that while each man is a free, subjective being, he is first and foremost a man. The human condition is the same for all. It is the individual nature of each person which is different. The fact than man's choices affect other men inhibits irresponsible behavior.

These profound concerns can lead a person into what Sartre calls "bad faith." Bad faith occurs when an individual begins to treat himself as an object (in-itself) rather than a free, subjective, and responsible being (for-itself). Rather than accept, without reservation, responsibility for what one is (remember, we create ourselves through our choices), the temptation for self-deception is an easy way out. To claim that heredity, social forces, poor upbringing, subconscious or unconscious motivations, have contributed to our shortcomings is acting in bad faith. Each person is responsible, completely and utterly for his actions—complete freedom requires this to be so, and the self deception of bad faith is invalid.

Sartre spent the better part of his life describing a philosophy which can only be called "pessimistic." His terminology—nausea, despair, condemned to be free, responsibility, nothingness, anxiety is full of words which connote a negative view of life in this world. In *Nausea* his hero Roquentin concludes that "existence is contingent, gratuitous, unjustifiable." Life is absurd in that there is no purpose, no direction, no meaning. Roquentin lives in the continual frustration of not being able to escape this "obscene superfluity."

Also, Sartre contends that "man fundamentally is the desire to be God." He desires to be "some thing" rather than nothingness. Since that is impossible (it's impossible for God to be God—God would be for it-self and in it-self by definition), man is engaged in a struggle which can only frustrate him. In the face of this bleak philosophy, why should one struggle to achieve the impossible? Why should one show kindness and charity if the end is the finality of death?

In *Existentialism is Humanism* Sartre contends that existentialism is not a pessimistic philosophy, but rather one that lauds action, elevates man as a creator of values, rejoices in the fact that man makes the laws for man, and finally places man at the center of the universe as he ought to be. One of his last statements about his philosophy maintains that man can find self-fulfillment in this life.

PART 3

POLITICAL THEORY: THE RELATIONSHIP OF MAN AND THE STATE

CHAPTER 12

Introduction to Political Theory

Political philosophers conceive of the nature of the state in forms that will conform to their view of the nature of man and of good societies. Political philosophy must deal with questions about the state and man's relations to and within the state. Most people discuss the state and problems related to the state without ever having answered the question, what is the state? In this chapter we will deal with the elements which comprise the state, the origin of the state, its nature, and its sovereignty. In Chapter Thirteen we will discuss law; what it is, where it comes from, its role in society, and why it is so important and integral to the study of political theory. In Chapter Fourteen we will address five problems of government which affect all states. The ways in which particular states deal with these problems determines what form the state will take. Finally, in the next several chapters we will deal with some of the political thinkers who have contributed greatly to the subject in their search for the ideal state.

The state is an institution, the origin and nature of which we will discuss later. There are five elements which are necessary to comprise a state. A state consists of *people, territory, government, unifying factors,* and *sovereignty.* Obviously, people are a necessary requirement for the existence of any state. Territory is another crucial element; there are boundaries, either natural or political, and states exist within certain geographical limits. Small islands are often limited by the simple fact of their isolation from other land masses, and the state is limited to the confines of that island. Political boundaries are set by sovereign states in relation to one another, according to treaties, pacts, or agreements between the parties involved.

Government, the means by which states function, is another essential element. Government is to the state as the board of directors is to a corporation. In order for the states to carry out their function, government is necessary. In Marxist philosophy, where one of the tenets calls for the "withering away of the state," i.e., the government, one of the questions posed asked "How can the necessary functions required by a society be carried out without government?" The answer given refers to a system of organizations which would run the operations necessary to serve the people. Organizations or government, or even board of directors, call it what you will, there is an entity which will exist for the purpose of carrying out the necessary services a society requires.

Unifying factors are also a necessary element of the state. Some of the more obvious factors that tie the people of a state together are: language, religion, culture, customs, common history, money, standards of weights and measures, and symbols. It is obvious that a state with several different kinds of currency would have some serious problems. The standardization of a money supply simplifies, expedites, and indeed makes possible an economic system, which is essential to the material well-being of a society. A common language is an obvious unifying factor, since language is the basis for cultural, historical, and moral values. The history of problems within bilingual nations (with Switzerland as the obvious exception) is very *religion* evident. There is still a great deal of animosity in Canada *not just* between the French- and the English-speaking people. Religion, *for* sometimes in conjunction with language, is also a divisive factor *common* if there is no common ethic. Witness the problems of the *beliefs* Catholics and Protestants in Northern Ireland, the Catholics and *but also* Moslems in Lebanon, the Jews and Arabs in the Middle East, the *common* Hindus and Moslems in India—the examples are many. *ethics*

There are within every state, many unifying factors. If those important factors are undermined or come into conflict with new *enemy* or different concepts, the tranquility of the state will be upset. *to the* This is not to say that the state might not be better off due to the *state* conflict, or that when tranquility is restored progress will not *new* have been made. It simply means that unifying factors are *Concepts:* necessary to the existence of an effective state. *ex. Jesus,* The final element of the state is the one which distinguishes *Ghandi,* a state from all other entities—sovereignty. A school has people, *martin* territory, unifying factors, and a government or organization to *luther* meet the needs of the school community. A church, a town, a fraternity, a corporation, and a family have all the elements of a

Def. Sovereignty

[handwritten margin note top: Sovereignty—what makes a state unique from other institutions. Final authority.]

state—except one. Sovereignty is that quality which makes a state a power unto itself. Sovereignty is the final authority, the highest authority, the last court of appeal. Sovereignty is what makes a state different from and superior to a school, a town, a corporation, or any other institution. Sovereignty resides in a state, somewhere, as defined by that state and is where "the buck stops."

Jean Bodin, in the sixteenth century, set forward a definition of sovereignty which can shed some light on the concept. Bodin claimed that sovereignty was *absolute, comprehensive, indivisible,* and *nontransferable.* Much of what he said was in a historical context which is important, but not germane to this discussion. What we are interested in are the implications of his theory which transcend his particular time frame. Let's examine each term. Absolute means without question, free from limit or qualification. When we speak of an absolute monarch we are talking about one who is free to do whatever he pleases in regard to his subjects. Comprehensive means all-inclusive, covering all aspects of the society. There are no favored elements, no exceptions to the rule—sovereignty is exercised and has jurisdiction over all. Indivisible was a term used by Bodin to indicate that a king could not share power with a legislature. Obviously a king and legislature can share power, but sovereignty itself cannot be shared—it must rest somewhere, indivisible. Finally, the concept of nontransferability deals with the idea that if an absolute ruler transfers (gives) that sovereign power to another, he can not, of right, reclaim it. To transfer an absolute power to another, makes the other an absolute power, and a return of that power would be at the largesse of the holder, not at the demand of the former holder.

[handwritten margin note right: in depth def of elements in sovereignty]

The point of using Bodin's concept of sovereignty, is to make clear the importance of the concept, and the power of the idea. In every aspect of government or government-like organization, there is the opportunity for appeal. In every scheme of levels of authority, a higher authority can overrule a lower one. There is a hierarchy of authority in every organization known to man. *[handwritten margin: sovereignty]* The state is the only entity where that hierarchy ends, finally and completely, at some place, and that place is where sovereignty resides.

There are several theories which are held in opposition to

against Bodin's concept of Sovereignty

Bodin's concept of sovereignty, and we shall examine some of them. First is the concept of *dualism*. Dualists believe that sovereignty can be shared, so long as the areas to be shared are carefully delineated and defined. Probably the most important experiment in dualism has been the one which has been in effect for the last two hundred years in the United States, where the federal government shares power with the states. Another concept that challenges Bodin's is *internationalism*. Internationalists contend that no nation is *truly* sovereign. In a world of nuclear weapons, economic interdependence, treaties and alliances, sovereignty is an illusion. No nation is free to do whatever it wants to do. No nation, says the internationalists, does what it chooses to do. It does what it *must* do to survive in a totally interdependent world.

true on a global scale now but on a state wide basis sovereignty can exist.

Also, there are people who claim that *law* is sovereign. They contend that no one, no entity, is higher than the law. The impeachment of Andrew Johnson is an example of an American president, one of the most powerful men in the world, being subject to law. Likewise the resignation of Richard Nixon, at the time probably *the* most powerful man in the world, was brought about by the force of law. At the other extreme there are those who say that *power* is sovereign, and in the final analysis power exists in the barrel of a gun. Those who accept the idea that power is sovereign contend that sovereignty is the final authority. Authority requires power of enforcement, and enforcement requires superior force. If Nixon were the most powerful man in the world, he would not have had to submit to the Congress. As Commander-in-Chief, he could have mobilized the army and maintained power. Those who subscribe to the power school of thought would say that the only reason he resigned was because he chose not to *use* the power at his command, since he did, in fact, *have* the power.

Now it doesn't because of other Sovereign nations.

Another group believes in the idea of *popular sovereignty,* which claims that after all, the people are sovereign. This group contends that law is not sovereign; if all the people want a law changed, it will be changed. They believe that if the people truly want something, regardless of the pressures of the international community, the people will prevail. Finally, they say that if the people want something, dualism doesn't matter and force cannot prevail over everyone. The popular sovereignty adherents claim

true to a certian extent and with certian issues.

people in the long run always win.

that even though the "people" are not organized, that although the "people" have no formal method of exercising sovereignty, in the long run, the "people" always win.

What then, is the function of this institution which is similar to most other institutions, yet because of sovereignty is stronger than any? The first and most basic function of the state is to maintain order. Each state's philosophy is based on a particular premise as to how best establish and maintain order. The structure of the state should be in harmony with that philosophy; any contradictions between the structure and the philosophy would probably lead to disorder, or at least, unrest. We should look to the philosophical premises about how a state should function, then examine whether the structure facilitates the implementation of that philosophy.

The Founding Fathers used the Preamble to the United States Constitution to set forth certain philosophical goals: "to establish domestic tranquility" (maintain order); "to form a more perfect union" (refers to the problems of the Articles of Confederation and how the structure failed to carry out the promise of the philosophy); "establish justice" (a very important goal of most states, to insure that the citizens can reasonably expect fair treatment); "provide for the common defense" (another primary purpose of the state, to provide for the people's security); "promote the general Welfare" (order is not enough; order is the basis for progress, and the state's role is to provide an atmosphere for individual and group progress); "And secure the Blessings of Liberty to ourselves and our Posterity" (a basic philosophical statement about a high American priority, liberty). The Constitution is the document which creates the structure and provides the means (laws) by which the government will carry out its function in accordance with the philosophical goals.

How did the state come into being? Theories about the origin of the state, coupled with speculation about the nature of the state, become important as premises upon which to base theories of how the state should function, and what structure will best accomplish the goals set forth by the philosophy. We will briefly study the *kinship* theory, the *force* theory, the *social contract* theory, the *divine* theory, the *organic* and *organismic* theories.

The kinship theory of the state explains the origin of the state as the outgrowth of the family. If one were to accept the father

the making of States is in our nature- we have a pack mentality saftey in numbers.

as the sovereign, then the family would fit the description given earlier of a state. It would grow by the joining of many related families, and at that point would be called a clan. The joining of clans with one another into a larger, more effective unit brings into being the tribe. The unification of many different tribes under the ruling umbrella of a council, or patriarch, or similar system, would create a nation. The evolution from the family to the present system of nation states, can be explained according to the scenario just presented. Those who accept this theory see the family as the basic unit of the state, and the modern state simply an extension of that family.

The force theory is one whose adherents claim is the only viable answer to the question of the state's origin. They contend that, in the earliest times of human existence, the cliché of the cave man with a club was not nearly so humorous as it was true. Man in nature is akin to all other animals, and the survival of the fittest is nature's law. After the use of simple brute force to subjugate others, man, having a well developed mind, sets up a system which allows him to rule more easily. The state, then, is one of man's many improvisations. However, if the rules set up by the strongest are violated, he always employs that strength (force) to command obedience. And, of course, the threat of that force is always present. The force theorists claim that the modern nation state is no different today than in the days of the cave man. The bottom line is, "When the rules fail, when persuasion fails, when consensus fails, force does not." All unresolved conflicts of opinion then and now, are and can only be resolved by the stronger imposing his will on the weaker.

The social contract theory of the origin of the state is a product of the Age of Reason. The proponents of this theory contend that man is different from the animals in nature, and it is man's mind which makes that difference. Man in nature did have some of the same problems as did the animals, but recognizing those problems was within man's ability, and doing something about them was also within his competency. So, men got together, expressed their concerns, and devised systems to deal with those problems that result from human interaction. The state, the government, the rules of behavior and methods of enforcement of that behavior, the establishment of systems of justice, the means to change the rules, all this and more was the product of man's mind, his ability to reason, to discuss and to implement. In short, men recognized the need and created the state by coming together and agreeing to do so for their own mutual benefit.

The divine origin theory is one which comes in many different modes. Some say that God created all: man, the family, nature, the very universe. If all, then, is God's creation, why would the state be the exception? Also, there is the idea that man was created to lead the good life according to God's will. If this is so, then the family is God's creation so that man can come into the world and be nurtured. The church is God's creation to teach man about how to live the good life in a spiritual sense. The state is God's creation also, to help man live the good life in a material sense. All three entities have their origin in a divine plan, and to that extent each is of a divine origin. In the middle ages this concept was extended to include the ruler as God's representative. If the state was a divine creation, the head of the state must have some divine sanction. Thus the theory of the divine right of kings came into being. Usually, however, adherents of this theory contend that the state is of divine origin because it is part of the divine plan for man.

The organic theory is based closely on concepts of natural law. Aristotle said, "Man is, by nature, a political animal." Thus, the idea that man is born into the state, that the state is as natural as the family, is the basis for this theory. To drive home this idea that the state is a natural institution, into which all men are born and within which they must exist, Aristotle said, "For a man to live alone, he must be either a beast or a god." To the adherents of the organic theory, then, the state is as natural to man as is the need for food, water, clothing, and shelter. Just as man cannot exist without food, clothing, and shelter, so also he cannot live without other men within the context of the state. The implications of this theory are important for understanding concepts of authority, the relation of the citizen and the state, the theory of revolution, the rights of an individual in relation to the group, and man's role within the state.

There is one other theory of the origin of the state—the organismic theory. Often this theory is considered to be essentially the same as the organic theory. There are, however, differences which are not only essential, but have grave implications for how the state will function. While there are similarities with the organic theory, the differences will be apparent.

In the organismic theory the state is thought to be a living organism—not just similar to a living organism, but in fact a living organism. Mussolini advanced this theory of the state and considered the people to be the cells, the government to be the limbs, and the leader the brain. A state then, like all other living beings is born, grows, matures, peaks, declines, and eventually dies. The implications of this position are obvious. Imperialism is considered a sign of growth. Militarism becomes necessary for the implementation the imperial impulse, thus chauvinism almost always must accompany the other two in order to sustain them. This theory compares the state to a biological organism, and contends that the state is indeed a biological organism.

George F.W. Hegel put forth a theory which while organismic, dealt with the birth, life, growth, decline and death of the state as a spiritual entity. He claimed that a particular state, as a spiritual organism, rises and falls within a historical context.

Obviously, one's conception of the origin of the state will be reflected in the notion of the nature of the state. Briefly, let us discuss the nature of the state. If the state came into being by force, as a social contract, or as an imitation of a family—then it's nature is mechanistic. The state is simply a tool, a device, a mechanism which men use to provide for those needs we have enumerated earlier. The mechanistic theory thrusts man into the crucial role—man determines what the state will be. If however, the state is organic or divine in origin, or if the family is the unit which developed naturally into a state, then the state is natural to man. If the state is a natural entity, of which man is a part, then the whole is greater than any of its parts. Finally, if the state came into being as a living organism, then its nature is the same as all other living things, and as an organism poses the same implications for the state as it does for all living beings.

CHAPTER 13

Law:
Understanding the Rule of Reason

How many times have we heard the phrase, "There ought to be a law." Usually we find ourselves using that phrase, not because we have carefully thought out the need for a change in our legal system, but because we are annoyed, offended, or otherwise upset. Conversely, when we are stopped for running a stop sign or driving forty miles an hour in a twenty-five mile-an-hour zone, the lament is usually, "What a stupid law, what a ridiculous place for a stop sign—twenty-five miles an hour on this road is ludicrous." Luckily law is not enacted at the whim or whine of unhappy or recently arrested citizens.

Law is a basic concept which is vital to the study of political philosophy. Laws are the product of complex forces and factors which are important to understand. Simply stated, law is rules for the guiding of human conduct. There are all kinds of law— we speak of moral laws, natural laws, scientific laws, divine laws, political laws, criminal laws, civil laws, and international laws—to name but a few.

There are two important concepts about law that we should examine first. Law must be enacted and enforced. Enactment and enforcement, however, can be very different, since there are many different types of law. Scientific laws are enacted and enforced by nature; man discovers such laws and seeks to understand them. Often men seek to defy them, and when they do, the price they pay is high. The only times men can seemingly defy nature's laws are when men in fact cooperate with nature and use the laws to achieve the ends desired. The flight of an airplane is not in defiance of scientific laws, but is possible due to the use of scientific laws.

The Ten Commandments can be referred to as divine law or as moral law. In the final analysis, the individual enacts divine or moral law. By the process of determining one's moral values, one is enacting the law he will live by. When one considers transgressing the laws he has determined to be right or wrong, conscience comes into play. Conscience is the enforcer. In fact, when the conscience prevails, the law is not broken; if the law is broken and the conscience is truly touched, the law will probably not be broken again. If, indeed, the divine or moral law is broken routinely, and the conscience never prevails, or is never sufficiently touched to prevent a reoccurrence, then for that person, there is no moral or divine law.

Natural law is law which its adherents contend is universally valid, is discoverable through reason, is a "higher law," and violations are thwarted by the censure of reasonable men or sometimes by nature itself. Aristotle defined it as the understanding that a "thing must fulfill the essence of it's being." From this he concluded that for man to be man, he must be rational, since reason is the essence of man. Hobbes saw self-preservation as a natural law, justifying man's contract with the state for protection. Such concepts as justice, private property, permissible sexual activity, equality, and liberty have their basis in natural law.

The law which is enacted and enforced by the state is called political law. Simply stated, political law is a set of rules for the guiding of human conduct, enacted by a legal body, enforced by the state, with prescribed punishments for its violation. Within this context there are two types of political law, substantive law and procedural law.

Substantive law is law which bestows, enhances, or actually creates, a right. Those basic rights which we enjoy under law such as freedom of speech and freedom of religion, are examples of substantive law. Procedural laws are those laws which deal with the process of securing, defending, enforcing, and dealing with citizen's rights. The right to due process is a substantive law, the particulars of how due process is carried out is procedural law. Usually substantive law has its basis in moral, natural, or divine premises which are considered essential to the citizen/ citizen and citizen/state relationship. Procedural laws are often arbitrary laws which set speed limits, drinking ages, voting ages, and other rules which are not basic to the citizen/state relationship, but are practically necessary.

All the laws of a state, whether substantive or procedural,

have the authority of the state behind them and are all equally valid. Those laws exercised when the state assumes the role of the aggrieved and prosecutes offenders are called criminal law. Criminal law most closely resembles the definition stated earlier, which calls for rules enforced by the state with prescribed punishments for their violation. Civil law deals with relations or disputes between individuals; in these instances the state takes the role of the arbiter. If individuals feel that they have been unfairly taken advantage of by another, if they have been hurt, defrauded, or in any way have been injured, the state, under its rules, determines how an equitable settlement of the dispute is to be made.

To illustrate further the concept of law requires a brief discussion of international law. International law is law which governs the dealings between nations. These laws are enacted in the United Nations, by treaties which bring large numbers of states into agreement, or in conventions of nations called to decide on important issues. Much of international law is based on customs which nations agree to observe as law. The problem of international law rests then, not with the enactment, but with the enforcement of law. There is no law-enforcement agency within the international community that has the power that national states have (sovereignty). Therefore, in a very real sense, there is no such thing as international law. What there is, is a system that is designed to encourage international cooperation. The system usually works, but if a nation chooses not to go along with the international community, there is no sovereign power to force compliance.

Law, then, in large measure, holds the community together by forcing compliance with the rules that the community deems necessary and good. But where does law come from? To the average observer it may seem that law is the result of votes in councils, senates, congresses, meetings, courts, and all manner of assemblages. But, in fact, law is the product of a terribly complex, interwoven, interrelated, evolution of social and historical forces. The United States Senate has been called "the greatest deliberative body" in the world. The organization of that body was designed to encourage its members to consider those forces and to consider the sources from which law evolves.

One source of law is custom. Men living in communities

develop a *modus operandi* to facilitate achieving one of their important needs, the need for predictability. Imagine some of our earliest ancestors walking along a path towards one another. How many times there must have been accidents, conflicts, or wasted time and effort determining who should move aside, and which way each should move to facilitate passage. Without the force of law, without any necessary requirement to do so, the custom of moving to the right to pass, developed through common consent and mutual agreement. After a while, the custom began to have the force of law, i.e., those who passed on the left were considered to be in error if an accident occurred. Eventually states enacted political laws to conform to those which had their origin in custom. Many laws which have their origins in custom evolved for very good and necessary reasons, and were meant to make living in a social setting better, and in some cases, possible.

Religion is another source of law. Religious laws deal with moral ideals which men as value-setting animals require as guides to the good life. Just as law based on custom has a good and necessary basis for enactment, often the religious laws evolve from man's needs. The concept of adultery as being a moral wrong is not frivolous. The importance of the family as a stabilizing force in society is a generally accepted premise. Adultery is an obvious threat to that stability and the initial moral prohibition has great implications for political law. In most societies adultery has been a violation of moral *and* political law. Even in this age of no-fault divorce, adultery is still considered grounds for divorce, and in contested cases the adulterer, according to law, is liable.

Judicial interpretation is a source of law which emanates from the decisions of third parties in cases where the issues are not clear. In America, judicial decisions are attempts by the courts to clarify and resolve conflicts with our most basic law, (the Constitution) and to determine the intent of the framers of the law. A simple example of how the concept of judicial interpretation works follows. Consider the problem of the apple tree and the fallen apples. The owner of the tree considers, reasonably, the apples to be his. The next-door neighbor, into whose yard the apples fall, considers reasonably, the apples to be his. "My tree, my apples." "My yard, my apples." Can the two positions ever be reconciled? Both parties, sooner or later, must realize that the issue will not be settled between them. Perhaps, in an earlier age, men decided to ask a third party, an impartial arbiter, one whom they both respected, to decide the issue. The decision becomes a precedent, so that in all future cases, there is an example to refer to, and the whole issue does not have to be resurrected again and again.

Scientific revelation changes law by bringing into the process new and irrefutable evidence, which was previously unknown. The rules of procedure in criminal cases were changed radically when it was discovered that there are no two fingerprints alike, and that the similarities and differences between fingerprints can be identified. What was once not evidence at all, became evidence of the highest quality; what was not a part of the law became an integral part of the law. There are many areas of the law which have changed because of the discoveries of science and technology, and new law has been enacted to deal with those advances. One can only speculate on how many people have been arrested for drunkenness, when in fact they were suffering from a diabetic reaction or some other physical problem unrelated to alcohol. The invention of the breath-testing devices to measure the alcohol content in the blood has resulted in the creation of a whole new set of laws.

Codifications, while not a major source of law, have resulted in some new laws. Codifications are usually the product of a conscious attempt on the part of a government, or government agency, or head of government, to bring the body of law into some organized form. Over the years laws become outdated; they overlap, contradict, and often confuse those charged with creating, enforcing, and interpreting them. Perhaps the most famous historical example of codifying law is the Code Napoleon. Napoleon called for the codification of French law, and in the process many archaic laws were retired, contradictions eliminated, and the need for new laws became apparent.

Commentaries are an infrequent, but interesting, source of law. Occasionally some lawyer, judge, or scholar writes a commentary on the law which is so insightful or profound that the legal establishment take heed of those insights and rushes to incorporate the ideas into law. Gladstone's commentaries and Brandeis' sociological brief are examples of how commentaries contribute to the evolution of law.

The most basic law is the law of constitutions. Constitutions are created for the purpose of enacting the basic law upon which the state will rest. Constitutional law creates not just laws, but actual government entities, rules not only for the citizens, but for the government itself. The first three articles of the United States Constitution create and define the role of the three branches of the government. The first ten amendments of the United States Constitution are substantive laws which protect some of the most important rights citizens have. It is interesting that the average person tends to think that the Bill of Rights give citizens such rights as freedom of speech, press, and religious expression. What they do, in fact, is limit the federal government from interfering with these basic rights. They are basic laws which define the rules under which the government will operate. Constitutional law is difficult to enact and difficult to change; since it is very basic law these difficulties are intentional.

Decree law is that which is the product of the action of a person or entity with the power to promulgate law by fiat. The president of the United States, governors of particular states, the heads of government at many levels have this power. In the case of the president of the United States, one of the constitutional prerogatives he has is the power to pardon. By simple decree, he can pardon people convicted of crimes and revoke their punishments. An example of decree law occurred when President Lyndon Johnson, soon after John F. Kennedy's death, decreed that Cape Canaveral was to be renamed Cape Kennedy.

Legislation, earlier defined as political law, is law enacted by a body empowered to do so, with prescribed punishments for its violation, and is currently the most popular method of enacting law. In America legislation accounts for the great body of law because the philosophy and structure require it. America is a democratic nation, and representatives legislate on behalf of the people as part of the function of this government. Historically, legislation is a new method as a source of law. In the past kings enacted law by decree, theocracies used religion as the primary source of law, custom was an important source of law, and law changed according to new discoveries. Whatever source of law dominates at a particular time in history, all sources come into play and the great body of law in any society is the product of all these forces. Law, therefore, is a result of various complex forces which combine to produce not only law, but a spirit, an ethic, a reservoir of knowledge, a national character into which that law must fit.

The importance of law in society cannot be overstated. The contention that the primary purpose of the state is to maintain order has been challenged seriously only by those who contend that the primary purpose of the state is to make law. With the understanding that law is the product of many forces, all of which are essential elements of the society, we must seek to understand the purpose of law. The stock answer to the question, "What is the purpose of law?" is "To provide justice." But, the answer is more complex.

Justice, simply defined is, that each person receive his due; that we get what we deserve. That, however, is a definition only in an ideal sense. Justice in the state must be predicated on that idea, but as stated before, the complexities of the law and the administration of justice require that we pass laws that truly reflect the customs, morals, religion, and perceived rights of the citizenry. But the vital element is that law is or ought to be the rule of reason. That law is reasonable is the only valid justification for demanding compliance. Governments which pass laws which are unreasonable, to the extent they are unreasonable, will reap a bitter harvest. Enforcement of such laws requires a disproportionate amount of effort. Imagine a stop sign put up on a road where there is no reason for it—no intersection, no access road, no hill, no curve, no reason at all. Those who drive that road often will soon learn to go right through the sign. And to enforce the law will require constant police surveillance of that part of the road. In a just society, one could expect that the sign would be removed when violators explained to judges and/or juries why they ran the stop sign. If such a sign existed, and there was no reasonable justification for erecting it, it would soon be removed.

That the law is reasonable does not mean that all reasonable men will agree as to what should or should not be law. But reasonable men should be able to agree that the law is reasonable according to some point of view, and to that extent is not lacking in reason. There are many reasonable yet disputable and even contradictory views as to how the AIDS epidemic should be dealt with. But no one seriously suggests all AIDS victims be quarantined, or that the society do absolutely nothing about the problem. Reasonable men will differ, but they will all suggest remedies to the problem which have some merit. And some of those suggestions will be enacted into law.

It is then, one of the primary purposes of the state to see to it that good (reasonable) laws are passed. The passage of good laws fosters respect for the law, respect for the law fosters compliance, compliance with the law welds the fabric of the society, and a stable society fosters the well being of the citizenry. Similarly, one of the primary purposes of the state is to enforce laws well (reasonably). That the punishment fit the crime is essential. That the law be enforced equally among all the citizens is also vital. Firm, fair, swift, and effective enforcement of the law is the complement to the enactment of good law. Thus, the intelligent enactment and enforcement of law is a vital component of a just society. The failure of either aspect of this dualistic concept of law will result in the failure of the law and, more important, the failure of justice and, most important, the failure of the state to achieve its purpose.

CHAPTER 14

Problems of Government: Five Great Issues

Living in a state, as with living in a family, poses many problems, and these problems have been the subject of political philosophy ever since men began to think seriously about the state. The problems that arise which governments must attempt to solve can be numbered in the hundreds, if not thousands. And these problems are constantly changing, evolving; often the solution of one problem results in the creation of others.

In 1954, Leslie Lipson of the University of California, published a text called *The Great Issues of Politics*. The text covered the traditional subject matter of political theory; in addition, he devoted ten of the fifteen chapters to an in-depth discussion of five issues that he maintains are basic to all governments. These five areas, into which all the many particular problems can be generally placed, are:

Elitism vs. Egalitarianism
Monism vs. Pluralism
Freedom vs. Authority
Dispersion of Powers vs. Concentration of Powers
Small State vs. Large State

While the issues are stated in terms of extremes, they are in fact, usually problems of degree—more freedom, less authority; more authority, less freedom. Also, there is a great deal of overlapping; these issues are often connected and interacting—they are not separate, static, and isolated. And while the issues are not "black or white," governments must make conscious decisions as to which of the alternatives meets the demands of their philosophical premises and can most probably achieve the desired goals. Like Alice in Wonderland, governments must decide which path to take and make the judgments as to why that path is best.

To synthesize Lipson's ten chapters into a brief introduction to the five great issues will not do justice to his analysis. He not only introduced the issues but presented historical examples to document his thesis and then presented cogent and insightful commentary. Also, some of the material presented here will differ in scope, emphasis and interpretation. However, the basic concept is so important that if students can begin to understand what the great issues are, what the basic premises are, and what their particular goals are, then perhaps they will begin to recognize what structures will yield the results they seek. Lipson himself maintains that analyzing governmental issues through the five great issues will" 1)...break down complex issues into simple components, 2)...provide understanding of government because it reveals the factors that undergo change and the area of choice within which the changes occur, 3)...make the political process meaningful by interpreting the actual forms and functions of the state in the light of valued ideals."

Elitism vs. Egalitarianism

The question posed in the issue of elitism vs. egalitarianism deals with the problem of who should rule. The extreme position of each of these views could be either "the best man or woman in the state should rule," or "every man, woman, and child should rule." As stated earlier, the issues are not usually addressed or resolved by dealing with the extremes, but rather by leaning towards one postulate or the other. Each of the postulates must be justified on the basis of some premise, some liberal or conservative view of the nature of man, the nature of the state, the nature of the relationship between the two.

The elitist contends that men are not all alike. Some are better than others. Some people are more intelligent, more capable, better administrators, more deserving than others. If the governing of a state is important, and it is, then the best should govern. Elitist theory requires that there must be criteria to determine who should rule, and on the basis of those criteria, the rule of those chosen is justified. Historically, nine criteria have been used to justify rule by an elite. They are:

1) *Race*: This concept is manifest in such terms as "The White Man's Burden," "The Master Race," "The Chosen People."

2) *Ancestry*: The ideas of monarchy, pedigree, heredity, and family name, are based on this concept.

3) *Age*: Councils of elders, voting age requirements, and age requirements for office holders are examples of of this concept.

4) *Sex*: The history of male dominance in governing, kings, primogeniture (when the eldest son inherits), and the child-rearing role of women are historical examples of this idea.

5) *Religion*: Consider the role of religion in ancient Egypt, India, the medieval church, and recent theocracies such as Tibet, Iran, Israel.

6) *Military Strength*: The concept is "Might makes right," and some historical examples are South American coups, Sparta, and Prussia where the military has been idealized.

7) *Culture*: Consider the definition of culture, and language, scientific achievements, literary pre-eminence as validating a superior culture.

8) *Wealth*: The concept of plutocracy, Aristotelian citizenship, Hamiltonian policy, and Marxian philosophy all recognize wealth a justification for governing.

9) *Knowledge*: Platonic philosophy and the value placed on intellectualism, college degrees, and literacy tests are examples of the belief in the value of knowledge.

The egalitarian maintains that while there are differences among men, the similarities should be emphasized. Since government affects us all, we all have a stake in governing. Also, the egalitarian considers the idea that "All men are created equal" to be the basis for a valid political philosophy. Thus, the egalitarian seeks to find basis for man's equality rather than criteria for differentiation. The classical roots of egalitarianism are:

1) *The Stoics*: They believed each man had a spark of the divine in him (reason), and to that extent all were equal.

2) *Roman law*: The development of the Roman concept of *jus gentium* and the extension of citizenship were historical movements toward equality.

3) *The gospel of Jesus*: His teaching of the equality of each

person's soul, the body as the temple of the soul, and all men as brothers was a religious egalitarianism.

The modern roots of egalitarianism are:

4) *The English, French, and American revolutions*: Each of these revolutions attacked hereditary rights, monarchy, class privilege, and other elitist concepts.

5) *Suffrage in England and America*: The extension of voting rights through laws which eliminated property qualifications (wealth), through constitutional amendments (race), (sex), (age), all served to advance egalitarian notions.

Monism vs. Pluralism

As with all the great issues, the problem of monism vs. pluralism deals with premises and goals. If, indeed, the premise and goal of one was clearly superior to the other, the issue would not really exist. The problem arises because each has advantages as well as disadvantages, each goal is worthy, yet each attempt to achieve it is beset with pitfalls. The goal of the monist is unity, while the pluralist values diversity. The problem is that one is often achieved at the expense of the other. How should the many different social groups in the state function, as one or separately?

The monist sees unity as the high goal. The advantages of harmony and order, the ability to easily set and clarify goals and to determine priorities and work together toward them, are just some of the advantages of monism. Monists see progress as the result of a stable society, unified in purpose, with minimal internal conflict. The family, religion, and economic theory are often the basis for monism.

In ancient Greece the concept of the city-state was the outgrowth of the kinship theory, a monist position. All social groups came under the umbrella of the state, as members of the family came under the paternal leadership of the father. Little weight was given to the idea that social groups could work against the goals of the state or in contradiction to the city's stated purposes. Socrates was tried, in part, for undermining the unity of the state.

The pluralist values diversity. Independent social, political, *friction state within a state necessary.*

and economic entities within the state, even sometimes in conflict with the state, are seen as the means to progress, creativity, and freedom. Conflict, or at least friction, is seen as necessary to stimulate a society and the forces within that society to a progress that only competition can inspire.

From about the 4th to the 15th century there developed a moderate experiment in pluralism based upon the Christian concept of dualism. From the beginning of Christianity when Christ said, "Render unto Caesar that which is Caesar's, and render unto God that which is God's," to the contention of St. Augustine about the two cities, "The City of God and the City of Man," the concept of dualism, as it relates to church and state, predominated.

During the 15th century the concept of monism regained prominence when the Pope rejected dualism and claimed the unity of church and state, with the church dominant. As problems within the church began to weaken the political power of the Pope, and the temporal power of European king's began to grow, the failure of dualism seemed apparent. With the appearance of Thomas Hobbes and his theory of absolute monarchy, monism was reinstituted, albeit on a basis other than family or religion.

In 1776, the concept of *laissez-faire* economics was introduced forcefully by Adam Smith, and the resurgence of pluralism began. Beyond the economic justification by Smith for pluralism, there appeared ethical and political theorists such as Thomas Jefferson, who justified pluralism on all three premises (economic, political, and religious). Pluralism dominated the world scene until 1914.

From 1914 to the present, monism and pluralism have been, as Lipson says, "in conflict and crisis." The obvious monistic system which dominated the twentieth century was the Soviet Union. Based on a Marxian economic premise, the Soviets were the best example of a monistic system. The collapse of the Soviet Union represents a forceful movement toward pluralism within that society. Perhaps the most obvious example of pluralism existing today is the United States. Mr. Jefferson's principles seem to have taken hold and dominate American's thinking. However, there are critics who think America is pluralism run amuck, and a reaction may drive the United States into monism.

Authority vs. Freedom

The problem of freedom and authority, once again, cannot be dealt with in the extreme. Total freedom is anarchy, and complete authority is dictatorship. The ideal is a delicate balance between the two, which maximizes freedom when freedom is best for the individual and the group, and maximizes authority when authority best serves the needs of the individual and the group. Each exists in a mutually exclusive relationship—the more freedom, the less authority, and vice versa. Both carry with them grave risks—too much freedom and the security that authority provides is threatened, too much authority and freedom is threatened.

The problem of terrorism poses an interesting example. The free access to airports and nations makes it easy for terrorists to do their work. Restrictions on travel, access, or free movement would limit terrorism. A particular example took place in the city of Norwalk, Connecticut, in January, 1986. The superintendent of schools cancelled several school-approved trips to Europe which were to take place during the spring vacation. The one trip he did not cancel was the one to the former Soviet Union. "It's safe to travel there," he said.

Lipson lists several types of authoritarian principles which justify authority that does not originate with those over whom it is exercised. They are: 1) divine right, 2) ancestral lineage, 3) military rule, 4) the Communist party, 5) Fascism and Nazism. He also lists some of the types of authority which emanate from the people over whom that authority reigns. The philosophical principles enumerated in the Declaration of Independence, in part transferred to the Constitution, are foremost examples of the philosophy of freedom. Constitutionalism, judicial review, and the rule of law are primary examples of authority originating with the governed, free from the constraints of authoritarian principles.

So, authority imposed, based on some premise other than the consent of the governed can be justified by one of the five authoritarian concepts listed above. Authority which is not imposed but is shared must take some form such as those listed as written, enumerated law.

Here let us depart somewhat from Lipson to discuss the

philosophical rather than political question of freedom and authority. Regardless of the form a government takes, rule of the one, rule of the few, or rule of the many (see Aristotle)—it must exercise authority. Too much authority exercised—less freedom for the citizenry. Too little authority exercised—more freedom for the citizenry. Thus, the question of justification aside, no system guarantees the ideal relationship between authority and freedom. This point is made to make the student aware of the fact that simply because the many have a role in the making of the law, that does not insure that the law will be effective, beneficial, or even just. One need only look at the excesses of the French Revolution to understand that point.

Concentration of Powers vs. Dispersion of Powers

The issue of concentration of powers vs. dispersion of powers deals primarily with how a state is constituted in order to carry out its function. Once again, the issue deals with matters of degree and the pitfalls are similar to those discussed in the previous issues.

To concentrate power in one group, one entity, one territorial sphere will usually yield certain results in terms of administration. The primary advantage of concentrating power is efficiency. Expenses are kept to a minimum, duplication of effort is eliminated, the ability to translate communicated needs into action is easier, and unified action once decisions are made is assured. The obvious problems revolve around the tendency of a person or group acting without opposition to become isolated, to lose sight of the common purpose, to use the power for their own purposes, and to use the structure to become authoritarian.

To disperse power to different, often conflicting, groups will usually result in much wasted time, duplication of effort, greater expense, slow, plodding resolution of problems, and conflict and friction in the carrying out of the governmental actions resulting from the final decision. The value of such a system is that conflicting views can often yield better solutions to problems, and time and deliberation in the discussion process give opportunities to reflect and make more informed judgments. Also, the prospect for a more independent, freer society, while not assured, is more probable. Finally, it should be noted that the fact is in most countries there are many combinations of separation and centralization.

At the extremes there are unitary and confederate systems of organization. The unitary form is one in which centralization is the key. Authority resides in one central organization where sovereignty resides. England is one of the great modern examples of the unitary form—all the power is centralized in parliament, and there are no independent entities of any equal power in the society. The confederate form is one in which individual states retain sovereignty yet relate in a loose organization with a central agency. The Confederate States of America were organized to escape from the authority of the central government in Washington. A modern example of a confederacy is the United Nations, in which each state is fully sovereign but meets together as part of a centralized agency and conforms to the rules and regulations of that agency so long as sovereignty is not threatened.

The federal form is meant to be a kind of compromise. In a federal government sovereignty is shared between individual states and a central agency. The example of fifty sovereign states and one sovereign nation as defined in the Constitution of the United States is probably the best example of this form.

Beyond the system of separation of powers, as manifested in the federal form, is the concept of separation of powers within governmental entities. In American government, for example, the central government's power is separated into an executive branch, a judicial branch, and a legislative branch consisting of two houses. Each has its own particular sphere of activity and power. Also, the concept of checks and balances exists in America so that each branch can thwart, to an extent, the actions of the other.

Some systems of government, then, are organized in order to facilitate speed, efficiency, and simplicity in carrying out their function. Others value what they see as the safeguards that are inherent in separation, discussion, and tension. A small, homogeneous nation might usually choose the benefits of concentrating power. A large, heterogeneous country might often need to disperse powers to serve the interests of the various constituencies.

Large State vs. Small State

The question at issue about the size of the state like all the issues before it, seeks to create the ideal within the limits of practicality. The extremes, of course, would be one world state vs. a state for every populated geographical entity, down to the smallest island. History, geography, transportation, communication and politics have all had an effect on how people have viewed this issue.

How large can a state be? Can a state be too small? Which is more important, territorial or cultural considerations? What may, can, must relationships between states be? As with all the previous issues there are many questions, and throughout history those questions have been answered very differently. An axiom might be, "the state should be big enough to be self sufficient, and small enough so that its members feel that they are an integral part of it." That axiom could be viewed very differently at different times in history or when conditions within that country undergo great change.

Obviously, the geographical basis has been used to determine the size of a state. Territory is one of the necessary elements of a state. Places like New Zealand and Japan can easily define their limits by geography. (Interestingly, one of the two chose not to be confined by its immediate geographic limits during the 1930's.) Within territorial limits, kinship can be the basis for a state, usually in a tribal, clan, or nomadic setting. The Greek city-state was a combination of both. There was a geographic as well as an ethnic basis, since the city-state tended to be located on the coast with a navigable harbor.

Throughout history the goal of some has been a universal order like the Pax Romana or the medieval period where the ideal sought resolution through the church. More recently the ideal has been expressed through organizations such as the League of Nations and the United Nations. Ideological premises which have sought to create a world order have been exemplified by the Nazi, Fascist, and Communist attempts to create a world-wide state. There are however, significant differences between the first two as compared with Communism—something which will be dealt with later.

The primary reasons that such dreams have not been realized, at least in Europe, have been the great cultural divisions, the religious differences, and nationalism. Language has been a thread woven within and throughout each of the three problems mentioned.

We live in the era of the nation state; for a world order to emerge, the concept of nationalism would have to be eliminated. In fact, attempts at world order within the context of the nation state have been through imperialism, conquest, and the ability to dominate through business and/or industry. In this regard the Nazi and Fascist attempts at a world order were based upon a concept of national superiority, and an extension of the nation through conquest and an imposition of that superior nation's values upon others. Ostensibly, the Communist ideology calls for a universal order so that the economic competition between nation states would cease and an economic cooperation which transcends national states would emerge. In practice Communist states such as the former Soviet Union have acted more in the tradition of the Nazis and Fascists.

At present the United Nations represents, at its best, an institution ideally suited to bring about the dream of a world state. At its worst it is an institution for bringing together immature, born-yesterday nation states into a forum where they engage in bickering, name-calling, and argument. In a very practical sense the United Nations may well serve to make clear the basic problem of this issue.

Should a state be just large enough to serve the economic, cultural, religious, and security needs of its people? Or should a world state, unifying all people, be the goal, eliminating in the process, the conflicts between nations? If we choose the former, how do we deal with the problems of conflicts between nations? If we choose the latter, on what ideological, cultural, and economic basis does this world state operate? Those who believe that men can and will cooperate with one another would probably choose the world state, seeking resolution to the problems within that context. Those who think that men cannot and will not cooperate with those whose premises differ probably foresee a continuation of the present arrangement, and would attempt to solve the existing problems and conflicts through negotiations between nations.

The 1990s has seen the most concerted (peaceful/democratic) effort in history to begin the process of unification in Europe. The euro-dollar movement is an attempt to bring Europe under a single currency standard. As noted earlier in Chapter 12, money is one of the crucial unifying factors that is inherent in every state. Years of negotiations have not yet been successful in taking this first small step towards union. It is interesting to note that none of the participants will admit that eventual union is the goal; so deep run the national feelings of the people in the countries involved. Yet, it is interesting to ponder - will the world ever see a "United States of Europe"?

So, we have briefly examined the five great issues of government. As we examine the political views of twelve great philosophers, we will see that they address each of those problems. Certainly time, place, and circumstance will color their analysis. Certainly the changes that have occurred which affect us all will have to be taken into consideration. But the basic premises, the universal concepts, the ideas which underlie their thinking and affect ours, will be worthy of consideration. Indeed, their thoughts are worthy of serious study, careful examination, honest discussion, and tolerant understanding.

CHAPTER 15

Plato and Aristotle:
Utopia and Polity

Plato (427-347 B.C.)

The state, to Plato, is a natural institution. It arises out of the need for man to live in groups, due to his inability to provide for his basic needs by himself. The family, which is the basic social institution necessary for the continuance of the species, is also natural. The state is the outgrowth of the normal and natural evolution of the family which is unable to provide all the needs that are required by a large community. Thus, the state is the means by which men can live in a community with one another. While the primary function of the state is to help man meet his economic needs, its function goes beyond that basic idea.

To simply provide the means for economic progress is not enough. Justice, the virtue that men must have in order to be good, is also the virtue that a state must have in order to be a good state. In Plato's moral philosophy, he contended that each person consisted of three elements, reason, spirit, and appetite. The just man was one who developed these three to their proper end, in their proper proportion, creating a harmony of wisdom, courage, and temperance. The state to Plato, was the "individual writ large." Thus, the ideal state was one in which all the members performed their proper function, creating a harmonious, a just, state. The *Republic,* Plato's most important work, is devoted, in large measure, to describing this ideal state.

Just as in the individual, then, the state was divided into three parts, three classes. The class which was to be responsible for governing, teaching, and otherwise directing the operation of the state was the "guardian" class, those who possessed the virtue of wisdom. Those who had the virtue of courage comprised the "warrior" class and were entrusted with protecting the state from all enemies. The "artisan" class, the vast majority of people, the farmers, merchants, laborers, and craftsmen, were meant to develop the virtue of temperance. This pyramidal structure, with each of the members in each of the three classes carrying out their respective roles in perfect harmony—this was the ideal state.

This ideal state would come into being by the application of Plato's highest good, knowledge. If knowledge, and it's virtuous realization, wisdom, were applied in the state as he envisioned it in the individual, the ideal could be achieved. Thus, the most important function of the state became the education of its members. To this end Plato devised a complex and all encompassing system of education, through which each member would find his proper place within the state.

All children were to be educated, boys and girls equally, in music and gymnastics. In ancient Greece, music included poetry and dance, while gymnastics was meant to produce good health. Thus the concept of a healthy mind and body was the goal this education was supposed to achieve. Beyond these basics was an academic program which would carefully weed out those who did not have the ability to achieve wisdom. Those who faltered first became the artisans, those who failed at the next stage became members of the warrior class, and those who could, continued on to become the guardians. Of the guardian class, the outstanding individual would become the philosopher king, or the few outstanding individuals would rule as an aristocracy of philosopher kings. The remaining members of the guardian class would teach and carry out the laws of the nation.

This educational process continued for the guardians throughout their life; those few who were to rule would do so only after a lifetime of study. Throughout their adult life the guardians were to live in a communal society, without property, without wives, without children, without any of the material goods which would distract them from their high calling. They would live simply, cultivating their minds, enacting the laws which would be the basis for the ideal, just state. Plato's theory that to know the good is to do it insures that these philosopher kings will rule in the interests of the community rather than their own. Also, the more the mind is cultivated, the less concern one has for the desire of the appetites. Thus the guardians would not desire the goods which power can obtain.

The communal life of the guardians would be total. Those in

charge would decide who would mate and when for purposes of procreation—the idea of breeding to improve the stock was more important than the concept of family. Immediately after birth, the newborn would be placed in nurseries, never to know their parents, and would begin the long educational process. This system served a twofold purpose: the guardians were left free to serve the community, and there was no possibility of favoritism towards the offspring of the rulers. Also, the Platonic concept of love elevated the ideal of spiritual, cerebral love, far above that temporary, insufficient experience of carnal love.

The "Allegory of the Cave" is in part a description of the path these philosopher kings would follow. They would "see the light" and come to know the good. Those who had not seen the light would not be able to understand the lifestyle, the commitment to truth, the disdain of the material world that these philosopher kings had obtained. That is why the self control of the artisans is the necessary virtue. They would obey the laws, and the laws would be just; they would also live in the material world, enjoying those temporary pleasures that were important to those of their station. Finally, there would be no attempts on the part of the guardians to convert the artisans to a life of contemplation. They all serve the state—the guardians, the warriors, and the artisans—when they take their rightful place, carry out their assigned duties, and live as a part of a harmonious whole.

In *The Laws,* one of Plato's last works, he modifies many of the particulars of this ideal state—perhaps his idealism became tempered as he grew older—but he insisted that this ideal, had in part, to be a pattern for the real. All states had to have a ruling class, and he considered his basis for governing a reasonable one. All states need harmony within the various classes. He considered his ideal one to be aimed at, if not achieved. He obviously believed that education was an important goal and one of the most important functions of any state.

The importance of the conditions of Socrates' death in Plato's political philosophy should not be underestimated. The excesses of the majority which condemned Socrates were of constant concern to Plato. The problems which are the product of ignorance or uncontrolled desires also were a cornerstone of his philosophy. Beyond his ideal state, he saw government taking four basic forms, each imperfect, and also tending to move in a cyclical manner. They are: Timocracy—rule by national heroes; Oligarchy—rule by a selfish few; Democracy—rule by the whim of a fickle majority; and Tyranny—rule by a one man dictatorship. Plato indicated that systems of government, when apart from the ideal, tended to follow a cyclical pattern which caused each form to deteriorate, develop into the next, going from good to bad to worst—then eventually to a short-lived good form.

Plato's political philosophy, like his moral philosophy, is a perception of the ideal. His premises are based on his concept of man as a cooperative, rational, and perfectible being. The priorities for the state are unity, harmony, peace and—according to his definition—justice. The state, an economic necessity, is natural and will always be with us; if this is so, then we must aim at the ideal and try to achieve it.

Aristotle (384-322 B.C.)

Aristotle's political philosophy, like his moral philosophy and unlike Plato's moral and political philosophy, is realistic, practical, and an attempt to reconcile extremes. His *Politics,* unlike Plato's *Republic,* is not a description of the ideal state but rather an analysis of existing states, their constitutions, their *modus operandi,* and his observations of the strengths and weaknesses in each.

The family—a man, a woman and their offspring—is the most natural of all organizations; the preservation of the race requires that man's natural instincts cause him to become a part of a family. Certainly, men did not deliberate about the relative values of the family. Rather the family unit was joined naturally, and its value determined in retrospect. The evolution of the family into larger units of organization progresses until the state is actualized. The state, according to Aristotle, is the highest form of community. In his moral philosophy Aristotle maintained that happiness was the highest good because it alone was self-sufficient. Likewise, the state is the only community which is self-sufficient, therefore, it is the best form of organization. "If all communities aim at some good, the state or political community, which is the highest of all, which embraces all the rest, aims at a good in a greater degree that any other, and at the highest good."

Man is by nature a political animal, Aristotle claims, because he is naturally gregarious. "A social instinct is implanted in all men by nature." This desire to interact with others is evident in every level of activity, from the family to the state. Also, no man can truly live alone; to live alone a man must be "either a beast or a God." Man, when separated from law and justice, is, at his worst, the worst of all animals, and at his best he is the best of all living things. Only through the state can man be his best; therefore, the state is necessary. Just as every individual activity aims at some good, the aim of the state is to make man good. To Aristotle there is no theoretical problem of the individual versus the state; the state exists prior to the individual, each man is born into the state, a part in relation to the whole. Thus, the state is organic, a natural and integrated whole, of which each man is a part, working through law and justice towards the good.

His major criticism of Plato's *Republic* revolved around Plato's communal organization and commitment to unity (monism). The idea of holding property in common was antithetical to Aristotle's thinking, and the holding of all things in common—even children and wives—and all the other peculiarities of the guardians seemed to be against nature. Aristotle believed that nature implanted a self-love in all of us which requires that at one time or another we glory in possessing something. "How much better to be a real cousin of somebody than to be a son after Plato's fashion," said Aristotle. Also, the state, while a unity of the whole, is a plurality in many respects—male and female, master and slave, buyer and seller, farmer, businessman, craftsmen, and professionals. Property, then, is a natural right, and if held and used with the moderation which is the hallmark of his philosophy, a good thing.

Aristotle deals with the question of who should rule by observing that there are only three possible types of governmental organization—rule of the one, rule of the few, and rule of the many. If then, there are only three possible forms, which is best? Or, is there no best form, just degrees of difference? Aristotle has a personal preference, but he believed that all three forms can be good, and similarly, all three forms can be bad. His good forms are Monarchy (rule of the one), Aristocracy (rule of the few), and Polity or constitutional form (rule of the many). The bad forms are, in the same order, Tyranny, Oligarchy, and Democracy.

The three good forms, monarchy, aristocracy, and polity are good because those in control govern for the common good. If a monarch rules as best he can for the common good, to make the subjects good and the state just—that is a good form. If the aristocracy, the rule of the best, govern in order that the public benefits through good laws, equal justice and honest administration—then the form is good. Finally, if the many, under a constitution which insures that the laws, administration of justice, economic climate and education are equitable and fairly shared, then the polity exists—a good form.

However, each form is subject to corruption. Tyranny is not the rule of the best, the most virtuous man, who rules for the common good, but rather one who rules by force for his own or his favorites' gain. Oligarchy is not the rule of the few wise men who dispense justice well and do their duty, but the rule of the corrupt few who manipulate their office for their own ends. Polity, the rule of the many under law, can become a democracy, in which the law of the many becomes the rule. When the masses use their numbers to make laws which are enacted, not on constitutional principles, but rather on the principle of the weight of numbers, the polity is corrupted into a democracy. Also, when many factions seek to enhance their particular group's advantage at the expense of the common good, democracy, the bad form prevails.

Ideally, the monarchy would be the best form of government, but the monarchy when corrupted would become a tyranny, which is the the worst form. Also, the monarchy is the most easily corrupted and therefore quite probably destined to become a tyranny. Since Aristotle is more concerned with the practical, and is skeptical of the ideal, he does not favor monarchy.

Citizenship, according to Aristotle, is different in different forms of government; the citizens in a polity will be different from those in a monarchy. The essential quality, however, that is a requirement for citizenship in the best form of government is the ability to govern as well as be governed. Therefore, in a polity where the broad middle class exists, the citizen will be one who is educated, has the time for civic duties, and is, in fact, virtuous. The person who is not only subject to law, but has a part in the administration of law can be a citizen. Children are not citizens, then, nor are slaves, nor are those who cannot share in the role of governing.

This, then, seems to be Aristotle's preference; a polity with a broad middle class, educated for citizenship, with a constitution to guide them. In such a state there would be three branches of government: the deliberative assemblies, the executive branch, and the courts of law. Each of these three branches would be differently constituted depending on which form is in effect. But in the polity, Aristotle recommends the middle class be the dominant force in the body that makes the laws. Those who execute the laws should have their duties very clearly defined. They should deal with particular subjects, i.e., be specialists rather than generalists, and have powers necessary to fit their role. The courts should be divided according to the type of litigation they will be dealing with, and the judges chosen by election or by lot, or in some cases, by both methods.

Education is one of the most important functions of the state. Primarily the "citizens should be molded to suit the form of government under which they live." Since the end of the state is self-sufficiency, children should learn the occupations which are required by the state in order to achieve this end. Education for citizenship is likewise important if the citizen is one who must be governed as well as govern. Aristotle is firm in the opinion that discipline is an important aspect of the educational process, since "he who has never learned to obey can never be a good commander."

Law should be the supreme governor of men's actions. Man is subject to temptations, desires, and personal preferences; the law is not. The law is neutral and objective, and to that extent should be respected because it conforms to Aristotle's great faith in reason. Law, the rule of reason, is superior to the whims of individuals. Good laws are to be revered. Judicial decisions should be made by groups of intelligent men capable of wise decisions. He seems to favor the jury over the judge in that he says, "As a feast to which all the guests contribute is better than a banquet furnished by a single man, so a multitude is a better judge of many things than any individual."

Aristotle's general view of the role of law in society tended to be based on a generally conservative view of man. He summed up his view of human nature by saying, "Human nature is, on the average, wicked, nearer to the beast than to the god." Therefore, his respect for the law is not simply based on its rational content, but because it is a primary force in holding a society together. And respect for the law requires that one understand that "the habit of lightly changing laws is an evil; and when the advantage of change is small, some defects in the law or in the ruler had better be met with philosophical toleration." Again, the realist, not the idealist, has spoken.

His political philosophy is very similar to his moral philosophy; a moderate, realistic view of the world. The nature of man, the theory of the family, the organic theory of the state, his view of the middle class, the role of law, his view of the different branches of government, his opinion on property—all have importance for us today. His opinions about slavery and women have few adherents in the world today, yet were consistent with the views held in antiquity. On balance, the political philosophy of Aristotle squares with his reputation as the philosopher of common sense, a man of moderation.

CHAPTER 16

Augustine and Aquinas: Platonist and Aristotelian

St. Augustine (A.D. 354-430)

St. Augustine was born in Tagaste, North Africa in 354. He lived in that part of the Roman Empire founded by Constantine and called the Byzantine Empire, during the time that Rome was sacked by the Goths. Persecution of Christians by Rome ended around 305, and it was under the rule of Constantine (323-337) that Christianity became the official religion of the Roman Empire. The rapid spread of Christianity set the scene for philosophical inquiry into the relationship between the theology of the Church and the philosophy of the ancients. Augustine is considered a Platonist who reconciled the pagan philosophy of Plato with Christian theology.

In his youth Augustine was was a pagan who lived the life of an insatiable hedonist. He studied at Carthage and was considered a brilliant student. In 387 he converted to Christianity, in 391 he became a priest, and in 395 he was named Bishop of Hippo. His search for truth, his acceptance of Neo-Platonic philosophy, his rejection of his youthful excesses, and his conversion to Christianity are all documented in his autobiography, *Confessions*.

Augustine was a prolific writer, but his most important work is *The City of God*. He began the writing of this series of statements three years after the fall of Rome. The impact of Christianity was so great within the Roman Empire, that when Rome fell Christianity was blamed for its fall. *The City of God* was written as a defense of Christianity, but covered a multiplicity of other topics. For our purposes we will be most interested in his views on the nature of man, his Neo-Platonism, and his views on the relationship between the Church and the state, and the relationship between the Christian and the state. His doctrine of the "Two Cities," the City of God and the City of Man, is his interpretation of the history of the world in the light of divine revelation.

Augustine contends that there are two realms in the world. One is the world of material, transient, and temporary things which the damned pursue at all costs. The other is the world of eternal values, the highest of which is God, which is pursued by those who wish to be saved and who are loyal to the Church, the vehicle for salvation. The greatest good is the search for God, and God is the ultimate truth. The similarities with Plato's dualism and the search for knowledge should be apparent.

The Platonic virtues of wisdom, courage, and temperance, culminating with the concept of justice, are totally accepted by Augustine. Augustine simply contends that the Platonic idea of "seeing the light" is incomplete. To Augustine, "to see the light" is to see God, and to see God is to love Him. Thus the ultimate goal of all men should be to love God, and through the Platonic virtues this is possible. With the attainment of the goal, will come wisdom. Wisdom is simply the ability to know good from evil. The major difference between Augustine and Plato in this area is the Augustinian concept of the will. Man is free, says Augustine, and freedom entails the concept of choice—thus one can will to choose evil even though the mind knows the good.

An important problem manifests itself here. If one can know truth, then truth exists. If one can know God, then God exists. Plato said, "to know the good is to do it." If one can choose evil, then evil must exist, and God the omnipotent, must have created it along with the good. Not so, says Augustine; God being all good, could not, would not create evil. Therefore, evil is nothing more than turning away from the good, the absence of good, a privation of the good. In a sense, all evil is a turning away from God, an act of the will. One does not turn to evil; one turns from good.

This dualism, coupled with the idea of the will, has implications for Augustine's political philosophy. To Augustine, man and civil society are inseparable; so, to the extent that man is a social animal, the state is natural. But since the state began as a result of man's choice (the fall of Adam), it is not so much natural as remedial, a product of divine intervention. Since, after the fall, man could not have survived without the state, it is through divine intervention that it was created, and by man's social nature that it endures. And by virtue of men's choices there are two states (cities), the City of God, and the City of Man. As Plato asserted, the state was "the individual writ large;" thus, the individuals who love the world are members of the City of Man, and those who love God are members of the City of God.

The state, then, exists for the sake of peace. Without the state there would be anarchy, a disorder brought about by man's fallen condition. This peace, however, is not a divine and complete peace as exists in the City of God, but one of convenience. It is an external one which yields the semblance of order, which allows the unredeemed men to pursue their temporal goals. Those who are the elect use the temporal order to facilitate their path to the City of God.

The tools for the enforcement of this peace are the laws. Augustine considered law that which has evolved or been imposed by a ruler to insure the maintenance of earthly order. Earthly law is concerned not so much with justice, but with order. True justice is impossible in the City of Man. If justice is that each receives his due, then justice cannot exist on earth. Full justice, like full peace, exists only with God in Heaven.

Law is vested in the power of the ruler. It is enacted to maintain order and a measure of justice. And though it is not necessarily just, it is binding. Since the state was divinely instituted, those in power hold, in a sense, a power that has been ordained from above. Society is a compact between the citizens and the rulers, and obedience to law is a part of that compact. It may be coincidental, but there is a similarity here to Plato's *Crito* where Socrates justifies obedience to the law even though it will mean his own death.

Obviously, the law of God is superior to all others. But Augustine believes that the natural law, innate in man since Adam, is the Golden Rule—"Do unto others as you would have them do unto you." Individuals must never violate this rule. Also, when there is a conflict between the state's law and God's law, the Christian must obey God. Therefore, the Christian must obey the state's law in all cases, except when there is a clear conflict between the state law and religious law. However, if for the sake of his religion the Christian must violate the law of the state, he is still subject to the secular law and must not evade the punishment the state imposes. How similar to Socrates, who violated the state's law for "God's sake" and yet submitted to his punishment willingly.

The role of the ruler is to insure peace and order, and to that end he may do virtually anything. Given man's terrible tendencies, leniency must be the exception, and often an active role should be pursued by the state to maintain the peace: "The heavy hand of the state and its dreadful instruments of repression are necessary because they are the only methods by which sinful men can be restrained; the fear of punishment is the only safeguard of general peace and security." There is no prescription limiting the state's activity. The state may, if it chooses or needs, do anything to facilitate its goal, with little consideration for the individual.

Two points should be made here: 1) The Christian is living in the temporal state as a transient; his journey is through the state to God. The eternal city will be his permanent home, so the inconveniences, even gross injustices, of this world are to be expected, and pale in the light of real values. 2) Augustine contends that because of original sin the state is a necessary institution and is bound to be immoral. This is not to say that the state should not be held to the same moral standards as individuals, but that the city of man will not be moral. The role of the Church, then, is to teach the moral virtues that the state should subscribe to, but a moral state can not exist unless it is a Christian state.

So, the Church is a superior society to the state, and it is the principles of the Church which should permeate the state. Thus, while the Church is separate from the state it has a responsibility to instruct the civil authority in the Christian principles which should be the standard for conduct. When left alone, the state is concerned with this world, and will rule by force. When instructed by the Church, the state would be more concerned with Christian principles and rule by love.

The final element in Augustine's political philosophy regards the role of the elect, or members of the City of God, living in the City of Man. As citizens of the earthly city, they are enjoined to obedience to the laws and the state just as the unredeemed are. They also have the obligation to obey God's law, and they must observe it as fully as possible.

If a citizen of the City of God should come to rule, he has a number of responsibilities. He first has the duty to earthly peace like any other ruler. He also must rule in the most Christian fashion possible, i.e., with an eye to mercy and charity. If he loves God he will be a member of a community which has the love of God as its *raison d'être*. However, because of the essential sinfulness of the City of Man, a Christian society similar to the City of God is impossible, unless the Church rules. Augustine states that at no time in the history of the world of men will a temporal state have only citizens of the City of God as its citizens.

Augustine's contribution, in addition to answering those who saw Christianity as the reason for the fall of Rome, consisted in taking a Platonic view of the world to its logical conclusion, in the light of Christian theology, to his City of God. Étienne Gilson's analogy sums up Augustine's concept of that community.

"To understand the origin of social life, let us look at it in the process of formation in a public spectacle, let us say, a theatrical presentation. When the spectators gather to attend the performance, they are unknown to one another and do not form a society. But if one of the actors plays his role with great talent, those who like his acting are completely carried away and even find in it the greatest pleasure the theatrical art has to offer. But they do more than love the actor who gives them such pleasure; a kind of mutual sympathy grows up at once between those who admire him. If the spectators love one another, they obviously do so, not for themselves, but because of the actor whom they love with a common love. The proof of this can be seen in the fact that the more we like an actor the more we applaud so as to induce the other spectators to admire him. We want to add to the number of his admirers, so we arouse the indifferent; and if any one should dare to disagree with us, we hate the contempt he feels for the object of our affections. Hence, love of an object spontaneously gives birth to a society which embraces all those whose love is centered in that object, and excludes all who turn away from it. This conclusion—and its application is universal—is verified in a peculiar way in the case of love for God. He who loves God is, by that very fact, brought into a social relationship with all those who love Him..."

St. Thomas Aquinas (1225-1274)

During the Middle Ages there existed a movement which brought the different branches of learning in the secular world together with the great body of Christian thought. The men who formed this movement were called the Scholastics, and St. Thomas Aquinas was the greatest of them all. His magnum opus, *Summa Theologica,* is one of the great systematic treatises on theology and philosophy.

After the Crusades, documents containing much of the learning from ancient Greece began to filter into Europe. During the early Middle Ages, little of Aristotle was known, but soon complete texts of his logic, science, and ethics appeared, culminating with the *Politics*. The Church was confronted with the problem of what to do with these impressive works of philosophy, pagan in source and substance, which might threaten Christian doctrine. Rather than ban these works, they were incorporated into Christian theology, and in fact became the cornerstone of the Roman Catholic philosophy. The man most responsible for the marriage of Aristotelian philosophy and Christian theology was Thomas Aquinas.

The state according to Aquinas is natural. Man is by nature a social being, endowed with reason, and with each person having a place in the hierarchy of that which exists with all things, from the highest to the lowest. Man is totally incapable of survival outside the state; his nature requires that he live in groups. His reason permits him to create governments, pass laws, and generally hold together the very delicate association of people. The division of labor is a requirement of the differing capabilities of different individuals. If there were no state, men, who are primarily concerned with self, would exist in a state of conflict and anarchy. Therefore, the state must exist for the common good, and the common good requires ruling power to direct individuals to an end beyond themselves.

Like Aristotle, Aquinas sees the state as an institution that exists to make man good. The common good requires that the state preserve the peace—peace is essential, as order in a classroom must exist before learning can take place. So must peace exist in a community. Also, the common good requires that the basic economic needs of the community are met—the government must insure some minimal level of subsistence for its people. Finally, the state exists to make man good—the laws, education, governmental edicts and programs should all be directed toward making men good. Aquinas agreed with Aristotle that the state is an institution in its own right with an end of its own. However, the Church, with a supernatural end is higher than the state. So, to make men good in this life is wonderful, but insufficient—the next life is of supreme importance.

The major difference between Aquinas, the Neo-Aristotelian, and Augustine, the Neo-Platonist, is that Augustine saw the eventual ideal as a unified world under the leadership of the Church, while Aquinas saw the Church and state as separate entities interrelating with one another. The operative concept would be "Render to Caesar the things that are Caesar's, and to God the things that are God's," and in the hierarchy of things in the universe there should be no question as to who is the more important. Aquinas has no great yearning for a church-state; he sees them as two separate entities.

Aquinas' opinion about the forms of government agreed with Aristotle's, and he too, believed that a monarchy was the ideal form. But given the nature of man and the state, a limited monarchy (constitutional) would be his preference. In the truest sense, though, all power comes from God, so the ruler of the state has sovereignty which comes from God via the people. Thus he must be limited, and in the final analysis the state's sovereignty rests in the commonweal.

What, then, is the role of the individual within the state, and what rights does he have? Aquinas despised the idea of tyranny, yet his thought was consistent with Greek and medieval thought, and he subscribed to the notion that the whole is greater than any of its parts. The state has the right to punish those who break the law since the common good is superior to the individual when the two conflict. So, to a very great extent the individual is subject to the state. Even if the rule becomes tyrannical, rebellion is considered a great evil, as is all violence, permissible only if the better part of the whole of the people rise up to replace the tyrant for the common good. The better method would be to have a limited government, based on law, which would prevent the absolute tyranny that would engender rebellion.

If violence within a state is vigorously condemned, what then does Aquinas think about international violence, i.e., war? The natural law allows individuals to use force to protect themselves as the right of self-defense. States also have this right. Aquinas set down what he calls the conditions for a just war. First of all, a war must be fought for a just cause, for example, when one nation is invaded by an another. The war must be fought by a legitimate authority; self-appointed groups of terrorists, or special interest groups have no legitimate authority to engage in war. Also, it must be reasonably determined that the resulting evil that will come from fighting the war will be less than the evil that would result from not fighting. In this regard, a war should be brought to a conclusion as quickly as possible.

Obviously, it is easy, according to Aquinas' criteria, to judge some wars as just or unjust. Some wars, however, seem just at the start, but as time passes, become unjust. Some wars, just in most respects, result in injustice by virtue of their length or the excesses of the participants. Reason and an objective regard for the facts are crucial to the making of the judgment. The terrorist does not become a freedom fighter simply because we agree with his ideology, nor does a freedom fighter become a terrorist because we disagree with his objectives. Clearly, in most cases the reasonable application of the criteria can aid in making the judgment.

Aquinas' concern for the importance of law is evidenced by his careful and complete treatment of the four types of law. Eternal law is the law of the universe, the physical laws which reflect the divine order, pattern, and rationality of the universe. Natural law is the tendency of living things, as Aristotle said, "to fulfill the essence of their beings." In man, this is to live as a rational being. Divine law is the law revealed by God through his commandments and scripture and most importantly through Christ. Human law is "an ordinance of reason for the common good made by him who has care of the community, and promulgated." In a very real sense, human law is a corollary to the natural law. The natural law, discerned through reason, tells us that murder is wrong. Human law is meant to define, prescribe penalties for, and otherwise distinguish murder from other forms of homicide.

Human law, then, should be consistent with natural law in all societies. It should be consistent with natural and divine law in those societies which have been exposed to divine revelation. Any human law which violates the natural law need not be obeyed in conscience, unless the non-observance would create a greater evil. Any human law which violates divine law must never be obeyed. Any law which is enacted against the common good would be a violation of natural or divine law, and therefore would be a bad law. This is similar to Aristotle's contention that a good government is one that governs for the common good, and a bad government is one that governs for selfish or personal ends.

This view of human law and divine law allows Aquinas to accept states as natural institutions which were moral prior to Christ because their laws conformed to the natural law. States which have not heard Christ's word, can also be moral through reason, by promulgating human law which is consistent with the natural law. Since there is no contradiction between natural and divine law, modern states can and should develop laws premised on the natural law. But rulers and citizens alike should now realize that the good life lived in adherence to natural law is incomplete, because it serves only the purposes of this life. The good life lived in adherence to natural and divine law serves the purposes of this life and the next.

Aquinas' political philosophy is part of a total, systematic theological/philosophical system. It begins with God and ends with God. The state is a natural institution, a part of a divine plan. The natural law teaches us the why and how of the state, and guides us in the making of judgments about human law. The ruler has great powers and serious responsibilities, as do the citizens of any state.

Both are obliged to work for the common good in accordance with natural and divine law through their reason. While the state is legitimate in the truest sense, man has a final end, a supernatural end, to which he must be true. In a good state, there will be no conflict with the natural and supernatural end. If however, the state requires, in violation of the natural law, that an individual jeopardize that final end, the individual is justified in refusing to obey. Violence on the part of citizens against the state is almost never justified, in that violence itself violates the natural law. In that rarest of moments when violence against the state may be justified, it must be justified on the basis of the common good—

never on the basis of personal, particular, or emotional premises. Men and states have the right to self-defense and all other rights which the natural law and our natural reason dictate—life, property, freedom, equality before the law, and moderation on the part of the ruler and those ruled.

St. Thomas Aquinas, a thirteenth-century Christian, restated the political philosophy of Aristotle in the light of that tradition. He did not compromise Christian theology nor Aristotelian philosophy, rather he married the two. As in all marriages, there are some disagreements and some minor incompatibilities—but it was a good marriage and it has lasted.

CHAPTER 17

Machiavelli and Hobbes:
The Prince and the Leviathan

Niccolò Machiavelli (1469-1527)

Machiavelli was born in Florence, Italy on May 3, 1469. His father was the poorest member of a wealthy and prominent family. Therefore, his education was informal compared to that of the elite of his time, but he read voraciously as a youth and as a result developed some original thinking about political theory.

The Italian city-states of the Renaissance were constantly involved in competitions and intrigues. Families ruled the cities through force and cunning; the stability of the Middle Ages gave way to the new political, social, and moral perspectives. Also, some of the philosophical givens of the Middle Ages, such as divine, eternal, and natural law came into question. Machiavelli, as a child of the Renaissance, formed many of his views as a result of first hand experiences in government. He rejected the concept of natural law as a basis for political philosophy, and developed his philosophy accordingly.

When the Medici family, the rulers of Florence were overthrown, Machiavelli became secretary to the Second Chancery in the new republican government. He worked in the government for fourteen years until the Medici were restored to power in 1512. With the return of the Medici, Machiavelli was arrested and jailed. After his release from prison he retired to his farm and began to write about the thing he loved most—politics. In fact, the rest of his life was spent yearning to return to a position in government.

His two major works, *The Prince,* and *Discourses on the First Ten Books of Titus Livius,* contain a political philosophy which is more practical than theoretical. Actually, Machiavelli is called the "Father of Political Science" in that he dealt less with the "ought" and more with what "is." He was the first major thinker to distinguish the facts of *realpolitic* from idealistic conjecture. His *Prince* is a handbook for ruling, and was dedicated to Lorenzo II in the hope that the Medici family, restored to power in Florence, would return him to a position in government.

Ben Franklin is reported to have said, "You get the kind of government you deserve." Machiavelli would not only agree with that statement but would also add that the vast majority of men, during most periods of history, deserve to be governed by an iron-handed leader (Prince) to protect them from their own inadequacies. Most men, unhappily, Machiavelli observes, are stupid and irrational. All men seek their own self-interest, but their emotions often lead them in the wrong direction. Human desires are insatiable: men seek wealth and power, yet are fearful, envious, and ambitious; they seek security from outside forces and yet when they are secure, they attack others.

If men were good, then a republic would be the ideal form of government. Reasonable men, with an understanding of the nature of the state, the purposes of the state, and the importance of the state to their own well-being, could create a republic. In fact, once there was such a republic. It existed in Rome and was Machiavelli's ideal state. The Roman Republic succeeded because the people were virtuous, and it was the virtue of the whole which allowed the republican government to function. But the fall of Rome, and the reasons for the fall, convinced Machiavelli that the ideal was beyond realization for any period of time in a world comprised mostly of dolts. The qualities of courage, reason, patriotism, along with the value of citizenship, the family, and a healthy work ethic, brought Rome to its moment of glory. Only man's irrational nature could cause him to abandon the qualities of character which allowed him to reach the ideal.

If the republic is the ideal, the practical reality is the principality. Human nature is, by definition, unchanging, the same in all societies, and men with all their vices can be restrained only by the state. The state is the vehicle which creates order out of chaos, which allows progress among competing entities, which prevents factions from destroying one another, and generally allows for conditions which make life bearable, and in the best of times, pleasant. The role of the prince is to see to it that the ends of the state are successfully achieved—at all costs. There are several premises which Machiavelli postulates which make such a prince necessary.

The state, according to Machiavelli, is organismic; man can not live without the state, man is a part of the state. The state is a living organism. It is born, grows, matures, ages, withers and dies. The implications of the organismic theory of the state follow logically for Machiavelli. If the state is a living organism, then growth and strength, as in a human body, are signs of a healthy state. Thus, three terms are necessary to understand— chauvinism, militarism, and imperialism. Chauvinism is love of one's state over another, and can be compared to self-love or self-interest. Militarism is necessary if the state is to be strong, and imperialism is evidence of the growth which healthy organisms display.

New states replace the old, and the cycle continues. However, while the state lives, within it are the means to attain that which all men desire—fame, power, and glory. Fame, power, and glory are Machiavelli's primary virtues. They are not the traditional virtues of the Christian society of which he was a part, but rather the pagan virtues of antiquity which he admired in ancient Rome. To distinguish his pagan concept from the traditional, he referred to those qualities as *virtù*. *Virtù* is what he wishes for all men, but in the prince, the state's leader, *virtù* is a necessity. Without the state there is nothing. So it takes a prince with *virtù* to do all that is required to maintain the state, at all costs, by any means. Machiavelli lists some of his most important rules for a prince with *virtù*:

1. *Be ruthless in the use of force.* He advises the prince to "commit all his cruelties at once." Men easily forget the cruelties that are committed if there follows a period of peace and tranquility. Time heals the worst of wounds; certainly the memory of a past cruelty fades. Conversely, the prince would be wise to pass out favors piecemeal, so that the pleasure is often received and therefore, by proximity, remembered.

2. *Use persuasion well.* The art of ruling requires that the people feel catered to, whether or not it is so. Force is best used to acquire power, but is not the best means to maintain power. The display of guns, bayonets, soldiers, only serves to remind the *populus* of the force that was once used upon them. But the results that propaganda can achieve act to soothe, comfort, and

thereby pacify, a people. Religion is the most important means to achieve this goal. Therefore Machiavelli places a high premium on religion in the state. The use of religion as a part of public policy is absolutely necessary to maintain a stable community.

3. *Act decisively.* It is much better to make a mistake than to hesitate. Of course, in most cases, to act without hesitation is probably the best way to avoid making the mistake. In war, for example, if you have the advantage and you hesitate, the battle can be lost. Not attacking because the opposition is better prepared, or in a better strategic position, is not hesitation, but simply good planning. Once the plan is settled and the decision made, do it.

4. *Maintain a strong army.* In order to use force ruthlessly and act decisively, a large standing army is necessary. Machiavelli is opposed to the use of mercenary armies and gives several reasons why they are undependable and therefore useless to his prince. A large citizen army is the best, if not the only way, to insure power of the prince and the safety of the state. No doubt the concept of the citizen-soldier as it existed in the Roman Republic became the pattern for his thinking about this issue.

A prince must also have certain qualities and be able to put those qualities into action. He must be both a "lion and a fox," cunning enough to recognize the traps and strong enough to frighten off those snapping at his heels. Both qualities are required. Brute strength is not enough. Where brute strength fails, cunning will generally succeed. The prince must also present himself as a highly moral person. He must have a "public and private morality." In his private life the traditional values that the average citizen must conform to are encouraged—being a good husband and father, living according to the laws of convention, church, and state. When it comes to the public good, however, the only morality is the morality of political pragmatism. Whatever works to benefit the state is good; whatever works to subvert the state is bad.

If, however, a prince must choose one of two courses, being feared or being loved by his subjects, he should choose the former. Love, says Machiavelli, is a fickle emotion, and can easily change. Fear, on the other hand, is a constant—those who fear, act on the basis of that fear, for their own well-being. Love also seems to be a condition which requires constant reaffirmation, while fear, once experienced, has a staying power by virtue of its own inertia. We tend to give our love easily and easily withhold it, and probably more easily change from one condition to the other. Fear once acquired, is hard to change.

The term "Machiavellian" has become synonymous with the idea that "the ends justify the means." To the extent that one is talking about the state and the ruler of the state, the association is correct. However, the concept of the ends justifying the means as a postulate of moral philosophy is not so. To Machiavelli, only the ruler is, and ought to be, above any law, moral law included. A prince's only concern is the well-being of the state over which he rules. A ruler must be judged on the success or failure of his actions as they apply to the state. If the state benefits, the action is good; if the state is hurt, the action is bad. He believed that politics is a science and that its laws are independent of morality. His conviction that fortune (luck) and necessity, not morality, controlled men's lives contributed to his generally pessimistic outlook about the world.

The Prince is simply a handbook for rulers, the *Discourses* less so. But they are also filled with the practical wisdom of governing. In *The Prince* Machiavelli, in addition to providing a "do-it-yourself kit" for governing, sends a message consistent with his total philosophy. He hoped for the unification of Italy. His patriotism, his theories of imperialism and militarism, his deep affection for ancient Rome, touched a sentimental chord in him. Italy, unified by a resurgent Rome leading the way, seemed to be one of the final wishes of this "mellowed" old Florentine farmer.

Thomas Hobbes (1588-1679)

Thomas Hobbes was born in Malmesbury, England in 1588. He studied at Magdalen College of Oxford University, but was not really turned on to learning until after college. During the thirty years between 1610-1640 he made three trips to Europe to study, write, and meet with the leading intellectuals of his day. On his third voyage he met and studied with the foremost Italian and French scientists, and probably with Galileo himself. He was a prolific writer and translator, but his major work, *Leviathan, or the Matter, Form and Power of a Commonwealth, Ecclesiastical and Civil,* contains the political philosophy for which he is famous.

Perhaps the two most important events in his life, which affected his thinking about the nature of man and the nature of the state, and his vision of what man is and how he lives in the state, were his European studies and the English Civil War. While on the continent he came in contact with the new scientific theories that were to become the basis for his materialistic philosophy. The English Civil War was so violent, so unforgiving, and so cruel that, having witnessed it, he could conceive of no condition so terrible as anarchy.

Hobbes was a personable and witty man, but with a penchant for argument. His views brought him into conflict with the scientific, political, and religious communities, yet he seemed to find patrons wherever he went. He was an active, productive man who played tennis well into his seventies, and during his mid-eighties translated the entire *Illiad* and *Odyssey*. He lived to be ninety-one years old, and it is said that he was still writing until the year of his death.

To Hobbes, everything in the world is matter, and all matter is in motion. All sensation is a product of this matter in motion, and can be explained according to the laws of physics. Since all of us are the products of this motion and matter, we are determined beings. Free will is an illusion; we choose on the basis of an idea which is the product of a material cause.

What causes us to choose one thing over another is what he calls "appetites and aversions." Objects which attract us, objects that we move toward, are called appetites. Objects which repel us, objects which we move away from, are called aversions. Since we ourselves are objects, each different from another, good and bad become relative terms. Our appetites we call good, our aversions we call bad, while, in fact, they are simply preferences based on the interaction of material forces. All morality, then, must be subjective.

Among the basic drives that men have which bring them into contention with one another are diffidence, desire for glory, and competition. Diffidence is the natural suspicion men have of one another. The desire for glory, then, coupled with this natural diffidence, brings men into competition with one another. The competition, in the state of nature becomes the basis for the anarchy that exists in the state of nature. Each man has the right to pursue his own goals. This places him in competition with others, and since each man is roughly equal to another, serious conflicts develop, and without rules anarchy reigns.

Man, then, is an animal like all others, albeit a much more complex one. Hobbes sees man as an animal in the state of nature, where the survival of the fittest is the rule. Thus, the first and most important natural law is the law of self preservation. This concept of natural law is quite different from the idea of natural law as a law of morality. All men desire peace, but their basic inclination for power puts them in conflict with all other men. Hobbes contends, then, that the state of nature is the state of war. The anarchy of the state of nature must give way to the authority of an artificial state, or there will be no culture, knowledge, art, literature, or society, and all men will live in "continual fear, and danger of violent death; and the life of man (will be) solitary, poor, nasty, and short."

But man has intelligence; he can reason. That ability to think leads him to realize that the state of nature, while allowing him his natural rights, deprives him of the benefits that peace can provide. To insure peace, men enter into a contract in which they give up the natural right to self-preservation to an entity powerful enough to protect each individual from those who would abuse him. This social contract is the basis for Hobbes' government, where, in trade for their very lives, the people relinquish their natural rights to a sovereign power. For this sovereign to exercise the power necessary to protect the members of the community, he must be above the law, with the absolute authority to act in accordance with the contract. The sovereign may be an individual or an assembly, but in terms of personal preference Hobbes opts for a sovereign individual. Because of this preference Hobbes has been called the philosopher of Absolute Monarchy.

What then, in the most simple terms, does this contract do? It gives absolute power to a monarch to protect the lives of his subjects. It gives the people the ability to live in the peace of civil society without fear of returning to the state of nature. The responsibility of the subject is to obey the laws; the responsibility of the sovereign is to protect their lives. The contract is made by the people for their mutual security, but the sovereign is not a part of the contract, which is an agreement among equals. The sovereign is simply the enforcer. Despite the absolute power of the sovereign in carrying out the terms of the contract, there are certain things he may not do. He may not force a citizen to go to war, testify against himself, or do anything that violates his right to self-defense or self-preservation. However, so long as the sovereign does provide this security, he rules and is to be obeyed in all other things.

The people, for their part, must obey the law. The peace, security, and tranquility that are the goals of the covenant result from obedience to the terms of the contract. Therefore, individuals who would try to assert themselves against others for their own interest, violate the law, challenge the sovereign, or in any way disrupt the community, are in violation of the terms of the contract and are subject to whatever punishment the sovereign imposes, with, of course, the obvious exception—no man need willingly go to his death at the hands of anyone, including the sovereign.

Hobbes' great concern is not only for security, but for unity. To that end he calls for a state religion. The religion of the sovereign should be the religion of the community. His materialism required that he reject religion as being able to explain God to man. God might exist but since there is no scientific way to explain God, dogma, and theology, religion's only value is in its pragmatic use as a tool of the state. Religion is a great means to help unify a state, but not a credible way to find and/or know God. Its credibility, however, was not Hobbes' concern. He believed that religion was the most important force in maintaining the unity of the state. Conversely, if not under the careful control of the sovereign, it could be and often was, the most divisive force conceivable.

There are two means by which states come into being. Hobbes calls them Commonwealth by Acquisition, and Commonwealth by Institution. A Commonwealth by Acquisition is, according to Hobbes, natural. It occurs when a superior force subdues his enemies and they, as a condition for maintaining their lives, submit to his will. The reason that the people submit to a ruler in the Commonwealth by Acquisition is because they fear him and what he may do to them if they do not submit. The only major difference between a Commonwealth by Acquisition and a Commonwealth by Institution is that in the latter the people fear one another; in the former they fear the ruler.

However, the Commonwealth by Institution is a bit more complex. Here men come together and by an act of the intellect recognize the advantages of peace over the life in the natural state, and they institute a government. The power is invested in a "man or an assembly of men," preferably in a man. The sovereign must have unlimited power in order to maintain the peace and protect the lives of the subjects. This, then, allows for one exception to an all-powerful ruler, for a citizen can defend his own life even if it means opposing the sovereign. The contract, once established, cannot be violated; the people come together out of fear of anarchy. If the ruler maintains a peaceful civil society, the quality of that society is not the issue. The fact that the state is relatively peaceful fulfills the only responsibility of the sovereign.

Hobbes' philosophy begins with a concept of man as a material being, determined by the interaction of matter in motion, governed by appetites and aversions. The state of nature is a state of war, and out of fear men make a contract to institute a sovereign to provide the peace they cannot provide for themselves. That sovereign must be absolute in all matters but one (he may not place a subject's life in jeopardy). He is above the law, and his role is basically utilitarian. There should be one religion in the state, controlled by the sovereign, and that religion should be the basis for unity. The concept of the social contract as the basis for the state, and the concept of absolute monarchy are probably his two most important contributions to political theory.

CHAPTER 18

Locke and Rousseau:
The Social Contractors

John Locke (1632-1704)

John Locke was born in Wrington, England in 1632, into a liberal Puritan family. He attended Oxford University and, after obtaining a B.A. and M.A., lectured in Moral Philosophy. By 1661 both his parents and his only brother had died, and he was left alone, but with a small inheritance. He later obtained a medical degree, but did not practice except as the private physician to the statesman Anthony Ashley Cooper, the Earl of Shaftesbury. It was this association with Lord Shaftesbury that brought him into direct contact with the political events that helped to shape his political philosophy.

The political turmoil in England caused Lord Shaftesbury to move to Holland, where Locke followed in 1683. Shaftesbury died in that same year, and Locke remained there until England's Glorious Revolution had run its course. He returned to England in 1688, and soon thereafter his two most noteworthy works, *An Essay Concerning Human Understanding* and *Two Treatises of Government,* were published. In his *Essay* he rejected the notion of innate ideas, claiming that just because reason discovers universal ideas, it does not follow that they are innate.

Locke was an Empiricist. He maintained that the mind is a *tabula rasa* (blank slate) and that all ideas come from experience. Simple ideas come from sense experience or reflection, combining in a variety of ways to become complex ideas. Truth, according to Locke, is the agreement of ideas according to three types of knowledge—intuitive (self-evident), demonstrative (logical relationships, rational proofs), and sensitive (observations of probable truths). He accepted the cosmological proof for the existence of God, and saw natural law as an extension of the will of God.

Unlike Hobbes, Locke rejected absolutism, and his *First Treatise* was an attack on Robert Filmer's *Patriarcha,* a defense of the theory of divine right. His *Second Treatise* was the major exposition of his political theory about the nature of man and the nature of the state. This basic disagreement with Hobbes and Filmer was most probably the product of his totally different opinion of the nature of man. Locke saw a "native goodness" in his fellow man and thought that mankind was generally decent, social-minded, and capable of self-rule.

Man in the state of nature, according to Locke, is equal to all other men. Equality, the law of nature, conforms to God's will, but this equality is not an equality of strength or intelligence. Rather it is a moral equality. And while Locke rejects the concept of divine right, the idea that God has somehow placed an individual on the throne to rule with His blessing, he does see the will of God manifested in the natural law, and insists that rational men can discover these natural laws and construct a political system that will work in accordance with these laws. Reason in the state of nature will prevail, not anarchy, for mature men are reasonable, and, with their "native goodness," capable of governing themselves.

In the state of nature, as Locke envisions it, the moral precepts which are divined from the natural law are known to all reasonable men. For example, in the state of nature it is obvious that murder is wrong, and as a wrong, punishment is justified. Yet if a murder takes place, who is to administer the punishment? The individual in nature has the right to administer justice according to the moral code contained in the natural law. But the problem inherent in this concept of the personal enforcement of the moral law is apparent. Thus, says Locke, a political institution to administer justice on behalf of the people is a necessity.

Thus the state is not a contrivance to save man from the horrible state of war (in nature). It is a device to provide "certain conveniences," such as the administration of justice, for the men who contract to establish it. Since man in the state of nature was relatively content, the state is charged with providing those "certain conveniences" which the citizens desire and need, as a condition for its justification. Men, by consent, establish a state. This social contract is an agreement which requires that the state serve the requirements of the body politic as a condition, not only for its justification, but for its continued existence.

The most obvious responsibility of the the state is to protect the life, liberty, and property of its citizens. The protection of life is a primary function of the state. Also, liberty is a requirement for carrying out moral dictates that a good life requires. Property, according to Locke, exists on different levels. First one has the property which is undeniably his own, his body. Next he has his immediate possessions, and then those things which he removes from nature by virtue of his own labor. Every man has a right to as much property as he can use, or store for future use. Any hoarding that would produce a surplus that would spoil or become unusable violates the natural law. The concept of money, however, complicates this issue, but Locke does not seem to consider the hoarding of money a violation of the natural law.

More important than the concept of the social contract as a technically correct description of an actual event, is Locke's concept of the moral justification of the state according to the concept of consent. Locke does not claim that every state came into being through the social contract, but he does maintain that no state has the moral right to exist except by the consent of the governed. Sovereignty must reside in the community as a whole and not in any power other than the people. The will of the people is, in the final analysis, the product of the will of the majority. A government must exist at the sufferance of the majority and in conformity with the desires of the majority. Locke sees government as the servant of the community, not the ruler of the community.

Locke suggests a structure for government which he feels will be responsive to the will of the majority and will be able to carry out the responsibilities which the majority has entrusted to it. The primary power resides with a legislative branch. The legislature has the right and the responsibility to pass the laws which provide for the common good. Legislatures are limited to just that end; they do not have arbitrary power to pass laws which are contrary to the public good. Also, the legislature is to be a separate branch of government and cannot exercise arbitrary power. The legislature cannot take a person's property without consent, and cannot transfer its lawmaking power to any other entity.

The second branch of government is the executive branch, which carries out the laws passed by the legislature. The executive branch also has the responsibility for the protection of the state from foreign foes. The federative branch sees to the state's relations with foreign countries, treaties, trade agreements, and all other international concerns. The whole of this structure of government is meant to provide, through separation of powers, a governmental structure meant to serve, not dominate, the people. There is, however, an interesting exception to this government of laws, with the prohibitions placed on each branch. It is called the prerogative power.

The prerogative power is the power which enables the king or prince to act when there is no law covering a particular situation. Not all conditions can be foreseen, nor can there be laws passed for all contingencies in advance, nor can a legislature always act with the speed that some emergencies require. Thus, a king in certain very special cases can act in the absence of law, or even against the existing law, for the public good. The action must always be for the common good, never for the particular interest of the king, or against the common good. If the executive exercises this power, it is left to the people to decide if the action was justified. If the legislative or executive branch abuse their power, they are answerable to the people.

Locke's next important concept follows logically. The people decide whether the government is serving the best interests of the majority. If the people determine that the government is, for whatever reason, failing in its responsibility, the people have the right to "alter or abolish" it. In a moral sense, when a government fails to serve the desires of the people, it has no moral rights and the contract of consent is, in effect, abolished. Locke, while considered the philosopher of the right to revolution, does not imagine that the right will produce the event. He thinks that people are more disposed to try to change existing problems peacefully, or bear the inconveniences, rather than to rush to the the barricades. The United States' Declaration of Independence echoes Locke's sentiment in this regard by stating, "governments long established should not be changed for light and transient reasons."

On the issue of religion in society, Locke, once again, differed with Hobbes. Hobbes required that the sovereign establish one religion, his own, to stabilize and unify the commonwealth. Locke calls for religious freedom and toleration. He bases his thinking on several factors: 1) a true Christian will be tolerant of others; 2) a state cannot enforce the beliefs of one religion on a person who believes in another; 3) the state will be more peaceful by tolerating different sects, rather than trying to impose compliance to a state religion; 4) the only role the state should have in religion is restricting practices which are inimical to the well-being of the state or other citizens. Once again, Locke's optimistic view of the nature of man produces a philosophy which results, not only in common consent as a basis for governing, but in religious pluralism.

Thus, Locke constructs a political system based on the moral equality of all men, which bestows upon them certain natural rights. The state is instituted by the consent of the people for the protection of those rights, and exists with moral justification so longs as it serves the desires and needs of the people. The government consists of separate branches, each serving a function necessary to a well ordered state. If the government ever violates its sacred trust, the people are justified in changing whatever offends them, and under rare and severe circumstances are even justified in dissolving the government itself. The state's responsibility to protect life, liberty, and property is a part of its obligation to the natural rights of its citizens. This obligation to protect natural rights also requires religious toleration of differing religious beliefs, while permitting regulation of religious practices which threaten the public good.

John Locke's life demonstrated the "basic goodness" he saw in humankind. He tried, patiently and thoughtfully, to determine the "ought" of political philosophy in the light of "what is." He died as he lived, quietly, peacefully, and well.

Jean Jacques Rousseau (1712-1778)

Jean Jacques Rousseau was born in 1712 in Geneva, Switzerland. His mother died soon after his birth; his father was a poor watchmaker who read romance novels aloud to the boy. His early youth was troubled and he had little, if any, formal education. He was brought up by his father until the age of ten, and then was left to an uncle who apprenticed him to an engraver.

He ran away from this situation when he was sixteen, met and was befriended by Mme. de Warrens and, as a means of maintaining her friendship, converted from Protestantism to Catholicism.

In 1750 his *Discourse on the Arts and Sciences* won an award from the Academy of Dijon. In it he contended that civilization had morally and physically weakened man and that the natural state was superior to modern society. Four years later he wrote *Discourse on the Origin of Inequality,* which claimed that man is naturally good but is tainted by institutions, and that the inequalities that result from social organizations are artificial and bad. His two most important works were published in 1762, *Émile,* a commentary on education and religion, and the *Social Contract,* a political treatise and his greatest achievement. His *Confessions,* an autobiography, is an emotional portrayal of an interesting but self-absorbed egotist.

After the publication of *Émile,* Rousseau fled from France to Geneva to avoid a hostile government and public. In 1766 he travelled to England where he stayed with David Hume until the temperamental Rousseau fought with Hume and returned to France in 1767. After travelling throughout France, he renounced his Genevan citizenship and settled in Paris in 1770. Rousseau was unlike most philosophers; certainly he was not like the stereotype. He was emotional, egotistical, undisciplined, moody, disputatious, changed religions whenever it suited his purposes, had numerous lovers, abandoned the five children born to his barmaid mistress, and probably took his own life. Yet, until his death, Rousseau believed that all men by nature were good, and that social institutions had corrupted us all.

Man, according to Rousseau, is a natural animal and as such has two basic governing principles, self-preservation and compassion. Self-love is the foundation for self-preservation, both natural and good, and man's social nature is the basis for his feelings of pity and sympathy with others. In the state of nature, man existed as a "noble savage," free and equal. Without institutions to corrupt him, man lives in a blissful harmony with others, eating, sleeping, making love whenever the moment dictates, like a happy, contented animal—but with the intelligence to appreciate his condition.

However, with the invention of tools and the coming together to use them, there developed an inequality based on the competition that ensued. Men's basic equality began to wane as competition caused some to become richer, stronger, and dominant. Institutions developed to protect those who, having achieved a superiority over their fellow men, desired to protect that which they had acquired. Society became a means to encourage selfishness and to bring about the fall of the natural, good, and decent "noble savage."

His *Social Contract* begins with the statement, "Man is born free; yet everywhere he is in chains." The chains he refers to are the restraints placed on individuals, on their freedom and their equality, by society. Since society has no right to impose these unnatural conditions on men—"Since no man has a natural authority over other men, and since might never makes right, it follows that agreements are the basis for all legitimate authority among men." Thus in two sweeping statements the reasons for and the necessity of the social contract is established.

Since man can never return to the natural state, and since by mutual agreement he enters into civil society, how to moderate the evil effects of civil society must be his main task. The answer to this difficult question rests with his concept of sovereignty—it rests with the people. Democracy however, must be an expression of the "general will," that is, what the body politic truly desires, and that desire must be for the benefit of the common good. He also uses the term "the will of all," which is quite different from the general will. When individuals vote for their own particular interest and a majority agree on a particular issue, that is the will of all, a corruption of the general will. The general will represents the equality of all, the understanding of the common good, and the effective enactment of law on behalf of the community.

It is interesting to note the paradox inherent in this concept. Rousseau begins the *Social Contract* with a statement about freedom, then creates a theory which demands individual subservience to the the common good. The general will, then, is whatever the common good demands, and what is good for the group is good. Freedom, then, is the freedom to do what is good, to conform to the common will. How does Rousseau then justify individual desires? He doesn't. If an individual goes against the common good he is, by definition, in error and thus not free. This thinking led him to talk about the state forcing "such an individual to be free."

Also, there is great confusion as to how the general will is to be determined in a practical sense. At one point he recommends a majority vote of the community. He also speaks of it as the theoretical ideal, an absolute truth. Thus, on the one hand he is a democrat, on the other hand, a totalitarian. The latter seems to be his practical solution. Since modern states are too large for a direct democracy, he favors an elected aristocracy. His opposition to the bickering of representative democracy, as a threat to the unity of the state, led him to call for the people's will to be exercised directly by the aristocracy or by a legislator. The legislator is an interpreter of the general will, a kind of intermediary, whose function is to perceive the general will when the community is confused and/or divided, and carry it out.

Further evidence that he was more the totalitarian than the democrat stems from his view of a state religion. Rousseau calls for a "civil religion" to which all people must subscribe or face exile or even death. This religion however, is not Protestant, nor Catholic; it is rather a kind of secular commitment to the state (God) and obedience to law (dogma), and failure to comply carries the penalty for sin (treason). All the while he maintains that all men should believe in God, a life in the hereafter, reward for the good and punishment for the bad.

The form that government takes is not of great consequence to Rousseau—government is simply the instrument by which the general will is carried out. When a state has more citizens who are performing an active role in enacting law than ordinary citizens, that is called democracy. When the government is put into the hands of a few and the mass consists of private citizens, that is called aristocracy. Finally, when the power of the people is put into the hands of one individual, who is called monarchy. Rousseau acknowledges that it is difficult to decide which of the three forms is best. In fact, one form may be best for one nation over another due to circumstances which are difficult to measure. Also, in practice all governments are mixed. A democracy has to have a head, a monarchy has to have many magistrates to carry out the functions of government. The question is which of the three forms dominates and to that extent is recognizable as one or the other.

Of course each of the three forms can become corrupt, and the size of the state can contribute to this problem. As with most philosophers, monarchy when corrupted, is the worst form. The resulting tyranny is most easily effected in a large state, so he opts for a small state, one in which the majority exercises sovereignty directly. The problem is not, however, limited to size. Obviously, the complexity of modern states compounds the problem and must be taken into consideration if the favored system is impractical.

Rousseau was a Romantic who placed considerably more faith in feeling than in reason. He considered instincts pure, and reason nothing more than clever manipulations for undermining man's natural goodness. Perhaps this is why his philosophy is often confusing. He can be the great democrat, talking about the general will being the product of an aware public voting on issues according to the good of the community rather than personal preference, and also account for the public's being deceived and call for a legislator and "interpreter" of the general will—and thereby sow the seeds of totalitarianism. Throughout, he seeks the moral supremacy of man unspoiled by progress, technology, and most of all, rationalism.

It is interesting to note that in this modern age of technology, complex and swiftly changing institutions, social alienation, and the myriad of problems that face us, nationally and internationally, many harken back to Rousseau's plea for a simpler life. The conflict between the romantic and the realist is joined today, as it was then. Can we go back? If not, can we save something from that earlier simple and uncomplicated life and incorporate it into the way we live today? Or is what exits the product of some vital force in time, and must we look ahead to new means to attack new problems?

CHAPTER 19

Burke and Hegel:
Conservatism and Absolute Idealism

Edmund Burke (1729-1797)

Edmund Burke was born in Ireland in 1729. His father was a lawyer who hoped that the son would follow the same path. As a youth he was sickly and spent several years in rural Ireland with his mother's relatives, who, like her, were Roman Catholics. He was educated at Trinity College in Dublin and graduated in 1748. He briefly entertained the thought of remaining at Trinity as a teacher, but felt that the life of a university professor was insular and stagnant. Armed with a classical education he left Ireland for London, ostensibly to study law, but began to write instead. His first major work *A Philosophical Inquiry into the Origin of Our Ideas of the Sublime and the Beautiful* was published in 1756 and was well received even though he criticized the prevailing opinion of absolute standards of beauty. His most important work, *Reflections on the Revolution in France,* contains some of the most important elements of his political philosophy.

In 1757, while living in London, he married, as his father had, a Roman Catholic. During his political career his position on Catholicism and Ireland was often criticized for being parochial, rather than principled because of the religion of his mother and his wife. Jane Burke, however, was a quiet and retiring woman who took no part in the political activities of her husband. During this period Burke moved slowly from literary pursuits towards a political career. In 1759 he became secretary to a minor official in the Whig party, rose in the party, and in 1766 took a seat in Parliament. He remained in Parliament for thirty years and his speeches, letters, and the *Reflections,* while not a systematic presentation, contain his political philosophy on virtually every important subject. He has become known as the "Father of Modern Conservatism."

Burke's conception of the nature of man is essentially a Christian view, that man is imperfect and imperfectible. This brought him into direct conflict with Rousseau and his concept of the "Noble Savage." Man in nature, according to Burke, would be more disposed to evil than to good. There is no such thing as a noble savage, so much as simply a savage, and all that the word implies. Civil society, in fact, is the force which brings some order, peace, security, enlightenment, and progress. Man is civilized by society, its institutions, laws, traditions, religion, and rational intercourse. There is a thin line between chaos and order, and that line is civil society.

Burke is not, however, a rationalist. Man, according to him, is too complex a being to be considered simply a rational being. He is much more. Certainly man is reasonable, but probably not so reasonable as he believes himself to be. There are in men natural sentiments, faith, inclinations and prejudices—all of which conspire to make the judgments of individuals suspect. There are few, if any, absolutes which can be perceived by an individual's reason alone. Perhaps the concept that "the individual is foolish; the species is wise" best conveys his position.

The state, then, is not a social contract in the sense that Locke and Rousseau consider it to be. Rather it is the evolutionary outgrowth of man's natural needs. Civil society, in itself, is a product of convention. But it is natural to the extent that it is formed for a natural need and for a natural purpose. Burke would argue against a social contract, but is committed to what could be called an "eternal contract," in that society is a "partnership not only between those who are living, but between those who are living, those who are dead, and those who are to be born."

Because of his vision of the limits of man's reason, and the abstract speculation about man in the state of nature, Burke is skeptical of theoretical political concepts. The political theories that men put on paper in the form of new constitutions that deal with concepts such as "natural rights," and words like liberty and equality in the abstract—these are an anathema to Burke. He is concerned with concrete relationships between men in civil society, and these relationships grow out of real experiences of people and institutions. Burke reveres law which has grown out of religion, tradition, experience, and the successful relationships that develop over a long period of time, rather than new law arrived at by philosophical speculation based on some abstract principle.

His opposition to concepts like natural rights does not prevent him from having some strong views on human rights which governments must respect. Also, the obvious requirements of our human nature must be observed. To Burke, the concept of freedom is not a natural right to do whatever one pleases. It is a human right which may be exercised so long as it does not interfere with another's human right to exercise that same freedom—in a concrete way. A mob in a street exercising "free speech" can often interfere, in a very real sense, with a person's right to cross the street. Similarly, human nature is such that the abstract concept of equality is not nearly so applicable as are the concrete realities of differences of intelligence, competence, height, weight, strength, and other qualities that make people, in a real sense, unequal. Thus, while Burke may approve of equality of individuals under the law, he would seriously disapprove of the concept that all are equally competent to make the law.

Burke, then, believed in a "natural aristocracy." He did not believe in the rule of an aristocracy as was commonly accepted. In fact, Burke took the position that if aristocracy simply meant the rich and powerful who dominated the poor, he would fight to the death for the poor if their human rights were being violated. Yet, he also maintained that if the poor banded together to avoid their responsibilities, and because of their numbers sought to be exempt from the moral and political restraints of civil society, he "...would join my hand to make them feel the force which a few, united in a good cause, have over a multitude of the profligate and ferocious." Those who naturally are best suited to govern, have the ability, the education, and the disposition—should govern.

A representative government was Burke's preference. In large measure he accepted the Aristotelian concept of governing for the common good rather than for narrow interest. When running for election from Bristol, he told his constituents that although they elect a representative, "he is not a member of Bristol, he is a member of Parliament." The implication here is clear. He is not going to represent the narrow interests of the part, rather the greater interest of the whole. Also, Burke set forth a concept of what a representative is, or rather, should be. He told his constituents, "Your representative owes you, not his industry only, but his judgment; and he betrays, instead of serving you, if he sacrifices it to your opinion." As a matter of principle, he supported the modification of penal laws against Irish Catholics. In anti-Catholic Bristol that, among other issues, caused his defeat in the election of 1780. He was given a safe seat, however, and continued in Parliament.

Burke lived during two of the three most important revolutions in human history. His position regarding the American Revolution and the French Revolution should provide further insight into his "realistic" philosophy. Burke fought in Parliament against the policies of George III, and gave speech after speech in defense of the position of the colonists against the King. His speech *On Moving Resolutions For Conciliation with America* put forward six points which probably most comprehensively states the colonists' arguments. He did not appeal on behalf of the colonists' natural rights. Rather he spoke of the rights of Englishmen, to which the colonists were entitled. *For Conciliation* used to be required reading in American high schools where student learned how Burke made America's case to the king. "The question is not whether you have a right to render your people miserable, but whether it is not in your interest to make them happy. It is not what a lawyer tells me I may do, but what humanity, reason and justice tell me I ought to do." He then asks the king if he refuses to relax his demands just because "your magazines (are) stuffed with arms to enforce them."

The colonists were simply defending their rights which had evolved over the centuries, from Magna Carta, to the English Bill of Rights, to the period in which their own institutions had matured into a stable, practical, and natural system of government. Burke believed that all revolutions were bad. They upset the natural evolution that was so important to him and his view of society. In a sense, Burke maintained that the American Revolution, like the Glorious Revolution, was "a revolution prevented, not made." Actually, George III was the revolutionary, attempting to return the monarchy to conform to some abstract concept of divine right. To an extent, history proved Burke right. After the War for American Independence, little of the existing institutions had changed. In a very real, practical way the political, social, educational, religious, and economic institutions of America were left virtually intact after independence.

The French Revolution was quite another matter for Burke. There he saw a revolution in the most frightening sense possible. A group of political theorists and sloganeers sought to overthrow the existing order, destroy it, and replace it with untried, untested political experiments. The attempt to destroy the historic, religious, cultural, economic, and social fabric which had been intricately woven over the centuries horrified Burke. To him, not only did the experiment fly in the face of history, and therefore was doomed, it set the stage for the "man on the white horse," which Burke predicted. Violent upheavals produce a social vacuum, and no one can predict what will fill that void. Those who sat down and wrote the theories and planned the political, religious, educational, economic, and social programs that were to be instituted after the revolution, were dreamers, according to Burke. Theoretical and abstract notions about men and institutions are nothing compared to the realities inherent in the evolution of both.

Thus Burke attacked the French Revolution, because it *was* a revolution and, by definition an evil. But Burke was not a reactionary, against change and reform. He was, in his writings and in his actions, a reformer. But he saw reform as a means to conserve. Change is a reality, and as such requires that men act accordingly; failure to act in response to real change jeopardizes the stability of society. Conversely, Burke would agree that "when it is not necessary to change, it is necessary not to change." The heritage of the past should not be lightly discarded, the wisdom of the ages should not be supplanted in favor of novel theories, and we should not experiment with the lives of the people who make up the nation.

Edmund Burke's legacy then, is one of conservative but steady progress, based on a respect for human rights as a practical necessity, not theoretical principle. He saw society as an evolutionary process based on religion, tradition, law, and representative government. He believed in a natural aristocracy, equality under the law, and political stability. He deplored abstract slogans and theories as they relate to men and institutions, and was the foremost opponent of revolution in modern history.

Georg Wilhelm Friedrich Hegel (1770-1831)

Georg Wilhelm Friedrich Hegel was born in Stuttgart, Germany in 1770. His family was of modest means and he studied theology with the intention of becoming a minister. He worked as a tutor, a teacher, a school administrator, a newspaper editor, and finally became a university professor. He taught at the University of Heidelberg and for the better part of his career at the University of Berlin. He became the outstanding German philosopher of his day and was renowned throughout Europe. His major works, *The Philosophy of Right* and *The Philosophy of History,* contain the most important elements of his political philosophy.

Hegel was an absolute Idealist. His most famous quote, "the rational is actual, and the actual is rational," is the basis for his position. Coupled with the concept that the absolute is the whole, it requires that one consider reality as a totality which can be achieved through reason. The momentary understanding of particular truths is only a part of a process. Thus, truth is not static, rather it is constantly evolving towards the totality. Reason is the supreme force in the universe and it operates through the dialectic.

The dialectic is the method by which this process operates. The dialectic consists of a thesis, antithesis, and synthesis. The thesis is an idea. Inherent in any idea is it's opposite—the antithesis. The combining of the two gives way to a synthesis— a newer, fuller truth—which in turn becomes a new thesis. This process is a continuum in which each new thesis is an improvement over the old one, so that all history is progressing on a higher and higher plane of truth towards what he calls the universal or world spirit.

The concept of the dialectic as it applies to Hegel's political philosophy begins with the family. The family is the thesis— representing the concept of unity. Within the family all the members are really one, not independent, but dependent, beings. The civil society is the antithesis—representing the concept of particularity. As children leave the family, they become independent entities in a social setting. The synthesis of the family and civil society results in the state. The state to Hegel is the highest realization of the dialectical process. The relationship of individuals with one another, and the relationship of families and civil society is the basis for the ethical life. Man cannot lead an ethical life outside the state. The state is a spiritual organism, and Hegel sees the state as the "realization of the ethical idea."

Also, the concept of the *Volksgeist* and the World Spirit is important to understanding the concept of the state as a spiritual organism. The *Volksgeist* is the National Spirit. It is not a mystical or theoretical quality; it is the whole of the natural, technical, economic, moral, and intellectual conditions that determine the nation's historical development. The *Volksgeist* is the sum total of the state's essence and personality, and the essence and personality of the people within it.

The World Spirit is reflected in the concept of ascendant nations. Since the course of history unfolds according to reason, the rational idea running its course according to God's will, the Idea in the world can be observed. At any given time in history a nation can be seen as being the dominant force in the world. Nations rise and fall; yet each time one nation rises, it does so as a manifestation of the realization of the force of the World Spirit. And each nation which replaces the previous one is an improvement over the last. This process is a part of the continuous march of history towards the Absolute Idea. The assumption that this march is ever evolving according to reason is based on Hegel's assumption that "God governs the world."

Hegel's theory of government is based on two premises— "the actual is rational, and the rational is actual," and "only the whole is real." Since each part of the state is actual, each part is also rational, in part. In a sound state absolute rationality is achieved. The state, then, is not a means to an end, it is the end, the supreme achievement in human affairs. The state is the absolute guardian of universal, not individual, interests, and it is the duty of each individual to be a member of the state. Each person who obeys the state is free, for he is obeying "the manifestation of God on earth."

Hegel divides his government into three distinct yet interrelated parts: the legislature, which represents the rule of the many; the executive, which represents the rule of the few; and the crown, which represents the rule of the one.

The legislature consists of two houses, Estates Assemblies. The first estate consists of members who are landowners. They are not elected but serve on a hereditary basis. The second estate has members who represent the different social, cultural, and professional associations. The aristocratic nature of the first estate is meant to represent the crown in its relationship to civil society. The second estate is meant to represent the interests of civil society. The role of the estates is to make general rules for the society and to educate the public and mold public opinion.

The executive branch is the most important in that the judicial and police powers are combined in it. They are part of the "universal class" and represent the general will and the reason of society. Hegel sees this group as a class of civil servants who do not view their position as a matter of right, but as a matter of duty. Formerly, aristocrats used their executive offices as a private club, and Hegel found that divisive, so he conceived of the idea of an executive corps of civil servants.

The crown is the branch in which "The physical embodiment of this organic unity is the monarch." The monarch personifies the state. The monarchy is a hereditary position and the main duties include appointing important officials. The monarch can pardon criminals, and as the titular head of the state represents the unifying force of the government. None of the particular elements of the state is sovereign, none is independent—their strength is in the unity of the state, and since the monarch is the state, he is sovereign.

It is difficult to sum up Hegel or his view of the world. He claimed not to understand himself. Schopenhauer accused him of purposely writing to confuse, and called him a "charlatan." John Stuart Mill claimed he got sick every time he read Hegel. Much of what he wrote has been interpreted in different ways, by different people, to serve their own purposes. But there are some concepts that seem to be worth repeating.

Hegel was an Idealist who believed that we live in a rational universe, directed by God to an absolute truth. The state is the highest expression of that truth. Truth exists only as a whole. Thus the state is a whole, and individuals are subject to it, and an ethical life cannot be lived outside the state. The Hegelian dialectic of thesis, antithesis and synthesis is the process by which truth is realized. The *Volksgeist* is the National Spirit and represents the essence of the state and its people. The World Spirit is the force of reason in the world and manifests itself through certain nations which are pre-eminent in the world at a particular time in history. Nations rise and fall, and each cycle represents a forward movement towards the absolute truth. Unity and harmony are manifestations of reason at work in a state which is a spiritual organism, growing and perfecting itself through that reason.

CHAPTER 20

Marx and Mussolini: Communism and Fascism

Karl Marx (1818-1883)

Karl Marx was born in Prussia in 1818 into a middle-class family. He studied at the universities at Bonn, Berlin, and Jena and received his doctorate in philosophy from the University of Jena. During his university days he came under the influence of Hegel's philosophy and later incorporated the dialectic into his own materialistic philosophy, creating Marxian dialectical materialism.

He married into the Prussian nobility in 1843, but at about the same time became a Socialist. He worked as a newspaper editor, wrote pamphlets, and engaged in various left-wing activities. Due to his radical writings he was expelled from Germany, went to France, was expelled from France, and eventually went to England where he lived out his life. His life in London was devoted to writing, and due to the meager earnings his writings provided, he was supported in large measure by Friedrich Engels.

Friedrich Engels, the son of a wealthy textile manufacturer, was his lifelong friend and collaborator. Together they wrote the *Communist Manifesto* which was published in 1848. Marx's major work, *Das Kapital,* was the product of years of effort and only one volume was published during his lifetime. The final two volumes were completed by Engels and published by him. The practical effect of these two works on the history of the twentieth century cannot be overestimated. Certainly the reality of Communism in this century can be traced back to the theories enunciated by Karl Marx in the middle of the nineteenth century.

Marx took the Hegelian concept of the dialectic, the idea of the process of thesis, antithesis, and synthesis, and transformed it into a materialistic dialectic. He claimed that the change inherent in the process is change in the material world, not the world of ideas. These material changes affect everything in human experience. The history of the world is the the history of the material changes which have resulted from changes in the means of production. The future history of the world is predictable according to the concept of economic determinism. During his lifetime, Marx saw feudalism as the thesis, capitalism as the antithesis, and communism as the final synthesis.

The material world is the only world, according to Marx. The most important aspect of this concept is what Marx calls the means of production. Whatever forces come into play regarding the means of production cause the political, social, and ethical principles which dominate a society at a particular time. Simply stated, all institutions of any society are the product of whoever controls the means of production, and the sum total of that society's ideology is the result. Political theory, art, literature, social mores, education, religion, are merely the outgrowth of ideological forces which emanate from those who control the means of production, and thus the society.

The history of the world, says Marx, is the history of the class struggle. Through the ages, because of the materialistic process of history, each stage has seen the conflict between the owners of the means of production and the exploited. Master and slave, lord and serf, landowner and tenant, factory owner and worker— the struggle has existed and continues to this day.

Capitalism is the stage in the concept of historical determinism which will give way to the final synthesis, communism. The process evolves as follows, beginning with:

1) *The labor theory of value.* The only value that an object has is the labor that went into its production.

2) *The surplus theory of value.* The factory owner pays his workers less than he receives for the goods he sells; the surplus, called profit, he keeps.

3) *The concentration of capital.* This profit is reinvested into new machinery, causing some owners to put other owners out of business and causing large number of workers to be put out of work.

4) *The new industrial army.* The large number of unemployed workers will grow, and their situation will become desperate.

5) *The inevitable violent revolution.* Since the owners will never willingly give up the wealth they have in their control, it will take a violent revolution to overthrow them.

6) *The dictatorship of the proletariat.* The workers will take over the means of production. (Note: The final synthesis occurs when the owners and the workers are one and the same, and the conflict ceases).

7) *The withering away of the state.* Since the state is simply a tool used by the exploiter-owners to dominate the exploited-workers, when the workers are the owners and the conflict ceases, the state withers away.

The scenario described above has not come to pass as predicted by Marx. The reasons given for the failure of the predictions—organized labor, enlightened capitalism, service industries, educated labor force, may or may not be valid. Let us however, analyze the major points which are central to his theory.

Marx contends that all societies up to this point in history have been in conflict, and the source of that conflict has been based on the economic disparity that results from the ownership of the means of production by the few at the expense of the many. The problem can be solved only by eliminating the cause. Thus the concept of common ownership, or the abolition of private property becomes the only viable means to end the conflict.

Capitalism is the logical and necessary step in the historical process which will lead to the final synthesis, communism. The process described earlier will lead to the violent overthrow not only of the capitalists but also of the social and political institutions which support them. It is the elimination of those institutions which will pave the way for a just society, beginning with the dictatorship of the proletariat—a small cadre (the Communist party) who will reorganize society—and ending with a classless society. With the advent of the classless society, the end of conflict will lead to a just economic order based on the maxim, "From each according to his ability, to each according to his needs."

In order to achieve the society that Marx considers just, ten measures to achieve the desired social reforms are put forth in *The Communist Manifesto.*

1. Abolition of private property.
2. A heavy, progressive, graduated income tax.
3. Abolition of the right of inheritance.
4. Confiscation of the property of emigrants and rebels.
5. Centralization of credit in a national bank monopoly.
6. Centralization of communication and transportation in a state monopoly.
7. State ownership of factories and means of production; planned use and improvement of the land.
8. Equality of labor; establishment of industrial armies, especially for agriculture.
9. Combining of agriculture and manufacturing industries; abolition of distinctions between town and country by distribution of the population over the country.
10. Free education for all children in public schools; abolition of child labor.

The world that Marx envisions will be a society without government. There will be no need for the state and the government the state requires, since the state is simply a device to enforce the will of the oppressors over the oppressed. Once the owner-worker delineation is eliminated, the social distinctions which follow naturally will also be eliminated. It is because of the social distinctions that class is pitted against class. In a classless society the main source of friction will be eliminated. Certainly there will be individuals who will go against the group, but there will be no state power needed to inhibit these misguided people. The force of the whole body of the community will keep them in line.

Also, Marx envisions a secular world in the future. Religion will not be necessary, since the use of religion emanated from the need of the oppressors to keep the oppressed content. The option of a happy life in the hereafter was an explanation for the pain of this life which the poor had to endure. Since man is a material being, the material needs of this life are of primary importance. The spiritualism of religion was "the opiate of the masses," and the drug runners were those who owned the means of production.

The final synthesis for Marx, then, is a classless society, where there is no state, no religion, no enforcing arm of government. The members of this society will live in a giant economic cooperative, where workers will not only produce the goods, but administer the factories and farms. There will be no distinctions between those who work with their hands and those who work in occupations which require mental acumen. The educational process will redirect people from a competitive, to a cooperative view of the nature of man—and since Marx's position is that human nature is not unchanging but rather created, the re-education of the population is not only desirable but attainable. This process will be in the hands of the Communist Party until the transition from political state to classless society is complete.

Benito Mussolini (1883-1945)

Benito Mussolini was born in Forlì, Italy in 1883. He was educated at the University of Lausanne in Switzerland, but was expelled from Switzerland for socialist agitation and returned to Italy. He was a member of the Italian Communist party, but had a policy dispute with the leadership and was expelled in 1914. He worked for several newspapers until he founded the Fascist party in 1922. From that time until his death in 1945, Mussolini was the main exponent of Fascism and the foremost opponent of communism and capitalism.

In a very real sense, Mussolini is not the philosopher of fascism. Rather, he is the synthesizer of several philosophies which combine to create the doctrine. His major work, *The Doctrine of Fascism,* is the compilation of several ideas presented by forerunners of the philosophy. Also, there is a real problem with approaching fascist political philosophy, in that there is a frequent lack of or contempt for, ideology. Fascists emphasize action and deeds rather than thought and principle. The very nature of fascism makes it difficult to study in the search of a definitive political philosophy, but there are several concepts which are consistent and necessary to understanding the theory—absolutism, irrationalism, imperialism, the organismic theory of the state, and the corporate state.

Absolutism requires that the government be in the hands of an all-powerful leader who can effectively direct the state towards the desired ends. This theory is not new—Machiavelli, Hobbes, and Bodin were early advocates of this position. However, it was

Vilfredo Pareto who most directly affected Mussolini with his "theory of elites," an explanation of mass behavior. Pareto claimed that all historical, revolutionary, and social changes were initiated by "vanguard elites," those who mobilized the sentiments of the masses behind a revolutionary ideal. This idea of a small group of elites who must lead the masses is very important to fascist doctrine.

Equally important is the concept of the "democratic fallacy," which views as incorrect the idea that the people are capable of governing themselves. Mussolini endorsed this concept, which had been put forward by Alfredo Rocco, who accused democracies of catering to private interests rather than rising above them for the "social collectivity." The ability to rise above private interests "in favor of the higher demands of society and of history is a very rare gift and the privilege of the chosen few." Thus, the fascist principle that only the qualified rule, because they "know better," sets up a condition which does not allow the expression of opinions contrary to those of the leader.

If democracy is invalid, then so is equality. Fascism delights in the concept of the inequality of men. Mussolini maintains that fascism "affirms the irremediable, fruitful and beneficent inequality of men." If this is so, then the one absolute quality that can properly separate the differences is power. The strong are better than the weak, and that is true for men as well as for nations.

The second major concept is that of irrationalism. The roots of this concept go back to the 19th century Romantics. Dosteyevsky, Nietzsche, and Freud all stressed the irrational side of man, and to that extent also contributed to fascist doctrine. Irrationalism denigrated the value of reason and used words like sentiment, inspiration, passion, intuition, which were used to replace reason in politics with emotion and faith. The most influential contribution to political irrationalism was found in the doctrine of the "social myth" put forward by Georges Sorel.

Sorel maintained that successful movements employed a myth which is not reasonable, but is rather a dream, a vision, carrying with it great emotional force. The myth cannot be refuted because it is defined according to the conviction of the group which is moved by it. Mussolini introduced the myth of the

Roman Empire and the glory that would return to Italy under fascism. The emotional ideal of the Roman Golden Age was the myth used to fire the imagination of the Italian masses.

The final aspect of irrationalism is the creation of the "new man." Mussolini saw communism and liberal capitalism as being simply concerned with man's economic condition, a superficial and inadequate vision which neglected the spiritual aspect of his being. This "heroic" man who was willing to sacrifice self for a higher good, who was strong, courageous, and disdained mere materialism, is the fascist ideal.

Imperialism, the third major concept, is an obvious outgrowth of irrationalism, since the violence, action, power, and human struggle are objectified in war. This driving force in man was incorporated into fascist philosophy as the struggle of good over evil, the strong over the weak. Mussolini saw war as desirable, because it cultivates moral strength and courage and "brings up to their highest tension all human energies and puts the stamp of nobility upon the peoples who have the courage to meet it." Through war a nation can bring a higher and nobler culture to others and fulfill a natural law. Imperialism, according to Mussolini, was "the external and immutable law of life."

A fourth major principle of fascism is the organismic theory of the state. This theory maintains that the state is a biological organism, similar in fact, not merely by comparison, to a human being. All the members of the state, like the cells in a human body, contribute to the whole and must function as a unity to maintain the health of the entire body. Thus, the state is not only a real person, but one whose reality is greater than any individual within it. Any elements which might jeopardize the health of the state may, therefore, be justifiably eliminated.

Just as with individuals, however, the state must be greater than just a mere economic or mechanical entity. The spiritual aspect of its being is of most importance. Hegel referred to the state "as the march of God in the world, the Divine Idea as it exists on earth." Mussolini not only accepted Hegel's idea, but expanded it. To him the state was a spiritual entity with an ethical will of its own, organically growing in form and substance. "Outside the state," he said, "there can be neither individuals nor groups ...the state is an absolute before which individuals and groups are relative. Individuals and groups are 'thinkable' in so far as they are within the state."

The idea of freedom, in fascist theory, is in accordance with the position taken by Hegel. Freedom can only be found in submission to the state. Physical submission is all that the state would require. The benefits of this submission would be found in the spiritual growth of each individual, since as the state grows and prospers, each individual grows spiritually with it. Mussolini uses the analogy of a soldier marching, in step, as a part of an army. The individual is not demeaned by submitting to the lock step of the group; rather, he becomes a part of a larger, greater, more powerful unit which glorifies the individual by making him part of something greater than himself.

The final precept of fascism is the idea of the corporate state. This concept has elements of the syndicalist movement (extreme left wing socialists) in it, and the term "national socialism" is very close to being the definitive term for explaining its meaning. Marxism on an international scale, and democratic capitalism on a national scale were seen by the fascists as divisive, encouraging class conflict and disunity. The corporate state was meant to abolish strife between the workers and the employer, head off international communism, and end capitalist exploitation.

In the corporate state all units of production would be united in a syndicate, or corporation, in which managers and foremen, owners and workers, would all be fairly represented, and in which all would work together for the national good. Private interests and union principles would be transcended, and the public would benefit with increased production and industrial harmony. This group would determine national priorities, cooperate in the achievement of agreed-upon goals, and eliminate conflicts which might impede national progress.

The corporation would work to insure the economic well-being of the state. The success of this program might not provide individuals with particular products that they might want, but it would provide the community with the goods needed to aid in the growth, strength, and progress of the state. Consistent with fascist theory, the economic well-being of the state is the primary goal, since if the state prospers, so does the individual. Also, the narrow individual desires that are satisfied by other economic systems do not contribute to the spiritual growth of the individual or the state.

Benito Mussolini took many different concepts from many different contributors, and not only articulated them in *The Doctrine of Fascism* but also acted on those theories. The short-lived Italian fascist state incorporated some, but not all, of the theories enunciated by Mussolini. The concepts of absolutism, irrationalism, imperialism, the organismic theory of the state, and the corporate state were not original with Mussolini, but probably best expressed by him in this century.

PART 4

ECONOMIC THEORY:
AN INTRODUCTION

CHAPTER 21

Introduction to Economic Theory

Economics is generally considered to be the study of man in relationship to his material needs. Alfred Marshall, who made a significant contribution to the study of economics, broadly defined the subject as "...a study of mankind in the ordinary business of life; it examines the part of individual and social action which is most closely connected with the attainment and with the use of the material requisites of well being."

Economists generally deal with the "what is" rather than the "ought," so to that extent the study of economics is not comparable to moral or political philosophy. Yet, there is a relationship between morality and political philosophy and economic theory which is important. For our purposes, we shall try to see economics as a part of the study of human ideas in juxtaposition to moral and political theory. Therefore, we will place emphasis on economic theory as it applies to the nature of man and the implications of that theory, rather than the statistical, speculative, and purely analytical aspects of the subject. Since economics is the study of the production, distribution, and consumption of goods and services, it is important to consider how to best accomplish the desired end within the context of acceptable moral and political postulates.

All economists agree that a basic concept necessary to understand economics is the law of scarcity. When one considers the world we live in, there are certain obvious observable truths. There is only so much land, water, iron, coal, or, for that matter, any other resources. Sooner or later those resources will be used, or used up in most cases. Considering that there are millions upon millions of people on this earth, all engaged in using or wanting to use some of the available resources, we are faced with the fact that in the long run all resources are in danger of being used up. Some say that sooner or later we are going to run out of everything. Others contend that the mind of man will prevail, and that technology as a response to scarcity will provide the means to provide for our insatiable wants. Therefore, man must always conserve and/or make the most efficient use of his resources, and/or come up with the technology which is required to maintain himself.

Man also recognizes that despite the law of scarcity, there is a side to his nature that demands one important thing—*more*! While a person can only wear one pair of pants at a time he wants *more*—dress pants, play pants, work pants, lounging pants, yellow pants, plaid pants, and on and on and on. If one considers that this simple example is multiplied by an infinite number of desires held by an infinite number of people, it becomes clear that all our resources would be used up—and then no wants could be satisfied. Since there is a limited number of resources and an infinite number of desires, the study of economics is essential in order to understand how to maximize the fulfillment of those desires in light of the limited resources necessary to do so.

What to produce, how to produce, and for whom to produce are the three questions which naturally grow out of this understanding of scarcity and human desires. What should we produce? Since we cannot have all things, we must prioritize our desires—and that becomes the choice of what to produce. Most people are concerned with the primary wants of food, clothing, and shelter. Thus production in these areas is high on our list of priorities. These things are produced first. People also desire goods other than these basic wants, and those choices are made according to taste, culture, and tradition. How should we produce? First we have to understand what are the component parts that production entails. They are land, labor, capital, and enterprise. We need the natural resource (land). The labor changes that resource into a good, the tools (capital) that aid labor in the production of goods, and the organizing ability to do so (enterprise) comprise those component parts. The law of scarcity demands the most efficient combination and use of these factors. For whom should we produce? Once we have the good—who is the recipient? Those people who have contributed most to its production? Those people who need it most? Those people who have surplus wealth? The answers to these questions are perhaps more moral or political than economic—but economic theory addresses them all.

One of the questions of primary importance deals with the nature of man. Is man's nature competitive or cooperative, or is he conditioned to be one or the other? The implications that follow from whatever postulates are accepted are important to economic theory. What one thinks about the nature of man has a direct relationship to the basic economic question of what to produce, how to produce, and for whom to produce, and economic philosophers have constructed elaborate systems based on their premises about the nature of man. We shall undertake to study and evaluate those systems.

There are six major goals that most people agree are valid concerns for any economic system. Economic theory generally deals with how we might best accomplish these goals. The identified goals are:

1) *Economic growth*—Each community seeks economic growth, to increase the production of goods for the improvement of individual and social well-being. There are, however, questions that are posed by the subject of economic growth. At what cost to the environment, individuals, or future growth may economic growth be considered good? When, and under what circumstances, might economic growth be considered undesirable? How do we make those determinations?
2) *Full employment*—Every community seeks full employment for its members, to provide jobs for all those able, eligible, and seeking to work. How to achieve that goal is the question. Does the private sector create jobs? Does the state have the right to force people to work? How is full employment best achieved, by the state or by private enterprise? If full employment is attained, who deals with the resulting threat of inflation?
3) *Price stability*—Wild fluctuations of price are universally acknowledged to be unhealthy for any community. The human need for some kind of predictability is not only a political postulate, but also an economic one. Should the state set prices? Is the desired stability a short or a long term goal? Does the supply and demand cycle require some instability?
4) *Economic freedom*—Choice is an essential aspect of the human condition. Most people would agree that to maximize economic choice is a desirable end. But, at what cost? Does

economic freedom require *laissez-faire*? Must all economic transactions be sanctioned—even drug dealing, pornography, prostitution? Are there political and/or moral constraints that may legitimately be placed on economic freedom?

5) *Economic security*—While there is a human need for freedom, the very concept of freedom implies some chance, thus an infringement on security. To what ends may we go to insure economic security? In the name of security should we retard the progress which comes from risky experiments? Is government the best means to insure security? Also, how are provisions made for those who are chronically ill, disabled, handicapped, aged or otherwise dependent? "Economic security" implies that somehow those who are unable to care for themselves fully, will be provided with some help.

6) *Equitable distribution of income*—One of the elements of the human condition is a seeking after justice. The question, of course, is what is just and how do we achieve it? Does equitable mean equal, or equal as a relationship of contribution to reward? If equality means each person receives the same, does it require each contribute equally? Is equality of condition ever possible? If each receives according to his contribution, who determines the value of the differing types of contribution? The goal is to promote prosperity and minimize poverty among the population. How to and who can best accomplish this is the question.

The goals stated above and the questions posed are properly the subject of economic theory. Of course there are many more questions than the few indicated here. We shall see that many of the economic philosophers presented in the forthcoming chapters pose more and different questions, all relevant to our understanding of the importance of the world in which we live.

There are, in fact, three basic types of economic systems: the command, the market, and the traditional. A command economy is planned and directed by government authorities through a central agency, and requires a large bureaucracy. The market economy is a system in which most economic decisions are made by individual buyers and sellers in the marketplace. The traditional is a rudimentary economic system in which change and growth proceed slowly; people do what their parents did before them, and most goods are produced and consumed locally.

The different economic theories that have developed have been attempts to answer some of the questions about how to achieve the desired goals of economic growth, full employment, price stability, economic freedom, economic security, and equitable distribution of income. These theories include capitalism, socialism, and communism. In fact most economic systems are a mixture of more than one of the three. However, there are premises which require that the system be more one than the other, e.g., basically socialistic with some elements of capitalism or vice versa. *Laissez-faire* is free-enterprise capitalism carried to one extreme of the pendulum, while communism is socialism carried to its logical extreme.

Some brief definitions of the major theories follow:

Capitalism is an economic theory which values the concept of private ownership of property, the right to engage in business for a profit, the legality of contracts between private individuals, and the primacy of private enterprise as the best means to insure the objectives of the community. Minimal government involvement is the goal; government regulation is acceptable, while government control is frowned upon.

Socialism calls for state ownership of the basic industries. Those industries which are considered basic to the general welfare should be owned and operated by the government. The more industrial, technological, and complex the society, the more industries that might come under the government control. The more simple the society the fewer industries that would become socialized. Interestingly, government control of a simple society's one or two industries would have the effect of considerable government control over the entire community. In a highly developed country with a great many different industries, the government ownership and operation of several industries would have the practical effect of less governmental control over the entire community.

Communism, simply defined, is state ownership of all productive goods and services and their means of distribution. Obviously the control of all the means of production and distribution will have a significant effect on the entire community. The state becomes integrally involved in every aspect of the lives of the people. The premise which is the basis for such a theory is that the government can better provide for the material needs of the people. Communism purports to eliminate some of the problems of unemployment, economic security, and economic stability that are inherent in a free-enterprise system.

The concept of man as a cooperative being is important to socialism. The idea that man is competitive by nature is the basis for capitalism. Capitalism has as a major premise the value of economic freedom, while socialism extols economic security as a more important value. Socialism looks to the state to provide full employment, while capitalism seeks economic growth as a means to full employment. All economic theories and their resulting systems are constructed with an eye to the improvement of man in the material world. The question, of course, is which system best achieves the desired results, and even more important which results are most worthy of being desired.

In addition to the theories about the nature of man, theories as to which economic values are superior to others, and what system is best for the individual, the group, or both, there are five great economic laws which have a bearing on what factors must be taken into account in our analysis of economic philosophy. The five laws are:

1) *The law of demand*—This law states that if the price of a product is reduced, more will be bought; if the price of a product is raised, less will be bought. For example, people will buy more at a sale than when the same item is offered at the regular price.
2) *The law of supply*—This asserts that producers will offer more for sale at higher prices than at lower prices. For example, more fans are produced and offered for sale in the summer than in the winter.
3) *The law of diminishing marginal utility*—This states that, given any consumption situation, as one consumes more of a good, the amount of usefulness or satisfaction derived from each consecutive unit used will rise, peak, and then level off or decline. For example, there is just so much of a food we can eat, even though we start out with a great hunger.
4) *The law of diminishing returns*—This says that, given any production situation, the more resources (input) that are used,

the more output will rise to a point where the output will level off or decline. An example of this concept is contained in the cliché, "Too many cooks spoil the soup."

5) *Say's Law*—This is the contention that the desire for products is infinite and the ability to purchase is also guaranteed, i.e., supply creates its own demand.

In the following eight chapters we shall attempt, from our readings and the ensuing discussion, to determine which economic premises seem most viable, which ideas square with our moral and political values, and which system or combination of systems seems to provide the best chance for attaining our goals. Obviously, we have to set priorities as to which goals are most important to us, what the ramifications of those priorities might be, and whether we must somehow moderate some of our goals in order to obtain others of value.

CHAPTER 22

Smith and Ricardo: Laissez Faire and Free Trade

Adam Smith (1723-1790)

Adam Smith was born in Kirkcaldy, a small town in Scotland, in 1723. He entered the University of Glasgow in 1737. He was offered a scholarship to Oxford, which he accepted, and studied there for six years. He returned to Scotland and taught Logic and Moral Philosophy at the University of Glasgow. In 1759 he published his *Theory of Moral Sentiments* which dealt with the problem of morality and how it related to man's self interest and his ability to make moral judgments in contradiction to that apparent dominant feature of his nature

Smith became famous by virtue of the success, if not controversy, that the *Theory of Moral Sentiments* inspired. He was asked to be the tutor of the stepson of Charles Townsend and in 1764 he and the young Duke of Buccleuch left for France. In France he met Quesnay, the great economist, and was introduced to many of the principles of the Physiocrats. Smith rejected the primary claim of the Physiocrats that all wealth sprang from agriculture, but did accept the idea wealth was the product of production and did circulate through the economy.

Upon his return to Scotland he worked for several years on his major work, *An Inquiry into the Nature and Causes of the Wealth of Nations,* more commonly known as *The Wealth of Nations,* which was published in 1776. During his lifetime Smith met with and engaged in discussions of moral and economic philosophy with men like David Hume, Samuel Johnson, Quesnay and Ben Franklin. Something of a character in life, he was the stereotypical absent minded professor, as well as a great intellect whose contribution has earned him the title, "The Father of Modern Capitalism."

The Wealth of Nations is divided into five books dealing with the problems of production, distribution, exchange, capital and public finance. Smith used each of these five particular problems to emphasize the supreme goodness of the natural order and to point out the imperfection of human institutions.

Smith's basic contention is that man is primarily motivated by self interest. This is not only his view of human nature, but is the point around which his economic philosophy revolves. Other characteristics which are controlling factors in determining human conduct are sympathy, a sense of propriety, the desire to be free, the propensity to barter and exchange goods, and the habit of labor. Man, according to Smith, is a very complex and dignified being. Each person is the best judge of his own interests and should be allowed to pursue those interests. Smith also contends that the effect of each man pursuing his own advantage will not result in chaos. He maintains that there is in this natural order of things, a delicate mechanism which transfers this personal striving into social good. The individual is "led by an invisible hand to promote an end which was no part of his intention."

The consequences of his belief in the natural order of things result in an negative view of the role of government. Generally, governmental intervention into economic affairs has a negative effect; actually governmental intervention into most human affairs has a negative result. If government allows each member of the community to seek his own advantage, the result will be the improvement of the common good. Obviously, the government does have a role to play in the natural order of things. The first is to provide for the common defense; second, to establish a system of justice, third, to maintain those public works projects which individuals and groups could not operate at a profit, and fourth, to maintain a monetary system. Outside of these four natural functions of government, Smith feels that government would do well to stay out of the affairs of individuals and thereby allow them to provide better for themselves and for the common good. Interestingly, Smith contends that monopoly is not the product solely of a business conspiracy; as a matter of fact, absolute monopoly could not exist for any length of time without government cooperation.

Thus, to Smith the natural order requires that economics be free from all forms of state interference with the ordinary business of industry and commerce. Each individual seeks his own greatest profit, but he is also a member of the community and his gain also helps the common good. Smith illustrates this point by his famous quote, "It is not from the benevolence of the butcher, the brewer or the baker that we expect our dinner, but from their regard to their own interest." The butcher, for example, must sell good meat, at a fair price, treat his customers courteously, and in general do all that he can to keep customers happy and thereby coming back. To the extent that he succeeds, he provides for his own family, thus provides for his own good as well as the good of others. All the butchers in a community are thereby looking to their own profit first, but the means to attain that profit is found in their service to the community. It is in this way that the natural economic order operates, and the natural competition which results in the greatest good for all concerned. Thus, the "invisible hand" guides the interaction of the market to an end the individual cannot anticipate.

Smith also considers this free market, this laissez-faire system, as a self-adjusting market according to laws of the natural order. The market automatically decides those important questions of what, how, and for whom to produce. Competition among the producers would naturally result in a pattern of production according to the needs and desires of the consumers. Every product has a real value, the combination of wages, rent, and profit. These factors result in what is called the natural price. Whenever the market price of a commodity differs from its natural price, certain market forces are set into motion to bring it closer to its natural price. It works like this. When the supply of a commodity falls short of the demand, some people will be willing to pay more for it. This competition among purchasers will cause the market price to rise above the natural price. If the supply of a commodity exceeds the demand, some people will wait before purchasing, causing the market price to fall below the natural price. When the supply is equal to the demand, the natural and market price will be nearly equal. Production automatically shifts to meet the demands of the consumers. Competition will drive the price down to the lowest possible level consistent with balanced production and demand.

Smith's primary considerations about labor dealt primarily with its division. The increase in the quantity of work done by the same number of people as a consequence of the division of labor is due to three things. 1) The increased dexterity of the individual worker. 2) the saving of time lost by going from one type of work to another. 3) The invention of machines to assists one man in doing the work of many. This last condition, Smith says, arises since machines are often invented by men who seek to save their own time and labor on whatever job occupies them. This division of labor, basically applicable to industrial production rather than agriculture, is responsible for the increase of production which benefits the entire society. Smith sees the increase of production as the source of national wealth, and a continual spiral of increasing well being for the entire community.

Wages, of course, are necessarily tied to labor. "The produce of labor constitutes the natural recompense in wages of labor." As a matter of fact, Smith believed that the entire produce of labor initially belonged to the laborer. But, as society became more complex, and concepts of rent and capital entered into the economic picture, wages became part of the entire package of economic enterprise consisting of rent, capital and wages.

Wages of course should be sufficient for the laborer to maintain himself and his family. In that way the continuum of economic prosperity will continue. Laborers are in that sense, a commodity which must be available for production. Smith maintains that if workers are not paid enough to raise a family the labor force will decline and wages would rise according to the law of supply and demand. The result of higher wages will be an increase in population. Smith sees a rise in population as a mark of national prosperity.

Smith's vision of the modern industrial state is an optimistic prediction of continued growth, prosperity, and improvement of the social conditions of the general public. Only the refusal of the government to allow the natural market mechanism to function can undermine this process. Also, the government must carry out its proper responsibilities regarding monopolies for Smith's vision to be realized.

Monopolies consist of four types: 1) Natural monopolies are those monopolies which exist as a resource of a particular area, produced by nature. Such natural monopolies as diamonds, oil, iron, or gold exist independent of man's ability to produce the commodity. 2) Necessary monopolies, often referred to as public monopolies, are those monopolies which the public good require. Public water supplies, roads, and other utilities which the private sector cannot economically provide are considered necessary. 3) Legal monopolies are those operations which exist by virtue of the ownership of patents, copyrights, and trademarks. 4) Artificial, or illegal monopolies are those combinations of forces which conspire to raise prices by collusion. Smith considered artificial monopolies as dangerous as government interference. He once said, cynically, that whenever people of the same trade meet, "the conversation ends in a conspiracy against the public." The government should step in, break up the conspiracy and step out again.

Thus, Adam Smith sees society as self-regulating through the interaction of self-interest and competition. Society is constantly improving, but the process is a long term evolution which will permit no tampering. The market must be left alone. In this process the consumer is the king and the monopoly (or government) the enemy. He saw order, design and purpose in society and believed that the process of laissez-faire economics would lead to real wealth. He created the first major systematic treatise of economic theory and still is the major philosopher of free enterprise capitalism.

David Ricardo (1772-1823)

David Ricardo was born in London on April 19, 1772. His father was a Jewish banker, who, when David married a Quaker, disowned him. Left to make his own way in the world, he quickly became a very successful stockbroker and amassed a considerable fortune. He became a rich man before he had reached the age of thirty. His *Principles of Political Economy and Taxation,* published in 1817, was his major work.

In the preface of his *Principles* Ricardo stated the three major aims of his text: first "to determine the laws which regulate... distribution" between the proprietor of land, the owner of stock or capital necessary for its cultivation, and the laborers by whose industry it is cultivated;" second, "to understand the effect of the progress of wealth on profits and wages;" and third, "to trace satisfactorily the influence of taxation on different classes." Specifically, the *Principles* was a treatise on Britain's growth prospects.

Ricardo was trying to identify some of the economic forces involved in the Industrial Revolution in England. He tried to set up a system of analysis whose core is composed of distribution and growth theories. The main categories of this system are the theories of diminishing returns, value, rent, wages, distribution, international trade and taxation.

All of Ricardo's economic theory is abstract, using as a model a giant corn farm. With this model, Ricardo demonstrates the law of diminishing returns by showing that if increasing amounts of capital or labor (variable factors) are applied to the land (fixed factor), the increase in corn, or total product—as each additional quantity of capital or labor is applied—will eventually decrease. In other words, successive inputs of capital or labor will result in decreasingly smaller increases of corn. Much of Ricardo's theory deals with corn; during his lifetime he argued vehemently against the corn laws which he felt were the cause of the high price of food in England. Obviously, if the law of diminishing returns was valid, and there were restrictions on the importation of corn, the price would have to be abnormally high.

Ricardo's theory of value is based on his contention that the exchange value of a commodity is determined by the amount of labor required for its production. There is a presumption here that a commodity has to be useful, before it can be considered valuable. The obvious exception however, are commodities such as diamonds, other gems, art objects, and rare items whose value is based on their desirability and the wealth and depth of desire of those who would pay for them. Since so few commodities obtain their value by desire, and so many gain their value through their usefulness, the importance of labor as value is important.

His theory of differential rent however poses another problem. Here labor does not determine price. If, he says, there is a great demand for corn, and there are two farms one of which is more fertile, the more fertile land will produce more corn with the same input of capital and labor, than the less fertile land. If the land of farm A can produce one hundred bushels of corn per acre, and in order to survive must charge one dollar a bushel, then if farm B is more fertile and yields one hundred fifty bushels an acre—farm A will set the price and farm B's landlord will be able to charge a higher rent—to the tune of fifty dollars an acre.

Because Ricardo subscribed to the labor theory of value, he smarted at the thought of landlords getting rich through this system of differential rent. Of the three elements which constitute cost—labor, capital and rent—Ricardo felt rent to be unearned.

Ricardo sees the economic world as expanding constantly and simultaneously with the population. More people means more food is needed which in turn means more fields are needed. The cost of grain will go up because the new fields that are cultivated to meet the growing demand for food will not be as productive. They are not as productive because wise farmers will have used up their good land first. As the cost of grain rises so do the selling price of grain and the rents of those landlords holding the most fertile land. Consistent with the upward trend, wages also increase because the laborer needs more money to buy enough of the more expensive grain to stay alive. This leads Ricardo to formulate his "iron law of wages."

The iron law of wages states that wages will always exist at a subsistence level, thus the laborer can never rise above that level. This gloomy forecast is based on his contention that "Profits depend on high or low wages. The natural tendency of profits then is to fall: for, in the progress of society and wealth, the additional quantity of food required is obtained by the sacrifice of more and more labor." He predicted further doom for wages with the advent of machinery.

In the area of international trade Ricardo took Adam Smith's assertion that it was advantageous for a country to produce those goods in whose production it has an absolute advantage and expanded it into a concept which stated that it would be beneficial to produce goods in which the country has a comparative advantage. The theory of absolute advantage calls for nations to produce and sell a good that it produces more efficiently than anyone else. The theory of comparative advantage states that nations have a shared ability to produce several goods more efficiently than other goods. He illustrated his theory by using Portugal and England as examples. If in England it takes the labor of 100 men to produce a certain amount of cloth and the labor of 120 men to produce a comparable amount of wine that will exchange for the cloth—then—if Portugal can produce an equivalent amount of wine with 80 men and cloth with 90 men—

these two countries should trade. England would get wine worth 120 men through the efforts of 100 men producing cloth and Portugal would get cloth worth 90 of her men through efforts of 80 men producing wine. This theory called for a philosophy of free trade which he felt would alleviate the problems caused by the corn laws and all nations could specialize in producing goods that they could produce efficiently.

Finally, Ricardo dealt with taxation. Simply stated he felt that all taxation inhibited progress. He served for a time in Parliament, and during his entire tenure he never voted for a tax increase.

Ricardo's view of man and his economic future was pessimistic. He believed that mankind was extremely greedy and competitive and therefore was doomed to live at subsistence level. He feared the landlord's increase in power would squeeze out the capitalist and continue to take advantage of the laborers. Thus, the two productive forces in society were at the mercy of the landlord, the sole beneficiary of unproductive labor. He suggests, but is not too optimistic, that men learn to restrain their natural bent towards insatiability. Free trade at home and free trade internationally holds out some hope, but the iron law of wages dominates his thinking and contributes greatly to his gloomy outlook.

CHAPTER 23

Malthus and Owen:
Gloom and Doom vs. Optimism

Thomas Malthus (1766-1834)

Thomas Malthus was born in Surrey, England in 1766. He was educated at Cambridge University with the intention of entering the ministry, which he did in 1798. For several years he served as a curate in a small parish in Surrey, but in 1805 he was appointed to teach political economy and history at the college in Haileybury. For thirty years he taught there and wrote two major works. However, his first and most important exposition of his economic philosophy, *An Essay on the Principle of Population as it Affects the Future Improvement of Society* was published in 1798. It is this work for which he is most famous.

His *Essay on Population* was written specifically as a rebuttal to the theories of William Godwin and M. Condorcet, both of whom wrote of a future devoid of the social ills that permeated the society of their day. In general, Malthus' essay flew in the face of contemporary economic theory which presented an optimistic view of the future of society. Malthus contended that life on earth could not and would not be perfected because of man's natural and instinctive urge to reproduce which would result in a continual assault upon his means of subsistence.

Malthusian theory begins with two premises. First, that food is necessary: every individual needs a sufficient amount of nourishment for survival. Second, that the human sex drive is the strongest passion. Couple these facts with what he sees as a necessary mathematical equation and he comes to a terribly pessimistic conclusion. Because of his views, Malthus more than any other person, caused economics to become known as the "dismal science."

Malthus' contention then, is that if men tend to procreate because of this very strong sexual urge, population will increase in a geometrical fashion i.e., population will grow in the following progression 1, 2, 4, 8, 16, 62, 64. But land does not multiply; so subsistence, with limited growing conditions can increase at best in an arithmetic progression i.e., 1, 2, 3, 4, 5, 6, 7. The obvious result of these forces is a world in a constant battle to maintain some minimal level of subsistence, and doomed to failure. Malthus projects what will happen or what can happen.

If men go about their merry way the population will outstrip the food supply and eventually famine will result. Many will die. This has happened often in the past and will continue in the future. Sometimes the famine is averted but only by means equally as horrible: war, disease, infant mortality. These "natural" checks on population Malthus calls positive checks. These positive checks however, limit population by inflicting misery upon mankind.

There are however, preventive checks, which man as a rational animal can employ. Animals procreate by instinct and when the environment for whatever reason cannot support them, they die in great numbers, sometimes becoming extinct. But man can use his reason and thereby limit procreation. Malthus calls for "moral restraint" on the part of individuals to limit population. He suggests a suppression of the sex urge until children can be supported, or a postponement of marriage so that the natural forces of age will limit the number of offspring. If men will employ moral restraint the situation can be moderated, but Malthus is skeptical of human nature and sees a gloomy future.

So—population can be limited by moral restraint, or by the misery of famine and disease. There is, however, a third factor which can limit population which Malthus refers to as vice. Population can be limited by the use of contraception, or by the unnatural release of passions (homosexuality, sodomy). Obviously, Reverend Malthus opposes vice as a means to limit population. His outlook for mankind in this world is bleak; if our short stay on earth is bound to be painful, how much worse it would be to compound the trouble by burning in hell forever. He leaves us with only one way out—moral restraint.

Malthus used this theory to develop his position in opposition to the Poor Laws in England. His contention was that the poor should not be given a dole from the state. His reasoning was two-fold in terms of specifics, but based on the general principle that to provide the poor with unearned money would actually increase their misery. First, Malthus claimed that to give the poor enough money on which to exist would result in increased procreation. He reasoned that the poor, without work, with nothing to do, idle, but with enough to eat, thanks to the state—would do the only thing they could to bring them some measure of pleasure. The result is an increase in the number of children in their family, thus an increase in their misery. Second, the distribution of money to the poor to see to their basic wants simply increases the amount of money which is available to purchase the limited amount of food. What in fact would happen is that the price of the food would go up in a direct proportion to the amount of money added to the supply to purchase it. Thus, the scarcity would remain essentially the same.

As a Christian minister, Malthus was not taking a cold unconcerned position on the plight of the poor. What he was doing was making a case for the argument that doling out money to the poor was not benefiting them, but in fact making their lives more miserable, and more miserable in greater numbers. He felt his philosophy would not end the suffering of the poor, but simply minimize it by limiting the number of people who would have to bear the suffering.

Malthus suggested a method for gradually abolishing the poor laws and alleviating the suffering of the poor. His proposal was for the government to get out of the business of trying to legislate help for the poor. He suggested that the government end the poor laws by setting a future date, after which, any child who was born would be ineligible for assistance. In conjunction with this governmental lack of involvement, Malthus foresaw a greater involvement of the clergy, who would be given the task to teach the value of moral restraint. Given fair warning, people would know that if they had children they could not afford to feed, they would pay a terrible price for their lack of judgment.

Malthus contends that after his plan is implemented there will be nothing left for the government to legislate in this regard—"nature will govern and punish for us." Those who choose to marry and consequently have children will live well or poorly based on their ability to support those children they bring into the world. To marry in poverty is obviously immoral and if children are born into this condition the punishment is want. Natural consequences will teach the lessons of moral restraint with untempered justice. The rise and fall of population in relation to food supply will always require checks, whether positive or preventative. But by leaving the population the alternative of choosing moral restraint or the suffering that will result—nature rules not man made laws. He maintains that if we let nature follow its course, and men do what is morally correct, all will be well (for Malthus, as well as can be expected). If men choose not to be moral, the natural and logical consequences will restrain men where they have not the will to do so.

It is interesting that Thomas Malthus, with this concept of laissez-faire economics, concludes darkly that the future is bleak. Adam Smith some years earlier, concluded that with this concept of laissez-faire economics the future is bright. Historical examples such as India and parts of Africa tend to validate the Malthusian theory. Historical examples of western Europe and the United States tend to validate Smith's theory. Does the answer lie in the value of industry, technology and production? Or despite the obvious benefits we have reaped in the progress of our ability to meet the needs of greatly increased numbers of people ... is the clock ticking down?

Robert Owen (1771-1858)

Robert Owen was born in Newton, Wales, in 1771. He was the sixth of seven children. His father was an ironmonger, and his early youth was spent in the relative isolation of a small market town. He was however, a precocious child, who at the age of seven had learned the body of knowledge required of students at his local school. So, for over a year he held the post of assistant school master, a position he retired from at the ripe old age of nine. He left home when he was ten years old to take a job in Stamford, England as a draper.

His career in the textile industry flourished. He progressed rapidly in the drapery business in London, left for Manchester at age fourteen, and worked in the mills there. Manchester was the center of the English Industrial Revolution and he was exposed to the workings of the cotton mills, and the factory system. By the time he was twenty, he was a master cotton spinner and was managing a large spinning mill. His work experience was not only successful in terms of advancement and monetary return, but it provided him with first hand observations of the factory system which triggered ideas which he developed into theories about the nature of man. By the time he was twenty nine he had amassed a large fortune, was a partner in the spinning mill he managed and was ready to embark on his most important venture.

During Owen's lifetime he was witness to the impact of the Industrial Revolution and the impact of that revolution on English society. The invention of the steam engine and the use of that engine for driving machines to spin cloth, coupled with the invention of the power loom launched the textile industry. People left the farms to come to work in the city's factories and brought with them the problems of overcrowding, disease, and the problems which accompany social disorientation. The social consequences of greater class mobility due to economic opportunity brought about by technology also became apparent. The conflicts between classes which did not exist a generation ago also became a problem which was manifested by the struggles between laborers and employers. The growing demand for factories, production and labor brought about by the war with France compounded the problems. Owen's observations and experiences in this fast paced environment led him to certain postulates which he developed, not simply into theories, but into a plan for action.

Owen's first principle is that a person's character is made for him and not by him. Second, that any community, small or large, can be made good or bad, based upon the way the government controls the environment. These two principles as presented by Robert Owen say much about his concept of the nature of man. Man is basically good, and can be perfected. Environment is the determining factor in the development of man's character. Properly controlled, the environment can not only make people good, but also entire communities good. Society is a social contract, and the rules for governing can be used to accomplish this Utopian goal.

Education is the key. Owen's view of education is an interesting combination of the ideas of Plato and Rousseau. Children should be removed from the family unit at an early age and educated in nurseries. A system of rewards should be instituted within a happy, loving framework to encourage children to succeed. While academic achievement is important it is far from the most important part of a child's development—moral education and character building are the primary goals of his system. Students in his school would not learn to read and write until they were nine or ten, but by that time they would be good citizens. Owen's school was meant to be a happy place, where children sang and danced and enjoyed themselves—a place where they wanted to be and where they would learn to be good.

Owen believed that through education based upon behavioral conditioning, a society free from misery, vice, crime and poverty was possible and he set out to prove his contention. Utopia was not simply possible; it was forthcoming.

When Robert Owen purchased the mills in New Lanark, he and his partners were primarily interested in an economic undertaking. But Owen had some big plans for this small factory town. He incorporated many of his ideas about education and factory reform into action in the New Lanark experiment and the results were dramatically successful. Within five years Owen had transformed a typical mill town into a showplace of clean, happy, productive people. The workers lived in small neat houses, which lined clean, well kept streets. The workers labored in clean, well-ventilated factories, under managers who had an "open door" policy encouraging suggestions or grievances. The children played and learned at school where teachers were kind and encouraging, where punishment was never administered and where any question was considered worthy and was answered immediately.

Within the factory he made many changes. He improved the organization of the mills to prevent dishonesty and theft and established a system of "silent monitors" to increase worker productivity. The silent monitor was a cube of wood which hung over the worker's station. Each side was painted a different color: white, yellow, blue, or black. An excellent day's work was rewarded with a white side showing, a good day produced a yellow side, a lesser day, the blue and for a bad day's work, the black was displayed. The improved working conditions, along with this system which encouraged pride in performance, produced not only happy workers, but huge profits. The Japanese factory system today employs a similar system to prod employees to produce more and better products.

The success of New Lanark encouraged Owen to plan for more Utopian communities. He was certain that with the proper guidelines and with adequate controls a series of ideal communities could be implanted throughout England. He petitioned Parliament with his plans for Villages of Cooperation, independent, self-sufficient planned communities to be built according to his Utopian ideal. Reaction to this Utopian scheme was negative. Owen the reformer was respected and admired. Owen the Utopian, worried people with his rigid plans, unbending rules, and hostility to religion and the family. Many considered the cost to human freedom too great to justify the implementation of his plans.

Owen however, was determined to implement his plans for his Utopian experiment. He sold the mills at New Lanark and set about organizing his ideal community in America. He bought thirty thousand acres of land in Indiana in 1825 and named the new community New Harmony. Within three years the community was determined to be an unequivocal failure. The community at New Harmony attracted a group of misfits and freeloaders who saw the experiment as an opportunity to get something for nothing. He lost most of his money, but none of his enthusiasm for reform. He returned to England where he continued to rail against injustice and work for economic reform.

He put his foreign experiment behind him, and once back in England he attempted to establish Villages of Cooperation, producers' cooperatives, consumer cooperatives, and exchange cooperatives where money was not allowed. Generally all of his attempts failed with the exception of consumer cooperatives, which had a modest success. His dreams of Utopian communities continued to be thwarted so he moved, with equal passion, from one reform movement to another. His final attempt on a grand scale was with the Grand National Moral Union of the Productive and Useful Classes.

The Grand National was a trade union, brought about in large measure by Owen's enthusiastic efforts, which sought to unite all the unions of England under one umbrella. The Grand National was not simply a union seeking higher wages and better working conditions, but a movement based in the laboring classes with an eye to radical social change. The program of the Grand National was a program of radical reform that went far beyond the traditional goals of labor unions. England was not ready for Owen's new assault on the social fabric of the nation and the union failed.

The rest of Owen's life was spent in continued writing and pleading the case for his Utopian ideas. He was not really an economist, nor was he a political philosopher. He was a moral philosopher only to the extent that he sought reforms to improve the human condition. He was rather, a zealot, who thought that the nature of man was such, that through the application of his ideas, men could work cooperatively, and would reshape the world. His life was filled with monumental failures and some significant successes.

His failures seemed to revolve around three ideas. First, the view of the perfection of man requires the rejection of God and most people accept God and reject the idea of the perfection of man. Second, his insistence on the abolition of the family as the first step towards the education of men to perfection engendered hostility towards his entire program. Also, most people rejected the idea that school teachers would be better prepared to mold their young children's character than parents were. Finally, Owen's continual attempt to abolish money antagonized some and frightened many. Most people accept money as a medium of exchange, a measure and a store of value and understand the economic significance of money as such. The misuse and abuse of money, by people, is consistent with many problems faced in the world. But to confuse the existence of money with the abuses that some perpetrate with it is another matter.

How is it then, with so much working against him, that he got so many things right? He was directly responsible for the laws which protected children in the labor force. Restriction on the number of hours children could work and the conditions of their work were two of his most important contributions. Working conditions for all workers were improved by virtue of his efforts. Consumer cooperatives are still a viable means by which people can use leverage in their buying. Laws affecting the education of young children, and methods used by their teachers are two more of his contributions. And finally, an awareness of the importance of the environmental factors which contribute to the formation of personality and character is part of Owen's legacy.

Robert Owen's failures and successes seem to be, in a very real way, very personal successes and failures. His rigid, narrow, dogmatic excesses were responsible, in part, for his failures. His enthusiasm, energy, and commitment to his causes were, in part, responsible for his successes.

CHAPTER 24

Veblen and George:
The Theory of the Leisure Class and
the Single Tax

Thorsten Veblen (1857-1929)

Thorsten Veblen was born in 1857 in Cato, a small town on the Wisconsin frontier. He moved with his family to Minnesota where he spent his youth, the sixth of twelve children. He lived in a very tight-knit Norwegian community and actually learned English as a second language; he spoke it imperfectly until he had completed college.

He attended Carleton College, applied for a scholarship at Johns Hopkins, which failed to materialize, and finally received his Ph.D. in 1884 from Yale. After his graduation from Yale he returned to his father's farm, where he spent several years reading or doing nothing at all. Throughout his educational career he earned the respect of his professors for his intellect and their disdain for his iconoclastic behavior. In fact his entire life was plagued by scandal, alienation, conflict, and outrageous behavior. He taught at Cornell and the University of Chicago, the University of Missouri, Stanford, and the New School in New York. His longest tenure was at the University of Chicago, where he wrote his most famous book, *The Theory of the Leisure Class*. He was dismissed from the University of Chicago because of his utter disregard for his students in the classroom, and his high regard for his female students outside the classroom.

Veblen considers the nature of man to be only slightly different from the savage barbarians who lived centuries ago. In primitive cultures the pillaging warriors, through strength, force and violence, seized the property of their enemies. Rituals and trophies became the means to identify those who had proved their strength in battle. They took the scalps of their enemies, their shields, their swords, their women. Their worth as individuals was counted in terms of their trophies, which were tributes to their predatory nature. Their standing in the community was elevated, not according to their contribution to the production necessary to maintain the group, but rather by their ability, through conquest, to stand apart from the group. Thus, conquest, not contribution, was the honored activity.

This predatory man, Veblen asserts, has not changed his nature, just his method. As time went on the struggle for existence became a competition for monetary strength. Money became the new trophy, and the predatory man became the pecuniary man, but his nature remained the same. Pecuniary man's successful aggression takes place in business, not on the battlefield. Thus the seizure of wealth is the role of the contemporary warrior, and money is the trophy. In contemporary society the predator, like his barbarian ancestor stands apart from the rest of society, and his conquest, not contribution, is also the honored activity.

In the present economic system, the industrial class produces the goods necessary to the survival of the group. Members of the group, like the primitive men of the past, are not looked up to for their contribution, but are considered drones involved in drudgery, and are looked down upon. The predators set up a non-industrial class, which is involved in the aggressive seizure of goods without any participation in the production of those goods. This non industrial class is called the "leisure class" because it does not perform useful work. Society has come to admire the leisure class as they had admired the powerful warriors in primitive society. In the eyes of society, those of the leisure class are the powerful members, and the common people seek to ape their betters.

The next development in Veblen's theory is that of "pecuniary emulation." Emulation is man's most powerful economic motive, with the exception of survival or self-preservation. Since contemporary industrial society uses money as its most important trophy, the common man seeks to emulate the leisure class by accumulating wealth. The lower classes seek to attain wealth, not as a matter of survival, but simply to emulate the leisure class. In this matter Veblen differs strongly with Marx, who thought the workers wanted to overthrow their employers. "The workers do not seek to to displace their managers; they seek to emulate them," says Veblen.

Although wealth is an important factor in pecuniary emulation, there are other characteristics of the leisure class that are examined and mimicked. The leisure class establishes certain norms and mores in addition to a certain standard of wealth that is considered minimal. Particular types of dress display wealth and indicate that the wearer is not engaged in physical labor. Certain sports, foods, drinks, and other activities are used by the leisure class and become the standard that the common man seeks to emulate.

Two of Veblen's most interesting concepts are the theories of conspicuous leisure and conspicuous consumption. The leisure class, Veblen asserts, is not satisfied in having attained a status which affords them leisure time; they can enjoy it only if it is conspicuously flaunted or demonstrated to the lower classes. Nor is the mere acquisition of wealth enough; it must be spent in such a way as to demonstrate the user's total unconcern for value and function.

The concept of conspicuous leisure, according to Veblen, requires an understanding of his definition of "leisure." Leisure is not time spent in relaxation or rest, rather it is the "nonproductive consumption of time." As Veblen states, "Time is consumed non-productively (1) from a sense of the unworthiness of productive work, and (2) as an evidence of pecuniary ability to afford a life of idleness." This requires that leisure time be spent in socially useless activities. Also, time taken for ceremonial reasons adds to the satisfaction of the members of the leisure class—the grand display of time to waste.

In addition to the many types of leisure activities that the wealthy develop to demonstrate their power, there is the system of vicarious leisure. Formerly the use of slaves, now the use of servants and women, is important in order to exhibit the extent of leisure the wealthy have. The sole aim of a servant is to wait upon the needs of the master. Because they are not performing an industrially useful function, these servants are technically at "leisure." The maintenance of servants who produce nothing, but serve another's whims, reflects back upon the master who receives the reward for the waste of their labor. This is called conspicuous waste; conspicuous waste and conspicuous consumption are condoned by society because it demonstrates the success of those who excel at those predatory activities which are a part of our nature.

Veblen sees the upper classes as exempt from industrial labor, but maintains that there are certain activities that are acceptable in place of productive work. Warfare, religious service, sports, and government employment are occupations in which the leisure class can engage without losing their standing in the community. These are the activities that "most reveal the traits of predatory man: political deceit and manipulation, military and athletic exploit and domination, and extravagant religious ornamentation and superstition." These, Veblen claims, are the modern occupations that conform to the role that the predatory man once played as a warrior, witch doctor, hunter, or tribal strong man.

Finally, conspicuous leisure is demonstrated by the development of a system of manners, tastes, and decorum. To the extent that a group can develop a sense of refinement and taste, and can create a set of rules for behavior—to that extent they can demonstrate that they are free from the constraints of practical life. Good table manners are not only impractical, they are totally undesirable for those men eating lunch deep in the shaft of a coal mine. Tea parties and the amenities that accompany them are demonstrations of conspicuous leisure by the upper class.

Conspicuous consumption is similar to conspicuous leisure—they both are based on waste. However, the difference is significant. Conspicuous leisure is the abstention from productive work, while conspicuous consumption is the consumption of what others have produced. Simple consumption is not enough. The social value of consumption is in the level of its conspicuous nature. The less practical the value, the greater the evidence of the owner's status. The gowns displayed at Academy Award presentations, each unique, rendering the owners incapable of facilitating productive labor, made of expensive material, and made for one night's use, are perfect examples of conspicuous consumption. Three-and four-hundred horsepower automobiles in a nation with a fifty-five mile per hour speed limit are also good examples of conspicuous consumption.

In his book *The Theory of Business Enterprise,* Veblen put forth another shocking yet interesting idea. Most people view the capitalist as the driving force in the process of industrialization. Veblen not only disagreed but also introduced a revolutionary theory into the discussion. Veblen considered the scientist, the inventor, the technician to be the driving force in industry. After all, the product must be invented before someone can invest in its production. Also, Veblen saw two totally different mentalities at work, each at odds with the other—those who make the goods and those who make the money.

The technician and scientist are interested in the product. Their very mentality is geared towards creating, producing, improving, and perfecting products. They begin the system of industrialization, and work within it. Each improvement, advancement, and refinement of a product is a source of personal satisfaction to them. Like a parent bringing up a child, they create, nurse, nurture, and bring to maturity, their brainchild. And Veblen sees them as the backbone of industry.

The capitalist, the businessman, or the investor comes from a different perspective. He is interested in making money, driving competitors out of business, selling ideas not products. The businessman is not the driving force of industrialization—he is the saboteur. His first concern is profit. His interests are salesmanship, marketing strategies, advertising gimmicks—whatever devices which can sell. Often the desire to sell, to increase income and profit, and to drive competitors out of business, comes into conflict with the integrity of the product. Veblen is certain that the businessman, consumed with self, threatens the product. His choices are made by considerations which are antithetical to producing the best product at the lowest cost. He seeks to sell the most products at whatever price he can get.

Veblen calls for a revolt of the technicians. He sees the technicians, engineers, machinists and industrial workers as the only hope for the future. The capitalist system is built on a structure that grew out of primitive, predatory man's *modus operandi*. It continues today in a sophisticated, industrial society to which it is ill suited. Only a scientific approach "can penetrate the origins and nature of the social compulsion of behavior and thereby lay bare the irrationality of an economic system driven by non-economic motives." Once the capitalist system has given way to a system owned and operated by the producers, the resulting improvement of product with the lowering of price will provide a higher standard of living for all.

Henry George (1839-1897)

Henry George was born in Philadelphia on September 2, 1839. His formal education ended at age fourteen but he ran away to sea and his travels stimulated his thinking about economic matters. The essential question which dominated his thinking, and later his economic theory was the question, "How can there be so much poverty among so much wealth?"

Following his experiences at sea, he settled in San Francisco and worked as a printer and free-lance writer. He also worked for several different California newspapers. While working for the Sacramento *Reporter* he led a vigorous attack on the land grant policy which gave the railroads a land monopoly. In 1871 he wrote a pamphlet, *Our Land and Land Policy,* in which he detailed his views about the railroad land monopoly and the resulting boom in California. He concluded that holding of land by the very rich few, extracting rent from the very poor many, was the basic cause for the great and unnecessary disparity of wealth.

His major work, *Progress and Poverty,* published in 1879, set forth his observations of the problem and his proposals to solve it. Simply stated, George contended that those who own the land, and can afford to hold it, extract unearned income in the form of rent, and unearned profits that accrue when they sell the land at an inflated price. His solution was a "single tax" on the value of land.

Progress and Poverty begins with George disputing two theories which he felt were not true, although they were in vogue at the time. The idea that employment was contingent upon existing capital, George claims, is false. Rather, it is the demand for consumption, or the needs of the people that really employs labor. Therefore, the claim that capital employs labor is really the reverse of the reality. Also, Malthus claimed that poverty was the result of overpopulation. Once again, George claims foul. It is observable that famine and underfed people exist in underpopulated as well as overpopulated areas. If this is so, then there must be reasons other than those advanced by Malthus which cause the problem.

Next, George analyzed the problem of distribution. The three factors of production—land, labor, and capital, are related to the three elements of distribution—rent, wages, and interest. Land and labor combine to produce wealth. Capital, the product of the wealth created by land and labor is returned to production. Taking Ricardo's concept of the "law of rent," George concludes that rent swallows up the gains of land, labor, and capital. Thus, we have the victory of unearned income (rent) over earned income (wages and interest). George winces at the thought that an individual on a large piece of land, working it as hard as he can, struggles to survive, while the lucky fellow who owns a small piece of land in the center of a large city grows rich on rent.

George sees the problem of speculation not only as the culprit but also as a preventable activity. Those who buy land and hold it out of production, by so doing bid up the price of that land. For example, if speculators purchase land near an expanding area, those who need the land will pay a premium to obtain it. Thus, nearby land increases in value as well. The idea that land purposely undeveloped, unused, and unproductive grows in value by leaps and bounds is at the heart of George's complaint.

The solution, however, is at hand, says George. Since monopoly in general, and land monopoly in particular, is at fault—end it. The power that is in the hands of the landowner is immense. The wealth that is generated by speculation and rent at the expense of the worker and capitalist will continue to prevent increased wages and industrial progress, but it will create an immoral and ever more powerful elite. If, however, land were held in common, such a condition could not exist.

Should, then, the government confiscate the land and institute a socialist form of government? Not quite, says George. Socialism, while admired as a concept by George, cannot be imposed on a society. He sees society as an organism, not a machine that can be built and adjusted according to someone's plan. Rather, the desired end can be achieved not by confiscating land, but by confiscating rent. The confiscation of rent can be achieved by a single tax on land. The end result of this process would undoubtedly lead to a situation wherein most of the land would end up in the hands of the government—but that land would only be the unused land. Productive land would remain in the hands of individuals, producing goods, wages, wealth, and capital.

If there were but one tax, and that tax were on the value of the land—not the buildings or the produce—no land would be held for speculation. The only land that could sustain the tax would be that land which was producing a good which produced earned income. George maintained that the low tax on unused land encourages speculation. Increase the tax on land to make it utterly unprofitable to keep land out of use, and George's goal will be achieved. Also, since the tax on the land would be so great, not only would unused land be forced into common ownership, used land would be used to the fullest.

Take, for example, a building on a piece of land in America today. The tax is placed primarily on the building, not the land. Thus, it is profitable for the owner to keep the building in disrepair, or to forego improvements on the building since to improve it would increase the taxes on that building. George's claim is that if the tax were being paid only on the land, competition would lead the owners to provide the best building possible, since a building of superior quality will not increase the taxes. Those who could not compete, work, produce, and use the land would have to abandon it. Thus, each man would have equal access to the land and the produce of his labor would be the determining factor as to whether or not he would keep it. In fact, the concept of owning land would give way to the concept of using land.

Henry George saw, in his philosophy, not simply a means to get the most out of the land, nor simply a means to end land speculation. With the end of land speculation would come just wages in relation to production, the end of periods of boom and bust, equal entry for all in the use of land, and the end of poverty.

During his lifetime Henry George was a colorful, diverse, interesting, and controversial proponent of an economic idea that has yet to be realized. Perhaps the single tax, with all of the intriguing predictions of its effect, is not possible. Probably the implementation of such a system could not be achieved. But the contribution of Henry George in pointing out the problem of land speculation and the problems that result from land monopoly, is a valuable one. Also, an understanding of his view of property taxation could be the basis for some creative ideas about how to deal with slums and deteriorating neighborhoods.

CHAPTER 25

Keynes and Friedman: Pump Priming and Individual Choice

John Maynard Keynes (1883-1946)

John Maynard Keynes was born in Cambridge, England in 1883. His father was an economist and logician and the first teacher of his son, who later attended Eaton College and Cambridge University. He worked for the British government's India Office and during World War I worked for the treasury department. He was part of the delegation which represented England at the Paris Peace Conference of 1919, but resigned because he opposed the terms of the Treaty of Versailles. He wrote *The Economic Consequences of Peace,* in which he predicted that the massive reparations that were demanded of Germany would result in economic nationalism and a return to militarism. He taught at Cambridge University, made a fortune dealing in international currencies, and generally succeeded in virtually every activity he undertook. He was a member of the Bloomsbury Group, an English intellectual elite, which exerted great influence in artistic circles.

During World War II he he wrote *How to Pay for the War,* in which he suggested that workers should have a part of their salaries deducted automatically and invested in government bonds. In 1936 he wrote *The General Theory of Employment, Interest, and Money,* which dealt with the problem of prolonged depression. *The General Theory* is considered to be one of the most important theoretical works of the twentieth century. In 1942 he was made a baron, and later headed the British delegation to the United Nations. He had a lifelong interest in the arts and helped form the London Artists Association. This interest carried over into his personal life and he married a famous Russian ballerina, Lydia Lopokova. The influence of his ideas on Franklin Roosevelt during the Great Depression was considerable. Keynes died of a heart attack in 1946 and was honored in services at Westminster Abbey.

John Maynard Keynes wrote his great epic, espousing "economic interventionism," at a time when American and most of the free world was experiencing a prolonged depression. In it he questioned some of the past assumptions of those he called "classical" economists, who claimed that capitalism had a natural mechanism which would maintain conditions of full employment and production. This assumption, which Keynes attacked, was based on Say's Law, which states that "supply creates its own demand." The classical economists believed that if businessmen increased production or supply, there would naturally be an accompanying rise in wages paid. The recipients of these wages would spend, and the spending would result in an increase of consumption or demand. Thus, the economy would always be balanced at the maximum level of supply and demand, which is the maximum level of production and employment.

Say's law is founded on three basic assumptions. First, a worker's wage equals the value of the product of his labor. If this is were not so, then an increase in supply would not produce an equal increase in demand. The second assumption is that wages and prices are flexible. Thus, as prices rise so do wages, and vice versa. This must be true, or else supply and demand would not be in equilibrium at the full employment level. Finally, if a person is unemployed it is either temporary or by his own choice. Since, if supply is at a maximum (as Say's Law presupposes), then all willing workers must be employed.

Keynes disputes these contentions by way of a practical illustration. What if prices were to rise and wages were to remain constant? The classical economist claims that workers would cut production or demand higher wages so that their wages would equal the value of the products of their labor. Keynes maintains that, in reality, the workers continue to work at the same wages. The employer, reaping higher profits, expands production by hiring more workers at the same wage. Thus, wages do not equal the value of the product of the labor—wages are not flexible— they do not rise with prices. Furthermore, unemployment must not be temporary or voluntary, since additional workers are easily obtained. Keynes then proceeds to explain the nature of involuntary unemployment, that which classical economists claim cannot exist.

To disprove Say's Law, Keynes points out that when wages are low in relation to prices, employers expand production by hiring new workers. Though this would seem to solve the problem Keynes is trying to emphasize, in reality actual employment is not increased. When all businessmen attempt to expand production, then all wages are generally low. This means, that although overall production may increase, the workers' overall propensity to consume will drop. Therefore, demand will decrease, and employers will not benefit from the expansion of production. New workers will not be hired, and employment will not increase. This concept of the public's overall propensity to consume Keynes calls "aggregate demand."

According to Keynes aggregate demand is determined by three main factors: government, consumption, and investment. He postulated that the government's net effect on aggregate demand was essentially neutral, since whatever the government takes from the economy by taxation, it returns by way of its expenditures. As for consumption, Keynes maintained that while men tend to consume more as their income rises, the increase in consumption is somewhat less than the increase in income. Since the government effect is neutral, the law of consumption deals with aggregate consumption alone and therefore does not explain the level of aggregate demand, so we are left with investment as the primary determinant of aggregate demand.

Investment, says Keynes, determines the flow of money in the economy. When investment is high, then the accumulated savings of the economy are borrowed and kept in circulation. This causes employment to increase, and subsequently, total national income to rise. As national income increases so does the volume of consumer spending. Thus, aggregate demand is high, and production and supply must be high to meet this demand, and the economy prospers. Conversely, when investment is low, the accumulated savings remain out of circulation. National income and employment drop along with aggregate demand. Production decreases and the economy becomes depressed.

Since investment dictates the state of the economy, it is important to note the factors which govern it. Keynes considers investment to be the risk taken by businessmen in the expansion of their production. The two primary considerations for investing are 1) the profit margin which business men expect from their investment (marginal efficiency of capital), and 2) the rate of interest, the amount of money businessmen will have to pay for the privilege of borrowing the original capital. Thus, only if marginal efficiency of capital exceeds the rate of interest will the investment be undertaken. Since the marginal efficiency of capital is not easily manipulated, Keynes focuses his attention on the more flexible factor, the interest rate.

According to classical economics, the interest rate determines the general supply of savings in the economy. Those who save feel that the interest rate is a sufficient reward for the postponement of consumption. Thus the rate of interest would adjust itself until it reached the point where the amounts of money saved and the amounts of money borrowed would be the same. Therefore, the rate of interest acts as a balancing force between consumption and investment.

Keynes, however, maintains that the interest rate is not related to savings or investment, but rather is the result of speculation. If speculators feel that stock prices are going to go up, causing interest rates to drop, they will invest large sums. The net effect of speculation tends to result in self-fulfilling prophecies; thus, interest rates are tied more to fluctuations in the stock market than to savings.

This observation was used by Keynes to explain how, during the Great Depression in America, when investment dwindled, there was not a significant lowering of interest rates due to the great supply of savings. Once the depression began, Keynes claims, people needed their savings and consumed them quickly. With no great supply of savings, interest rates never dropped, and the equilibrium between consumption and investment was not restored. Keynes saw that the economy was in balance but not at the previous high investment level. How then can a depressed economy be stimulated?

Keynes saw government involvement as the answer to the problem. The government alone was capable of both increasing the marginal efficiency of capital and lowering the interest rate. By providing men with work, even essentially non productive work, the government could put money into the hands of consumers, thus stimulating spending. This is called "pump priming." With aggregate demand increased by pump priming, it became more profitable for businessmen to invest. Also, the government could increase the money supply, thus bidding stock prices up, and thereby lowering interest rates.

While he was convinced that his proposals would help right an economy gone awry, he recognized that there could be some difficulties. First, by mismanagement, the government's demand for funds could drive the interest rate up and thereby lessen investment. Second, psychologically, government spending could damage investor confidence, resulting in a "let the government do it" syndrome. Also, government bureaucracies are notorious for their reluctance to withdraw once involved in an operation. (*See* Parkinson, chapter 26) Finally, in an economy where foreign trade plays a large role, some of the funds generated by government spending might flow right out of the country.

Keynes did not seek to replace free-enterprise capitalism with government control, but did want to repair what he saw as a technical flaw in the overall mechanism. He did not want permanent government interference, but wanted government to jump in and out in times of serious economic difficulties, to stimulate investment whenever the private sector hesitated. He probably would agree that, in the long run, a depressed economy would eventually right itself when investors regained confidence. Yet, he saw the Great Depression as a unique event, which caused so much unemployment and social misery that it was not worth waiting for those "natural forces" to take hold.

Milton Friedman (1912-)

Milton Friedman was born in Brooklyn, New York in 1912 of Jewish immigrant parents. He grew up in Rahway, New Jersey and was educated at Rutgers University. He graduated in 1932 and subsequently received a fellowship to the University of Chicago, where he studied under some of the foremost American economists. He was granted a Ph.D. from Columbia University in 1946 and began to teach at the University of Wisconsin. Later, he moved to the University of Chicago and has been associated with the economics department there for the past several decades. It is no accident that his major work is called *Capitalism and Freedom,* or that his book *Free to Choose,* which was also made into a television series, has in its title the word *freedom*. At the basis of Milton Friedman's economic philosophy is his faith in the free-market system. To him, when government power in economic matters is limited, individual opportunity is enhanced. He actually used Adam Smith's term in an interview when he claimed that "...the invisible hand of the free market, whereby men who tend to serve only their own interests serve the public interest, is a far more sensitive and effective source of both growth and freedom than the dead hand of the bureaucrat, however well intentioned he may be."

Friedman also contends that the relationship between economic and political freedom—they are integrally bound to one another. Economic freedom has a dual role in a free society. First, it is a desirable end in itself, and second, it is necessary to the maintenance of political freedom. The idea that an individual should be free to control his own economic activity is a self-evident truth, according to Friedman. For example, the idea that most Americans must contribute by law to a Social Security system, which deprives them of a percentage of their income that they might very well choose to invest elsewhere, is a limitation of personal freedom.

A free economic system is necessary to maintain political freedom, since it ensures a dispersion of powers that is the basis for political freedom. When economic power is separate from political power, the government is unable to coerce individuals through their pocketbooks. The threat of the loss of their jobs, or of a reduction of income, or other governmental pressures on individuals who are economically as well as politically tied together, can result in enormous governmental power and is a threat to a free society. During the 1950s several screenwriters were black-listed by the studio heads for alleged communist leanings. Most of them simply continued writing under assumed names and continued to make a living. The desire of the producers and directors to make good movies, and good profits, led them to hire these writers despite their political views. If the studios had been under government control, political considerations would have insured that these men, despite their talent, would not have been able to earn a living.

While Friedman is opposed to government control, he acknowledges a role for government. That role is to support the free market. The government's role is to enforce the laws which support a free market and to mediate differences between individuals, thus preventing the coercion of one individual by another. The government must enforce contracts, define and enforce property rights, and provide a monetary framework. Also, the government must prevent monopoly and regulate the problems brought about by "neighborhood effects." (An example of a neighborhood effect is when a person's pond is contaminated by an upstream polluter). Such activities as price supports, tariffs, rent control, minimum wage laws, price controls, import quotas, or any other interference in the free exchange of goods and services should be outside the role of government. He also opposes regulation of industry and railroads, licensure laws, subsidized housing and Social Security.

One of Friedman's major interests is in the area of money. He contends that the government's regulation of the money supply has been at the root of many economic problems. He blames government mismanagement for the Great Depression and sees the actions of the Federal Reserve Board, which incorrectly manipulated the supply of money and interest rates, as responsible for exacerbating the banking crises and the depression in general. When the Federal Reserve Board condoned a decrease in the supply of money and moved to make it more difficult for banks and for business to obtain it, the opposite action should have been employed. He concludes that rather than giving discretionary power to a few men in the Federal Reserve Board to regulate money in response to day-to-day changes in the supply, there should be a fixed rate of growth in the supply, with an eye to the long-range goal of stable growth.

As with his classical forerunners, Friedman calls for freedom in the area of international trade and finance. His view is that international trade and monetary exchange should be opened to the mechanism of the free market. Tariffs and fixed monetary exchange rates should be abolished. Without trade barriers and with a floating exchange rate, Friedman contends that there would be a rise in the standard of living for all countries, and that the people of all nations would have more and better goods available at lower prices.

Friedman attacks the theory, developed by John Maynard Keynes, of "secular stagnation." Following the Great Depression, Keynes and his followers held that the limitless opportunities for investment that had previously existed in countries like the United States were evaporating. Thus, the government should actively stimulate investment whenever it seemed necessary. Friedman maintains that to properly gauge the time and the need for such governmental intervention is so difficult that such intervention most often leads to inflation, or minimally makes matters worse. Once again, the private sector is most effective in determining when to invest, especially since, as Friedman claims, the opportunities for investment are as numerous as ever.

Among the many ideas that Friedman advances to achieve the goals of economic and political freedom, diversity, and growth are the voucher system, right-to-work laws, occupational licensure, and the negative income tax.

When the great mass of immigration took place, the public school was the great institution which contributed to the success of the melting pot, bringing unity to many diverse cultures. Today, however, with a huge public-school system monopolizing education, Friedman sees the need for diversity. He proposes that each parent with a school-age child be given a voucher, which would represent a portion of the taxes paid for public education. The parent would be able to cash the voucher in at any school of his choice, public, private, or parochial. The competition among schools to offer a better product would be stimulated, and the freedom to choose would be expanded. The roll of the government would be simply to determine minimal educational standards that each school would have to maintain, and the free market would do the rest. Friedman cites the excellence of private colleges over most public universities as evidence of his theory.

In the area of labor, Friedman seeks to expand the freedom of the worker to choose whether or not he should belong to a union. He claims that unions, exempt from antitrust laws, have become monopolies of the worst sort. Thus, laws restricting both "closed shops" (where one must be a member of the union to get a job) and "yellow dog" contracts (where in order to work one can not be a member of a union) are laws favored by Friedman. The objective is to maximize the freedom that employers and employees have in their relationship with one another.

Laws restricting the pursuit of certain occupations are supposedly enacted to protect the public. Friedman contends that in reality they are enacted to serve the interests of the members of the occupational group seeking to preserve their own economic well-being. Systems enacted to limit the number of doctors increase the income of those already licensed. The American Medical Association and the American Bar Association are the two biggest and most powerful "unions" in America, Friedman asserts. Their power over who shall be licensed, who may practice, who may be drummed out of the business, which colleges and universities shall be allowed to train such practitioners, contributes to creating an all-powerful monopoly—to protect, not the public, but the doctors' and the lawyers' economic status.

Friedman categorizes occupational licensure laws into three types: registration, certification, and licensure. Registration can be justified as a control device as a part of the state's police powers. Registration of pharmacists to keep accounts of drugs, or gun dealers to keep records of firearms sales, are examples of this type of regulation. Certification is less easy to justify, since the process is and can be done within the private marketplace. The Good Housekeeping Seal, *Consumer Report* magazine, and other independent rating agencies are examples of this process. There is, however, no justification for licensure. The exclusive club created by lawyers, of lawyers, for lawyers, assumes that people cannot choose; someone must choose for them. And then the lawyers decide that it is they who will choose. Certification would do the job just as well: a person achieves certain minimal competency in an occupation and then offers his services to the public—the market will do the rest.

The ethics of distribution in the free market rests on the premise, "to each according to what he and the instruments he owns produces." Of course, monetary rewards are not the only standard; some choose to work longer, harder, outdoors, for money; others choose to work at jobs which provide free time, travel, or other rewards. To attempt to redistribute wealth by a graduated, progressive tax on income without taking into account factors other than those which relate just to monetary value, is not only wrong, it doesn't work. People who feel unjustly taxed seek to create loopholes to avoid taxation. In particular, those who have the wealth tend not to pay nearly so much tax as those who are trying to become wealthy. Taxation becomes more a process of tax avoidance than paying one's fair share. To attempt to take from some to redistribute for others is to violate essential morality.

Despite his opposition to most government welfare programs, Friedman does support some governmental efforts to help the poor. First, programs to alleviate poverty should be directed towards the poor, not specific groups. Second, the program should not distort the operation of the free market, as do price supports, minimum wage laws, and the like. His solution is the negative income tax, which would provide cash to a person according to a system which would encourage work. For example, if a person were not working, he would receive a minimum payment; if he earned a portion of that minimum, he would continue to get a percentage of the minimum, not a full percentage but enough to encourage even more work. If the base figure were $600, a non worker would get $300, a person earning $300 would get $150, while a person earning $400 would get $100, and so on until the minimum was met, at which point, at $100 above the $600 amount the individual would begin to pay taxes. Thus, the incentive to work is incorporated into the payment, since it is never more profitable not to work than it is to work. Also, the government-provided funds come with no strings, the recipient determines how the money is to be spent, and the market is not distorted.

Milton Friedman is a modern-day Adam Smith, who has analyzed economics, and incorporated into his theory the complexities of modern society, while maintaining the moral premise of individual freedom. His contributions in the area of monetary policy, the negative income tax, and the voucher system are being vigorously debated at this moment. His views on unions, the graduated progressive income tax, right-to-work laws, and the relationship of economic and political freedom have become accepted theory in many circles.

CHAPTER 26

Parkinson, Webbs, Von Mises and Hobson:
Insights into Economic Theories

There are several other economic philosophers who have much to say about economic theory and will be included in this chapter. However, since much of what they have to contribute has been covered, in large measure, in the previous chapters, we will treat only their most important or unique ideas, rather than survey their comprehensive analysis. These philosophers are C. Northcote Parkinson, Beatrice and Sidney Webb, Ludwig Von Mises and John A. Hobson.

C. Northcote Parkinson (1909-)

C. Northcote Parkinson was an English historian and author. He cannot be considered an economic philosopher by any ordinary standard; his economic writings are humorous satires on business and governmental management systems. It is in his humor that his contribution to economics is important. Humor often deals with human nature, and we laugh easily when human foibles are exposed for our examination. Parkinson, in his book, *Parkinson's Law,* and other works in the same genre, tells us much about human nature and its effects on government and corporate institutions.

Parkinson's Law is, simply stated, "work expands to meet the time allotted for its completion." Parkinson demonstrates this truth with a story about a retired old lady who spends an entire afternoon writing a postcard. The importance of this humorous tale, with the seeming foolishness of the old lady, is that it is a commentary on us all. The teacher who assigns a paper knows full well that if the students are given two weeks or a month to complete it, the bulk of the work will be done the weekend before it is due. Those who run meetings know that if there is a time frame imposed on those in attendance, the agenda will be covered close to the schedule. If there is no time frame imposed, the first item or two will take all the time, and the last several items will be rushed through when it is evident that the meeting must end. Parkinson is validating the cliché, "if you want a job done, give it to a busy man." The implications for businesses are clear. In order for a business to prosper there must be quotas set, time lines drawn, and schedules which must be met.

As a result of the implications of this law, Parkinson states that in any institution subordinates multiply at a predeterminable annual rate, regardless of the work to be done. Parkinson demonstrates this phenomena by examining the British Admiralty during the years 1914-1928.

*PARKINSON'S LAW
ADMIRALTY STATISTICS

Year	Capital ships in commission	Officers and men in R.N.	Dockyard workers	Dockyard officials and clerks	Admiralty officials
1914	62	146,000	57,000	3249	2000
1928	20	100,000	62,439	4558	3569
Increase or decrease	-67.74%	-31.5%	+9.54%	+40.28%	+78.45%

It is evident from the chart that as the number of ships and men needed to man them decreased, the supervisory personnel increased. The bureaucracy in this case, the admiralty, increased the most. Why is this so? Parkinson claims that bureaucrats seek to multiply subordinates, not competitors. So, when a bureaucrat feels overworked, rather than hire someone to share the load, he hires two subordinates. This, Parkinson says, creates more work for all involved, since the bureaucrat is responsible for the work that leaves his office, and now finds himself having to check on the work of the two subordinates whom he hired to alleviate his own work load. Long-established business institutions and government agencies are the prime offenders in this process.

Parkinson's second law states, "expenditures rise to meet

Parkinson's Law. Boston: Houghton Mifflin Co., 1957, Pg. 8.

income." Governments have limitless public revenues, therefore expenditures rise eternally to meet them. The continual rise in government spending is the result of this law. Individuals have to regulate their spending within the budgetary constraints of their incomes. If government officials would apply the same standard for their agency as they do for their personal finance, this problem would cease to exist. Governments, says Parkinson, must learn to ask first what the country can afford, rather than begin by determining what they need. Parkinson claims that if a nation would limit its spending to a certain percentage of the national income, the problems of continual rising expenditures, and taxes would cease.

Parkinson takes several aspects of human nature and applies their implications to the problems of business and government. If business and government were to recognize these human tendencies and organize accordingly, many of the problems of waste, inefficiency, duplication of effort, ineffective use of time and money, and stagnation could be eliminated. Parkinson's contribution to economic theory lies in his attempt to have us recognize that the tendencies inherent in our human nature have profound economic implications, and to ignore the way human beings act is to avoid solutions to some of our serious economic problems.

Beatrice Potter Webb (1858-1943) and Sidney Webb (1859-1947)

Beatrice and Sidney Webb were English Socialists, who through their involvement with the Fabian Society contributed greatly to making socialism respectable in England. The Fabian Society was a small group of English intellectuals who saw socialism as the best means to organize an economic system and set out to convince others through their writings. George Bernard Shaw was perhaps the most famous member of the group, but the leadership was clearly in the hands of the Webbs.

Essentially, there are two kinds of socialism—revolutionary and utopian. Revolutionary socialists like Marx contend that only through violent revolution can capitalism be displaced. Utopian socialists like Owen claim that all the problems of society can be solved through the institution of socialist communities structured according to some behavioralist plan. The Webbs made the case that a socialist society need not come about through violence, and need not solve every problem facing mankind. Sidney, in his famous tract *Facts for Socialists,* stressed that education, propaganda, and persuasion, were the best means to convert people to socialism. Also, he believed that such persuasion should be accomplished on an issue-by-issue approach rather than by a comprehensive ideological stand.

The Webbs sought to solve many of society's problems, not only by addressing those obvious failings of big business, but also by seeking to bring about change in all institutions which affect people's lives. While contemporary capitalism seemed to ignore the human factor in the production of wealth, concern for the human factor in all institutions seemed to the Webbs to be lost, or at least lacking. Churches, unions, even families must be concerned less with the functioning of the institution, and more with the concern for the people that form it. The end result of this concern for the people would be a political, social, and economic equality that was among the main goals of the Webbs' socialist philosophy.

Beatrice's main concern was with unions. She felt that democratic labor unions were the best means to improve the condition of the working man. Sidney looked to collective ownership of property, democratically controlled, as the best means to help the common man. Both agreed that education was the best means to convince the public of the need for socialistic measures. And both agreed that a certain minimum standard of living for every person was necessary to achieve the end that they believed was contained in the maxim, "The greatest happiness for the greatest number."

For each problem they confronted, they proposed a solution in accordance with the basic premise of socialism—state control or ownership. For the problem of maintaining the elderly they proposed a state pension system. The problem of medical expense and quality was to be solved by instituting socialized medicine. For those who were unemployed they suggested national and local public-works projects. A minimum wage law was their answer to help the working poor.

The single most comprehensive statement of the Webbs' economic philosophy is contained in the *Fabian Essays,* written by Sidney in collaboration with G. B. Shaw. The British Labor party was founded, in large measure, on Fabian principles, and its constitution was drafted by Sidney Webb. He later served in Parliament as a member of the Labor party. It was through the political power of the Labor party that England nationalized the coal mines, medicine, and transportation.

The major contribution of the Webbs was to establish that socialism could exist without having to subscribe to Marxist theory or Utopian planning. The concept of democratic socialism, through education and within existing political, social, and economic institutions is the outstanding legacy of their philosophy. The success of their ideas has been indicated by the number of laws the Labor party was able to enact, thus making England a Democratic Socialist nation. (It is interesting to note, that in recent years, a slow but steady repeal has occurred, and much that the Labor party had entrusted to government is being returned to private enterprise.)

Ludwig Von Mises (1881-1973)

Ludwig Von Mises was a classical economist. He has been associated, for the better part of the twentieth century, with the Austrian School of economics, and has written several tracts on history, philosophy, and sociology. His major economic work, *Human Action,* is a comprehensive view of his philosophy. We shall touch on some of the most important concepts which dominate his thinking.

Von Mises asserts as a historical fact that civilization and private property are indispensable to one another. He claims that not one example in human history disputes that assertion, and that government's attempts to eliminate private property are doomed, not only to failure, but to the destruction of civilization as well. The implications for the role of the state, based on this premise, are clear. Von Mises abhors state interference in all economic matters. He decries state interference with all individual actions.

Praxeology is Von Mises' term for the science of dealing with human action. His philosophy rests on the principle of the supremacy of the individual. Praxeology deals with the actions of individual people. Action is always the action of individuals.

There is no such thing as a social collective, there are simply individual members acting. The relationship of praxeology to economics is at the basis of Von Mises' philosophy. Economics deals with the physical universe, with things and tangible material objects, not with people and their actions. Value is within us. It is how we react to the physical universe; it is in action. In a sense, Von Mises is making economics into a moral rather than an economic matter.

Man is a choosing animal. It is that ability to choose which separates us from the other animals. Our moral worth exists in that fact. Any governmental activity which limits our choices is morally wrong. In addition, governmental interference in the economic operation of the free market will only harm rather than help the process—which is dependent on freely choosing individuals. The market, then, is entirely the product of human action, and all market phenomena can be traced to the decisions of choosing individuals. Every day, every individual votes with his purchases, and some businessmen get rich, others become poor. The justice of the marketplace is not absolute in a moral sense, according to merit, but rather according to how well it satisfies the public. Those who satisfy more wants, make more dollars. Those who satisfy fewer wants, make fewer dollars. If one wishes to write unpopular poetry, one will be poor. Happy, maybe, but poor. If one wishes to get rich, all one has to do is satisfy a public want—build a better mousetrap, perhaps.

Man's quality of insatiability is also a determining factor which justifies the market economy. Since men are constantly searching and wanting, their choices are always changing. Planned economies cannot take those individual value changes into account, and therefore cannot work. Thus, those who seek equilibrium in an economy, however reasonable it might seem, a) cannot attain such a goal, and b) in the attempt will throw a wrench into a system that is meant to be dynamic, changing, and filled with ups and downs.

Von Mises claims that the two most important forces in the last hundred years have been socialism and state interventionism. He blames both for intruding on human freedom. Socialism determines what is best for people and plans accordingly. State interventionism is simply the use of force and coercion to control human action. Both are wrong, both are doomed to failure. The best and the most moral system is the free market economy; human nature not only requires it, human nature demands it.

John A. Hobson (1858-1940)

John Hobson was a social reformer, a teacher, and an author. His entry into the field of economics caused great controversy, since he brought the views of a reformer to the study and attacked nationalism, imperialism, and capitalism. His major interest was in alleviating the suffering of the poor and much of his writing deals with the equalization of the distribution of wealth.

His major contribution is considered to be his concept of social cost. Hobson was the first to put forth the idea that the cost of production—wages, capital, and rent—was an inadequate measure. Poor working conditions, inadequate ventilation or lighting, or lack of safety precautions can cause illness, disability, slow production, and create unseen costs that traditionally have not been taken into consideration. Hobson insisted that those costs (to individuals and the community) must be included as real costs of production.

Hobson shocked the economic community with his assertion that economic slumps are the result of excessive savings. He concluded that the workers were being paid at a wage that precluded their buying anything but the meager essential goods. The unequal distribution of income led to the rich having to save an inordinate amount. Since neither the rich nor the poor were consuming enough, new markets had to be found lest economic downturns take hold. Hobson's conclusion from this analysis is his most startling and important contribution to economic theory.

In his book *Imperialism: A Study,* Hobson maintained that imperialism was a necessary outgrowth of capitalism. Since capitalism on the domestic level could not survive, it had to look outward for markets, and imperialism was the result. The consequence of imperialism, in addition to the negative social affects on those conquered by the industrial nations, was war. War was the natural outgrowth of the competition between imperial powers and a world at war was the consequence.

While Hobson's theory has been taken to task by those who claim that war between nations existed long before industrial powers competed for foreign markets, Lenin took Hobson's theory to heart. Imperialism, its causes and the conflicts that result, became part of the official communist indictment against capitalism. This was not Hobson's intent. He was a heretic among his peers, but by no means a revolutionary. It is interesting that John Hobson, a meek, unassuming reformer, who wanted only to seek a solution to the poverty he saw in his native land, would provide a theory that has become a pillar of Marxist philosophy.

At this point, Marxism deserves mention. However one assesses its validity, the philosophy of Karl Marx has been the dominant political and economic force in this century. While recent events strongly suggest that his influence is on the wane, the effect of his ideas has been enormous. In Chapter Twenty the philosophy of Karl Marx was detailed: the labor theory of value, the theory of surplus value, the theory of concentration of capital, the theory of the new industrial army, the inevitable violent revolution, the dictatorship of the proletariat, and the eventual withering away of the state are all important in understanding Marxism. Dialectical materialism and historical determinism, coupled with his other theories are predicated upon his concept of the nature of man and it is upon that issue that we must begin to analyze Marx as well as the other philosophers.

Is man, by nature, competitive? Is man, by nature, cooperative? Does man have no human nature at all, in this regard, and is he simply conditioned to be one or the other? What is human nature and how powerful is heredity in determining it? How is our nature formed, and how powerful are the forces of environment? Is man basically self-interested? Or, is man basically altruistic? These questions are at the forefront of the investigation not only of economic, but of moral and political questions as well.

EPILOGUE

EPILOGUE:

Application of Ideas to the Modern World

During the previous twenty-six chapters we have attempted to present the *basic* ideas of several of the great minds of the Western World. The time spent studying these pages, with outside readings, and in discussion will have heightened our awareness of these ideas. Hopefully, the seed has been sown which will grow into a real and abiding interest in the philosophers presented here, as well as others and their ideas. If we can evaluate these philosophers, and in the process determine which moral, political, and economic ideas are important to us, we will have come far. Also, we should be able to use these ideas to help in the constructing of our own personal philosophy of life. We shall attempt, as a final project, to apply some of the ideas we have learned—but first, let us in a brief review, try to crystalize our thinking.

Each of us enters every study, every experience, with attitudes and prejudices learned in the home, the culture, the school, from peers, and the media. An awareness of this fact is an important step in opening the mind. Often, we organize these attitudes into classifications of a world view, the two most prevalent being the conservative and the liberal. Reflection on these two points is important in beginning the process of application of ideas to real situations.

Studying theories of truth, logic, and critical thinking is the part of the the process which leads us to making sound rather than poor judgments, accurate rather than vague statements, and thoughtful rather than capricious analyses. Understanding of fallacies is helpful in recognizing errors, both linguistic and logical. So, using positive measures to understand better, and developing the ability to recognize fallacies should help us to think more clearly and make more reasonable judgments. Finally, the ability to think and write clearly will be valuable not only to ourselves, but to others.

We have spent considerable time in the study of right and wrong—morality. If we do not subscribe to any one of the philosophers studied, at least we will be aware of the importance of moral choices, and that is a good beginning. Beyond awareness, however, are some important ideas which are worth considering. The *good* as knowledge, moderation, cerebral pleasure, apathy, God, feelings, sympathy, power, or freedom—which one or ones make the most sense? How do we apply these ideas to situations which require action? What have we learned from premises and the logical implications that follow? If we subscribe to any of the moral theories set forth by these thinkers, hopefully it has become apparent that our moral actions take place in a social/political context.

Thus, we have to consider and act upon moral judgments in the light of our understanding of the nature of man, the nature of the state, the type of government which will best serve us in our quest for the good life—moral and political. What we consider the state to be, and what we consider to be the rights of citizens, is important in making judgments about whom to support and whom to oppose. Our concept of the state and our role within it will help to determine what position to take on the issues.

Is the whole greater than any of its parts? Aristotle and Plato seem to think so, and we must decide whether we agree or disagree with them. If we do, what about individual rights? Men like Rousseau, and Locke have some interesting answers which we must consider. Augustine and Aquinas, Machiavelli and Mussolini, Hegel and Hobbes, Burke and Marx—all deal with the following questions, and we also ought to consider them. When does freedom become license? What does one do about unjust laws, or, if the process is just, can the resultant law be unjust? Should the brightest rule? What should be the relationship between the church and the state? Must we separate public from private morality? Is absolutism ever justified? Is the social contract a myth? How do we make our personal judgments about the basis for communism and fascism?

Assuming that we answer the important questions about the state to our own satisfaction—what do we do when the moral and the political come into conflict?

One of the valuable results of these exercises will be to humble us in the face of the difficulties encountered. Choices between good and evil are usually no great problem. Most people have little trouble with the question, "Should I rob that bank or not?" Morally and politically, the answer for most people is easy. But most of our problems arise when we are faced with choices between two goods or the lesser of two evils. Is the draft involuntary servitude? Does one serve the country or avoid the draft? If one is morally opposed to murder, must he also oppose capital punishment? Does a church leader have the right to speak out against abortion? When does the moral position take precedence over the political, and vice versa?

Most people would agree that there are great difficulties deciding between moral and political goods. Often those same people would say that there is little conflict between moral and economic choices. Some of these judgments are made without serious thought, and often we are surprised by the difficulties we have dealing with what seem to be obvious situations. Most of us have principles about what is the right and wrong of a given situation. However, how do we act in light of those principles in real situations? Do we return the ten-dollar overpayment that the clerk in the grocery store gives us as a part of our change? Does the policeman reject the fifty- or one-hundred dollar bribe, but accept the thousand-dollar offer?

Every year there are countless news reports about murder trials throughout the country. While the national news reports details about the trial and the accused and the victim, often the story focuses on the personal reactions of the parents of a young person who has been brutally murdered. An essential part of many stories concern the parents' conversion from opposition to capital punishment to favoring capital punishment. Reasons for the parents' reversal of opinion about capital punishment were contained in statements such as, "No one can imagine the suffering I've felt. I never knew I could hate this much. I want to see him (the murderer) dead." In addition, however, to this type of response, was the introduction of an economic argument. "The idea of my tax money being used to keep this murderer alive makes me ill."

No one can question the grief of a parent over the death of a beautiful young child. The question is, should we decide the issue of capital punishment on the basis of our own personal grief? Prior to the child's death, the parent was against capital punishment—did that parent fail to consider that many children had been brutally murdered in the past? Would they have been part of the consensus which prevented capital punishment for those who murdered other parents' children? Can we, dare we, make our judgments solely on our personal experience? How do we prepare ourselves to act when the unthinkable happens?

For our purposes such stories demonstrate that often we assume that we have a moral position on an issue, when in fact we do not. Or we think we have a position, but when tested find that, in fact, we don't. We can not always determine in advance how we will react to situations, but if we are truly committed to our premises, our response will not surprise us. Indeed, one of the purposes of philosophy is to teach us that there are many and serious implications in situations which are not always immediately obvious. Unless we try to recognize these implications, we will often find ourselves in confused and contradictory positions. The same holds true for political and economic premises.

What are our economic premises? First, we should reflect on our view of the nature of man; is man by nature competitive or cooperative? Or is man neither, but conditioned to be one or the other? Is *laissez-faire* the best way for man to provide for his material needs, or is socialism or communism? Who should determine what goods will be produced, how many goods will be produced, and how those goods will be distributed? All of these questions, and more, must be answered in conjunction with one's moral and political positions in order to address fully the problems of society.

Recognizing that whatever positions an individual holds at this moment may change, nay, will change—let us use what we know now and apply that knowledge to some concrete situations. Every day we must deal with the real world, and in that world there are some serious social problems. These problems are not easily solved, because there are conflicting ideas, conflicts between moral goods, political goods, and economic goods, as well as conflicts of contradiction. We shall try to analyze several different social problems, apply individual moral, political, and economic ideas, and attempt to moderate the problem through the application of those premises. What we will find is that this is a very difficult project. Not only will we find contradictions in our own beliefs, but we will find that we have to compromise certain positions we hold because of our priorities, which value some things more than others. Also, we should learn in the process which priorities should be held in higher esteem than others.

What follows will be a brief outline of how we will address any social problem. Let us take as an example the problem of capital punishment. Should the state use capital punishment, and if so, in what cases. If not, why not?

1) The first step in the process is to define the problem not only in terms of semantics, but in terms of the history of the issue.
2) The second step is to present our own moral position, first in a general sense, then in the particular as it applies to this issue.
3) The third step is to present our own political position, first in a general sense, then in the particular as it applies to the issue.
4) The fourth step is to present our own economic position, first in a general sense, then in the particular as it applies to the issue.

At this point we must analyze our moral, political and economic premises to see if they are consistent with one another; e.g., one cannot assert the majority-rule principle as a basic political position and simultaneously assert that the state can do whatever it chooses to do in regard to the issue of capital punishment. Nor can one assert that as a moral absolute the taking of life is always wrong, whether by an individual or a state, then justify capital punishment because the majority desires it, or introduce the concept of expense in maintaining convicts. If, indeed, there are conflicts of premises, then we must identify the conflict, determine the priority, explain the process for the determination—then make the choice.

Once all the moral, political, and economic premises have been determined, all the contradictions have been eliminated (or the priorities have been set and explained), then we are ready to apply the principles to the problem. This brings us to step five.

5) The fifth step, which is in fact a combination of the steps listed above, is to apply our own moral, political and economic premises, not just as an intellectual exercise, but with an understanding of all the complex factors which are a part of

the situation. We should arrive at an intelligent decision, but with a full awareness of all the emotional, social, personal and subjective forces which are a part of that decision.

More important, however, than the fact that one comes to a reasonable decision, is that this process should help each person come to terms with his own ideas, beliefs, and priorities. Certainly the conclusion that one arrives at is important, but the realization that the conclusion is the accurate reflection of the individual's most complete analysis of the situation is very significant. If we follow Aristotle's advice and create the habit of engaging in this thought process, hopefully, we will never (or almost never) find ourselves in a situation where our moral principles change simply because of a single experience which has caused us personal pain.

Or, if we apply this thought process to any problem, we will discover the contradictions that cause our thinking to be confused, or that bring us to foolish conclusions, or that lead us to solutions which are worse than the problem they were meant to solve. A classroom exchange may illustrate this point.

A student, very much into the back-to-nature, simpler life, organic food, and anti-technology philosophy, made a long, impassioned argument for the elimination of all motor vehicles in New York City. The pollution, traffic, psychological strain on motorists, dehumanizing effect of machines on men, and more, were dramatically and accurately detailed to the class. When he was finished the teacher said, "There are eight million people in New York City, and all those people require all kinds of goods and services which are provided in large measure by motor vehicles. How do you suggest that, if your plan is implemented, those eight million people will get those goods and services that motor vehicles supply?" The student thought for a moment or two and then replied triumphantly, "Horses!" To which the teacher replied, "Young man, the number of horses it would take to supply eight million New Yorkers with all the goods and services they require, would, within a week, insure that eight million people would be up to their knees in the product of your solution."

Hopefully, the product that results from the implementation of the process described here will free us from the results of poorly-thought-out schemes. This is not to say that the implementation of the process will solve problems. There are often unseen and unavoidable results which cannot be predicted. But the chances of success are increased by the application of a well-thought-out approach to the problem.

If however, we never solve a single problem that exists in the world, we still can develop our own ability to understand the problem, some of the causes of the problem, the difficulties in dealing with the problem, and also develop some tolerance for those entrusted with the responsibility for dealing with the actual problem.

Surveys have shown that many people have voted for candidates who were running for political office and when asked to articulate their position on the issues found that their opinions were contrary to those of the candidate. What was shown was that often, people vote for the wrong man—not the wrong man on the basis of another's opinion, but the wrong man, based on their own opinion. If we apply our well-thought-out premises to questions that arise, we many come up with the wrong answer in the eyes of others, but we certainly will be, to a large extent, at peace with ourselves. And that, hopefully, will lead us to the most important lesson of all.

If we cultivate our opinions with an understanding that they are based on certain reasonable premises and follow logically from those premises, not only on the particular issue confronted, but on all like issues, then we should be able to understand, appreciate, and be tolerant of the opinions of others who have, based on their own premises, come to a different opinion. It is because of this concept that we have been able to study the differing premises of a Plato, Aristotle, Aquinas, Hume, and Nietzsche while still recognizing the value of their individual contributions. Also, if we can recognize that individuals have different concerns—Plato with the ideal, Aristotle with the practical, Locke with the rational, Rousseau with the emotional, and Sartre with the subjective—and still appreciate their perspective—that is a sign of intellectual and emotional maturity.

Obviously, the process of becoming a reasoning, thoughtful person requires a lifelong commitment. It is not easy, nor is it always possible—but it is a goal that we would do well to pursue. Often, being able to recognize our mistakes or the mistakes of others can remind us that we can easily be sidetracked from the goal. The story related earlier in this chapter about the parent and her opinion on capital punishment after the murder of her child is one example of how we can abandon some seemingly well-thought-out positions. Other examples abound, and perhaps it would be well to end this text with some that might remind us of how often we are confronted by situations which test our character.

Imagine the person who constantly complains about the unemployed and the high rates of compensation awarded for not working. If that person becomes unemployed and soon takes the position that unemployment compensation is inadequate and should be increased, is this person's conversion the product of a better understanding of the problem, or is it simply the manifestation of the cliché, "It all depends on whose ox is getting gored."

Consider the person who constantly calls for higher taxes for those who have great wealth, "since those who have more can afford to pay more." If that person wins ten million dollars in the state lottery and soon begins to complain about and work towards the equalization of taxation because "to tax at unequal rates is unjust"—should we take note of this reversal and ask, "Why?"

These examples relate to individuals, but social consequences result from the acts of individuals. A generation ago, marijuana use was generally considered a serious offense. People caught possessing or using marijuana were often incarcerated. At the time, the perception of many was that most marijuana users lived in Harlem. Has the decriminalization (if not in fact, in practice) of marijuana come about because of public acceptance based on an understanding that marijuana is not really a seriously harmful drug? Or, has this decriminalization come about because suburban kids began to use it, and the power of that constituency caused the change in the enforcement of the law?

Finally, there was a young lady who was describing her boyfriend. "He is a kind, considerate, tender, intelligent, wonderful guy." During the week, however, the young man explained that he has met another girl, and although he held the first young lady in the highest regard, he did not have the deep feelings required for a continued romantic relationship. The next day the young lady described her former boyfriend as a "mean, inconsiderate, cruel, stupid, miserable wimp."

The goal of this process is to hear the young lady describe her former boyfriend as "a person who, yesterday, hurt my feelings to the core, has made me angrier than I can say, but is a kind, considerate, tender, intelligent, wonderful person that I am emotionally disposed to hate at this moment. However, these are emotions that I will try not to harbor, but to overcome."

BIBLIOGRAPHY

PART 1

Burns, J.M., and Peltason, J.W. *Government by the People*. Englewood Cliffs: Prentice Hall, Inc., 1966.

Chase, Stuart. *Guides to Straight Thinking*. New York: Harper & Row Publishers, 1956.

Copi, Irving M. *Introduction to Logic*. New York: Macmillan Co., 1972.

Copleston, Frederick. *A History of Philosophy*. Volumes 1-8. Garden City, N.Y.: Image Books, 1962-7.

Dupuis, Adrian M. *Philosophy of Education in Historical Perspective*. Chicago: Rand McNally & Co., 1966.

Durant, Will. *The Story of Philosophy*. New York: Simon and Schuster, Inc., 1933.

Durant, Will and Ariel. *The Lessons of History*. New York: Simon and Schuster, 1968.

Engel, Morris S. *With Good Reason: An Introduction to Informal Fallacies*. New York: St. Martin's Press, 1982.

Fagothey, Austin. *Right and Reason, Ethics in Theory and Practice*. Saint Louis: The C.V. Mosby Company, 1972.

Fearnside, W.W., and Holther, W.B. *Fallacy, The Counterfeit Argument*. Englewood Cliffs: Prentice Hall, Inc., 1959.

Feibleman, James K. *Understanding Philosophy*. New York: Dell Publishing Co., 1973.

Frost, S.E., Jr. *Basic Teachings of the Great Philosophers*. Garden City: Dolphin Books, 1962.

Fuller, B., and McMurrin, S. *A History of Philosophy*. New York: Holt, Rinehart, & Winston, 1955.

Key, V.O., Jr. *Public Opinion and American Democracy*. New York: Alfred A. Knopf, 1964.

Kreyche, Robert J. *Logic for Undergraduates*. New York: Dryden Press, 1954.

Lazarus, A., and Smith, H.W. *A Glossary of Literature and Composition.* Urbana: NCTE, 1983.

Lippman, Walter. *The Good Society.* Westport: Greenwood Press, 1943.

Manning, D.J. *Liberalism.* New York: St. Martin's Press, 1976.

McCall, Raymond J. *Basic Logic.* New York: Barnes and Noble, Inc., 1947.

Meyer, Frank S. *What is Conservatism?* New York: Holt, Rinehart, & Winston, 1965.

Mitchell, Malcolm G. *Propaganda, Polls, and Public Opinion.* Englewood Cliffs: Prentice Hall, Inc., 1970.

Oesterle, John A. *Logic, The Art of Defining and Reasoning.* New York: Prentice Hall, Inc., 1952.

Orton, William A. *The Liberal Tradition.* New Haven: Yale University Press, 1945.

Rossiter, Clinton. *Conservatism in America.* New York: Alfred A. Knopf, 1966.

Runes, Dagobert D. *Dictionary of Philosophy.* New York: Philosophical Library, 1960.

Sahakian, William S. *History of Philosophy.* New York: Barnes and Noble, 1968.

Sahakian, W.S. and M.L. *Ideas of the Great Philosophers.* New York: Barnes and Noble Books, 1966.

Schapiro, Salwyn J. *Liberalism: Its Meaning and History.* New York: Van Nostrand Co., 1958.

Smith, Vincent E. *The Elements of Logic.* Milwaukee: The Bruce Publishing Co., 1957.

Viereck, Peter. *Conservatism.* Princeton: Van Nostrand and Co., 1956.

PART 2

Acton, H.B. *Kant's Moral Philosophy.* New York: St. Martin's Press, 1970.

Adler, Mortimer. *Aristotle for Everybody.* New York: Macmillan Co., 1968.

Albert, E., *et al. Great Traditions in Ethics.* New York: Van Nostrand and Co., 1969.

Aquinas, St. Thomas. *Summa Theologica.* Garden City: Image Books, 1969.

Beck, Lewis W. *Early German Philosophy*. Cambridge: Havard University Press, 1969.

———. *Studies in the Philosophy of Kant*. New York: Bobbs-Merrill Co., 1965.

Bentham, J., and Mill, J.S. *The Utilitarians*. Garden City: Dolphin Books, 1961.

Bonforte, John. *The Philosophy of Epictetus*. New York: Philosophical Library, 1955.

Bourke, Vernon J. *The Pocket Aquinas*. New York: Washington Square Press, 1960.

Brinton, Crane. *Nietzsche*. Cambridge: Harvard University Press, 1941.

Buber, Martin. *Good and Evil*. Translated by Walter Kaufman. New York: Charles Scribner's Sons, 1968.

Cassirer, Ernst. *Kant's Life and Thought*. New Haven: Yale University Press, 1981.

Chappell, V.C. *The Philosophy of David Hume*. New York: Random House, 1963.

Copleston, Frederick. *Aquinas*. Baltimore: Penguin Books, 1955.

———. *Medieval Philosophy*. New York: Harper & Row, 1961.

D'Arcy, M.C., ed. *Saint Thomas Aquinas: Selected Writings*. London: Everyman's Library, 1964.

Descartes, René. *Descartes, Selections,* ed. Ralph M. Eaton. New York: Charles Scribner's Sons, 1955.

Everett, Charles W. *Jeremy Bentham*. New York: Dell Publishing Co., Inc., 1966.

Farrington, Benjamin. *The Faith of Epicurus*. New York: Basic Books, Inc.,1967.

Gilson, Étienne. *The Christian Philosophy of St. Thomas Aquinas*. New York: Random House, 1956.

———. *Moral Values and the Moral Life*. The Shoe String Press, 1961.

Greene, Norman N. *Jean-Paul Sartre: The Existential Ethic*. Ann Arbor: University of Michigan Press, 1966.

Grene, Marjorie. *A Portrait of Aristotle*. Chicago: University of Chicago Press, 1963.

———. *Introduction to Existentialism.* Chicago: University of Chicago Press, 1959.

Hayin, Gila J. *The Existential Sociology of Jean-Paul Sartre.* Amherst: University of Massachusetts Press, 1980.

Hicks, R.D. *Stoic and Epicurean.* New York: Russell & Russell, 1962.

Hollingdale, R.J. *Nietzsche.* Boston: Routledge & Paul, 1973.

Hospers, John. *Human Conduct: Introduction to the Problem of Ethics.* New York: Harcourt Brace, 1961.

Hume, David. *An Inquiry Concerning Human Understanding,* ed. by V.C. Chappell. New York: Random House, 1963.

Hume, David. *A Treatise of Human Nature,* ed. by V.C. Chappell. New York: Random House, 1963.

Kant, Immanuel. *Critique of Pure Reason.* New York: Willey Book Co., 1900.

Kaplan, Justin. *The Pocket Aristotle.* New York: Washington Square Press, 1958.

Kaufman, Walter. *Nietzsche: Philosopher, Psychologist, Anti-Christ.* New York: Vintage Books, 1968.

———. *The Portable Nietzsche.* New York: Viking Press, 1968.

Kemp, John. *The Philosophy of Kant.* London: Oxford University Press, 1968.

LaFarge, René. *Jean-Paul Sartre: His Philosophy.* Notre Dame, Ind.: University of Notre Dame Press, 1970.

Mack, Mary P. *Jeremy Bentham: An Odyssey of Ideas.* New York: Columbia University Press, 1962.

Magee, Bryan. *The Philosophy of Schopenhauer.* New York: Clarendon Press, 1983.

Mann, Thomas. *The Living Thoughts of Schopenhauer.* New York: Longmans, Green and Co., 1939.

Mill, John S. *Utilitarianism, Liberty, and Representative Government.* New York: E.P. Dutton and Co., 1951.

Nietzsche, Friedrich. *Beyond Good and Evil.* London: Penguin Books, 1973.

———. *The Birth of Tragedy and The Genealogy of Morals.* New York: Doubleday and Co., 1956.

———. *Thus Spake Zarathustra.* New York: Viking Press, Inc., 1966.

———. *The Will to Power.* New York: Vintage Books, 1967.

Oates, Whitney. *The Stoic and Epicurean Philosophers.* New York: Random House, Inc., 1940.

Parker, DeWitt H. *Schopenhauer.* New York: Charles Scribner's Sons, 1928.

Patton, H.J. *The Moral Law.* London: Hutchinson & Co. Ltd., 1948.

Pegis, Anton C., ed. *Basic Writings of St. Thomas Aquinas - Summa Theologica and Summa Contra Gentiles.* New York: Random House, 1945.

Ree, Jonathan. *Descartes.* New York: Pica Press, 1974.

Rist, J.M. *Epicurus.* New York: Cambridge University, 1972.

———. *Stoic Philosophy.* New York: Cambridge University, 1969.

Ross, W.D. *Aristotle.* New York: Barnes and Noble Inc., 1966.

Rouse, W.H.D. *Great Dialogues of Plato.* New York: Mentor Books, 1956.

Sartre, J.P. *Existentialism.* New York: Philosophical Library, 1947.

———. *Being and Nothingness.* New York: Washington Square Press, 1953.

Schneewind, J.B. *Mill.* Notre Dame, Ind.: University of Notre Dame Press, 1968.

Stocks, John L. *Aristotelianism.* New York: Cooper Square Publishers, 1963.

Taylor, A.E. *Plato - The Man and His Work.* London: Methuen & Co., Ltd., 1960.

Voegelin, Eric. *Plato.* Baton Rouge: Louisiana State University Press, 1966.

Vrooman, Jack R. *René Descartes.* New York: G.P. Putnam's Sons, 1970.

Wilson, Margaret. *The Essential Descartes.* New York: The New American Library, 1969.

PART 3

Aaron, Richard. *John Locke.* London: Oxford University Press, 1961.

Augustine, Saint. *The City of God.* New York: Modern Library, 1950.

———. *The Confessions of St. Augustine.* New York: Modern Library, 1949.

Babbitt, Irving. *Rousseau and Romanticism.* Cambridge: Riverside Press, 1919.

Barker, Ernest. *The Political Thought of Plato and Aristotle.* New York: Dover, 1959.

Buchanan, Scott, (ed.). *The Portable Plato.* New York: The Viking Press, 1948.

Burke, Edmund. *Reflections on the Revolution in France.* New Rochelle: Arlington House, 1966.

———. *Speech on Conciliation with the Colonies.* Chicago: Henry Regnery, 1964.

Canavan, Francis. *The Political Reason of Edmund Burke.* Durham, N.C.: Duke University Press, 1960.

Cassirer, Ernst. *The Question of Jean Jacques Rousseau.* Bloomington: Indiana University Press, 1975.

Chamberlain, William H. *Collectivism: A False Utopia.* New York: Macmillan Co., 1937.

Collier, Richard. *Duce!* New York: The Viking Press, 1971.

Cone, Carl. *Burke and the Nature of Politics.* Lexington: University of Kentucky, 1957.

Diggins, John P. *Mussolini and Fascism.* Princeton: Princeton University, 1972.

Ebenstein, William. *Great Political Philosophers.* New York: Holt, Rinehart, Winston, 1966.

Ellenberg, Stephen. *Rousseau's Political Philosophy.* Ithaca: Cornell University Press, 1976.

Fermi, Laura. *Mussolini.* Chicago: University of Chicago Press, 1961.

Foster, Michael B. *Masters of Political Thought* (Vol. 2, *Plato to Machiavelli*). Boston: Houghton Mifflin Co., 1941.

Gettell, Raymond. *Introduction to Political Science.* Boston: Ginn and Company, 1910.

Gilson, Étienne. *The Christian Philosophy of St. Augustine.* New York: Random House, 1960.

Gregor, A. James. *The Fascist Persuasion in Radical Politics.* Princeton: Princeton University, 1974.

Hook, Sidney. *From Hegel to Marx.* Ann Arbor: University of Michigan Press, 1950.

Jones, W.T. *Masters of Political Thought* (Vol. 2, *Machiavelli to Bentham*). Boston: Hoghton Mifflin Co., 1968.

Kaufman, Walter. *Hegel: A Reinterpretation.* Garden City: Doubleday Anchor Books, 1965.

Kirk, Russell. *Edmund, Burke, A Genius Reconsidered.* New Rochelle: Arlington House, 1967.

Kojeve, Alexandre. *Introduction to the Reading of Hegel.* New York: Basic Books, Inc., 1969.

Lancaster, Lane W. *Masters of Political Thought* (Vol. 3, *Hegel to Dewy*). Boston: Houghton Mifflin Co., 1965.

Lauer, Quentin. *Hegel's Idea of Philosophy.* New York: Fordham University Press, 1971.

Lipson, Leslie. *The Great Issues of Politics, An Introduction to Political Science.* New York: Prentice Hall, Inc., 1954.

Locke, John. *Two Treatises of Government,* ed. Peter Laslett. Cambridge: Cambridge University, 1960.

Loewenberg, J. *Hegel Selections.* New York: Charles Scribner's Sons, 1929.

Lowith, Karl. *From Hegel to Nietzsche.* New York: Anchor Books, 1967.

Machiavelli, Niccolo. *The Prince and the Discourses.* New York: The Modern Library, 1950.

Marx, Karl. *The Communist Manifesto.* New York: Washington Square Press, 1964.

McLellan, David. *Karl Marx.* New York: The Viking Press, 1968.

Nisbet, Robert. *The Social Philosophers: Community and Conflict in Western Thought.* New York: Thomas Y. Crowell Co., 1973.

O'Connor, D.J. *John Locke.* London: Penguin Books, 1952.

Ortega Y Gasset, José. *The Revolt of the Masses.* New York: W.W. Norton & Company, Inc., 1932.

Pareto, Vilfredo. *The Mind and Society.* New York: Harcourt Brace & Co., 1935.

———. *Sociological Writings,* trans. Derick Mirfin. New York: Frederic A. Praeger, 1966.

Payne, Robert. *Marx.* New York: Simon and Schuster, 1968.

Pennock, J.R., and Smith, D.G. *Political Science, an Introduction.* New York: Macmillan Co., 1964.

Rousseau, J.J. *The Social Contract,* trans. G.D.H. Cole. New York: E.P. Dutton & Co., 1950.

Smith, R.E. *Cicero the Statesman.* Cambridge: Cambridge University, 1966.

Sorel, George. *The Illusions of Progress,* trans. J. and C. Stanley. Los Angeles: University of California Press, 1969.

Strauss, Leo. *Hobbes' Political Philosophy: its Basis and Genesis.* Oxford: Clarendon Press, 1936.

Taylor, Charles. *Hegel.* London: Cambridge University, 1975.

Wilkins, B.T. *Hegel's Philosophy of History.* Ithaca: Cornell University Press, 1974.

PART 4

Barber, William J. *A History of Economic Thought.* London: Penguin Books Inc., 1967.

Bladen, V.W. *From Adam Smith to Maynard Keynes.* Toronto: University of Toronto, 1974.

Blaug, Mark. *Ricardian Economics.* New Haven: Yale University Press, 1958.

Cole, G.D.H. *Classics in Economics.* New York: The Philosophical Library, 1960.

Cole, Margaret. *Robert Owen of New Lanark.* New York: Oxford University Press, 1953.

——. *The Story of Fabian Socialism.* Stanford: Stanford University, 1969.

Cord, Steven B. *Henry George: Dreamer or Realist?* Philadelphia: University of Philadelphia Press, 1965.

Diggins, John B. *The Bard of Savagery.* New York: The Seabury Press, 1978.

Dorfman, Joseph. *Thorsten Veblen and His America.* New York: Augustus M. Kelley, 1961.

Ebenstein, William. *Today's Isms.* Englewood Cliffs: Prentice Hall, Inc., 1973.

Friedman, Milton. *Capitalism and Freedom.* Chicago: University of Chicago Press, 1971.

Friedman, Milton and Rose. *Free to Choose.* New York: Harcourt Brace Jovanovich, 1980.

Hansen, Alvin H. *A Guide to Keynes.* New York: McGraw Hill, Inc., 1953.

Hayek, Friedrich. *The Road to Serfdom.* Chicago: University of Chicago Press, 1960.

Heilbroner, Robert L. *The Worldly Philosophers.* New York: Simon and Schuster, 1967.

Hobson, J.A. *Imperialism.* Ann Arbor: University of Michigan, 1971.

Hutt, W.H. *Keynesianism - Retrospect and Prospect.* Chicago: Henry Regnery, 1963.

Keynes, J.M. *The General Theory of Employment, Interest, and Money.* New York: Harcourt Brace, 1964.

Klein, Lawrence. *The Keynsian Revolution.* New York: Macmillan Co., 1966.

Lekachman, Robert. *The Age of Keynes.* New York: Random House, 1966.

———. *Varieties of Economics.* New York: Meridian, 1962.

Malthus, Thomas. *An Essay on the Principle of Population.* New York: W.W. Norton and Co., 1976.

Morton, A.L. *The Life and Ideas of Robert Owen.* New York: Monthly Review Press, 1963.

Nemmers, E.E. *Hobson and Underconsumption.* New York: Augustus M. Kelley, 1972.

O'Brien, D.P. *The Classical Economists.* London: Oxford University Press, 1975.

Owen, Robert. *The Life of Robert Owen.* New York: Alfred A. Knopf, Inc., 1920.

Parkinson, C.N. *Big Business.* Boston: Little, Brown & Co., 1974.

———. *In-Laws and Outlaws.* Boston: Houghton Mifflin Co., 1962.

———. *Mrs. Parkinson's Law.* Boston: Houghton Mifflin Co., 1968.

———. *Parkinson's Law.* Boston: Houghton Mifflin Co., 1957.

Ricardo, David. *Principles of Political Economy and Taxation,* ed. R.M. Hartwell. Maryland: Penguin Books, 1971.

Roll, Eric. *A History of Economic Thought.* New York: Prentice Hall, Inc., 1946.

Schumpeter, Joseph. *Capitalism, Socialism, and Democracy.* New York: Harper Torchbooks, 1962.

Scott, William R. *Adam Smith as Student and Professor.* New York: Augustus M. Kelley, 1965.

Smith, Adam. *The Wealth of Nations.* New York: Random House, 1937.

Soule, George. *Ideas of Great Economists.* New York: Viking Press, Inc., 1952.

Spiegel, Henry. *The Growth of Economic Thought.* New Jersey: Prentice Hall, Inc., 1971.

Thomas, John L. *Alternative America.* Cambridge: Harvard University Press, 1983.

Veblen, Thorsten. *The Portable Veblen,* ed. Max Lerner. New York: The Viking Press, 1948.

———. *The Theory of the Leisure Class.* New York: The Seabury Press, 1978.

Von Mises, Ludwig. *Human Action, A Treatise on Economics.* Chicago: Henry Regnery, 1966.

———. *Omnipotent Government: The Rise of the Total State and Total War.* New Haven: Yale University Press, 1944.

———. *Socialism.* New Haven: Yale University Press, 1951.

INDEX

absolute advantage, theory of, 208
absolute freedom, 104
Absolute Idea, 180
Absolutism/Absolutist, 20, 187-188
Academy (Plato's), 56, 60
accent, 34-35, 36
accident, 36-37, 43
aesthetic contemplation, 97
affected ignorance, 51
aggregate demand, 229, 230-231
Albertus Magnus, 72
"Allegory of the Cave," 57-58, 140
alternative syllogism, 30
amphiboly, 33-34, 36
anarchy, 132, 148
antecedent passion, 51-52
apathy, 69
a posteriori, 48-49, 93
"appetites and aversions," 161, 164
a priori, 48, 91
Aquinas, St. Thomas, 49, 53, 72-78,
   151-155
  existence of God, 76-77
  laws, 4 types, 75-76, 153-154
  reason, types of, 76
  the state, 151, 154
  writings, 72, 151
argument from degrees of being, 77
argument from design, 77
argument from efficient cause, 77
argument from motion, 76-77
argument from necessity, 77
argumentum ad baculum, 41
argumentum ad hominem, 40-41

argumentum ad ignorantium, 42
argumentum ad misericordium, 41
argumentum ad populum, 41-42
argumentum ad verecundium, 41
aristocracy, 143, 172, 173
Aristotelian philosophy, 72, 73, 77-78,
   79
Aristotle, 15, 32, 49, 53, 56, 60-64, 72,
   73, 78, 81, 117, 120, 141-145, 151,
   154, 248, 252, 253
  criticism of Plato, 142
  governmental organization, 142-143
  governmental purpose, 143, 176
  law, 144-145
  moral act, qualities of, 49-50
  political philosophy, 141-145
  reason, 77-78
  writings, 47, 61, 141, 151
Arrian, 69
artificial monopolies, 206
ascendant nations, concept of, 180
association, forms of (Hume), 83
ataraxia, 67
attitudes, formation of, 3-11
Augustine, Saint, 131, 146-150, 152
  concept of the will, 147
  on the nature of man, 147
  the state, 147-149
  writings, 146
Austrian school of economics, 241
authority, 132-133

"bad faith," 106
begging the question, 38, 43